Open Query File Magic!

Open Query File Magic!

A Complete Guide to Maximizing the Power of OPNQRYF

Second Edition

Ted Holt

MIDRANGE COMPUTING
IIR PUBLICATIONS INC.

Second Edition

First Printing—December 1998

© 1998 Midrange Computing
ISBN: 1-883884-57-8

Midrange Computing
5650 El Camino Real, Suite 225
Carlsbad, CA 92008
http://www.midrangecomputing.com

V4R2

I dedicate this new edition of OPNQRYF Magic! *to my wife, Jerry Susan Holt, who has dedicated her best waking hours to the most important job on Earth—raising children—and to Kyle, Tabitha, Anna, Caleb, Amy, Nathan, and Jacob—the children to whom she has given birth.*

❖ Contents

❖ Introduction

I once heard a joke that goes like this, "What did God say after He created Adam?" The answer: "I can do better than that!"

I'm proud of *OPNQRYF Magic!* Since it was first released in 1992, it's helped a lot of people. But I've always felt that it could be improved. I hope you like the major improvements I've made, which include adding chapters. After *OPNQRYF Magic!* was first released, I wished I had placed date data type information in its own chapter; now it is. I've also added a chapter about ILE, which didn't exist when I did the first edition, a chapter about Y2K issues, which few people were concerned about in 1992, and I've added more examples and more techniques.

In certain sections of the book, I repeat information where I think it will be helpful. I wrote the original *OPNQRYF Magic!* as if someone would read it from start to finish. Of course, I knew then that would not often be the case. Now, some topics are repeated in selected places to help readers find information easily.

I hope you like this new book. I think it's an improvement over the prior version. Even so, I'm sure—within a short time—I'll be saying, "I can do better than that!"

Ted Holt
Corinth, Mississippi
June 1, 1998

1

❖ Overview

One of the greatest advances in the field of data processing is the invention of interactive query programs, which allow an end user to retrieve data from a database without having to write high-level language programs. Interactive query programs permit a user to see data sorted the way the user wants it, to see specific fields of interest, to calculate new fields, or to see data in summary form.

Open Query File (OPNQRYF) is a CL command that gives these capabilities to high-level language programs. OPNQRYF can present data to a high-level language program in a certain sequence. It can select records that meet certain criteria, create new fields, and summarize data.

Just as query programs have allowed users to be much more productive, OPNQRYF can make your programs more productive. Instead of writing two or more programs that do more or less the same thing, you can write one flexible program that will handle all foreseen (and many unforeseen) requests for information.

Imagine an RPG or COBOL program that can select any subset of records in a database file and print the same basic report in four different sort sequences. Now you have an idea of what OPNQRYF is all about.

To get a better understanding of OPNQRYF, suppose you work in the Information Systems Department of a factory. One of the most important reports—which shows what sales orders are in the system and their status in the shop—you provide for management is the customer order schedule. Sometimes the plant manager:

❖ Wants to know about all customer orders.

❖ Wants to know about orders for a certain customer.

❖ Asks to see the orders that are ready for final assembly.

❖ Requests an order schedule for all orders due by a certain date.

The plant manager usually wants the customer order schedule sorted by due date, but sometimes the manager asks for it sorted by customer number or by item number. Usually the manager wants the left-most column to show the date the order is to be shipped to the customer, but sometimes there is a need to see the date the order was entered into the system instead.

All of these preceding requests are variations of the same report. In many data-processing shops, such processing would be handled by a dozen different COBOL programs (11 of which would be clones of the original). A request for a new combination of conditions (such as orders for customer 60620, sorted by item number, with ship date in the first column) would cause a programmer to hastily make yet another clone of an existing program. All of this program cloning can get out of hand. In an OPNQRYF environment, however, an end user fills in a prompt screen with the proper values and soon thereafter has a report.

How Opnqryf Works

Now that you know about the purpose of OPNQRYF, the following sections describe how it works. Try to put OPNQRYF to work as you go through this book. Don't wait until you have read it all to start using this powerful command. Proceeding one concept at a time and building on what you know so far is the best way to learn. Refer to appendix A if you have problems. Appendix A has a list of the most common problems beginners have with OPNQRYF and some probable causes.

OPNQRYF acts as a filter between a high-level language program and database files. You can use OPNQRYF to select records, sort, create new fields, and summarize data before the high-level language program reads from the database. Although OPNQRYF does many of the same things logical files do, logical files are permanent. In contrast, the open data path created by OPNQRYF lasts only for the duration of the job.

A high-level language program must share the open data path created by OPNQRYF. If the queried file doesn't have the share open data path attribute, it must be overridden before the high-level language program opens the file.

OPEN DATA PATHS AND POINTERS

When the OPNQRYF command is executed, it creates an open data path through which data is accessed. Think of an open data path as an imaginary pointer that moves from record to record as a file is being read. The high-level language program opens the queried file as usual but—instead of reading the file with its own pointer—it uses OPNQRYF's pointer. OPNQRYF accesses only those records that meet the conditions given to it and returns them in the prescribed sequence and format. The high-level language program doesn't need to sort or select records. The high-level language program is coded as if it reads the entire file in its regular sequence.

COMPARING OPNQRYF TO LOGICAL FILES

Another way to understand OPNQRYF is to think of it as a builder of dynamic logical files. As you know, logical files can select fields and records and create an alternate key. Imagine building a temporary logical file, running a program against it, then deleting it, and you can see what OPNQRYF does.

Actually, this is what System/38 programmers did before the introduction of OPNQRYF. Many programmers had utilities that would change the select/omit and key-field specifications in the data description specifications (DDS) before the logical file was created. While that approach worked well, OPNQRYF has made that technique obsolete in all but a few cases.

CODING OPNQRYF

At first glance, OPNQRYF might look a little complicated. However, most of the parameters aren't used frequently.

Often you will need only the FILE, QRYSLT (query select) and KEYFLD (key field) parameters. The only required parameter is FILE, which names one or more database files from which the data is to be retrieved. For each file listed, you can specify the library in which it is found and the member to use. Both physical and logical files are permitted, but only one record type is allowed per file-parameter entry. A few examples of OPNQRYF FILE parameters follow.

The code shown in Figure 1.1 causes the system to search the libraries in the library list to find a file named CUSMAS. CUSMAS has only one record format. The first (or only) member is used.

```
    OPNQRYF     FILE((CUSMAS))
 or OPNQRYF     FILE((*LIBL/CUSMAS))
```

Figure 1.1: Specifying file CUSMAS to OPNQRYF.

As shown in Figure 1.2, OPNQRYF uses the first member of file CUSMAS in library DALLAS.

```
 OPNQRYF     FILE((DALLAS/CUSMAS))
```

Figure 1.2: Specifying file CUSMAS in library DALLAS to OPNQRYF.

As shown in Figure 1.3, OPNQRYF uses member PREVYEAR in file CUSMAS, which is found in the current library.

```
 OPNQRYF     FILE((*CURLIB/CUSMAS PREVYEAR))
```

Figure 1.3: Specifying member PREVYEAR in file CUSMAS in the current library to OPNQRYF.

CUSSALES (customer sales) is a logical file with more than one record format. OPNQRYF reads only the SLSDTL record type in the first member. See Figure 1.4.

```
 OPNQRYF     FILE((CUSSALES *FIRST SLSDTL))
```

Figure 1.4: Specifying record type SLSDTL in the first member in logical file CUSSALES to OPNQRYF.

OPNQRYF retrieves data from two single-format files: the order header file and the order detail file. If either file has multiple members, the first member is read. See Figure 1.5.

```
OPNQRYF      FILE((ORDHDR) (ORDDTL)) ...
```

Figure 1.5: Specifying two files, ORDHDR and ORDDTL, to OPNQRYF.

CL variable &FILENAME has the name of the file to be queried (Figure 1-6). The FILE parameter by itself won't usually achieve anything; you will need another parameter to make it do something useful. Rather than explain all the parameters at this point, they are covered as they are used. For the complete syntax of OPNQRYF, consult the *CL Reference* manual.

```
OPNQRYF      FILE((&FILENAME)) ...
```

Figure 1.6: Using a variable, &FILENAME, to specify a file to OPNQRYF.

CL REQUIREMENTS

OPNQRYF requires that the high-level language program that accesses the queried data must share the open data path it creates. Unless the queried file already has the share open-data path attribute, it must be overridden to SHARE(*YES) before the program opens it. For this reason, it is common to code an Override Database File (OVRDBF) command immediately before the OPNQRYF command. Throughout this book, it is presumed that files don't have the share attribute, and that an override will be coded.

The call to the application program usually follows the OPNQRYF command. Once the application program finishes, the file should be closed (with the CLOF command) and the override may be deleted. The typical OPNQRYF application, then, consists of five steps.

1. Override the database file to SHARE(*YES) .
2. Run the OPNQRYF command.
3. CALL the high-level language program.
4. Run the CLOF command to close the query file.
5. Delete the override to the database file.

A typical CL program executing OPNQRYF contains lines like those shown in Figure 1.7.

```
OVRDBF    FILE(SLSHIST) SHARE(*YES)
OPNQRYF   FILE((SLSHIST)) QRYSLT('CUSTNR=60620') +
            KEYFLD((ITEMNR))
CALL      PGM(HLLPGM)
CLOF      OPNID(SLSHIST)
DLTOVR    FILE(SLSHIST)
```

Figure 1.7: Typical OPNQRYF code with OVRDBF preceding the OPNQRYF command.

Some programmers prefer to open the query file before overriding the file as shown in Figure 1.8.

```
OPNQRYF    FILE((SLSHIST)) QRYSLT('CUSTNR=60620') +
             KEYFLD((ITEMNR))
OVRDBF     FILE(SLSHIST) SHARE(*YES)
CALL       PGM(HLLPGM)
DLTOVR     FILE(SLSHIST)
CLOF       OPNID(SLSHIST)
```

Figure 1.8: Typical OPNQRYF code with OVRDBF following the OPNQRYF command.

Either method is fine. The first method is used for most of the examples in this book because IBM uses this method in its AS/400 manuals. If you are querying a multi-member file, you must name the member to be queried in both the OVRDBF and OPNQRYF commands, as shown in Figure 1.9.

```
OVRDBF    FILE(CUSMAS) MEMBER(PREVYEAR) SHARE(*YES)
OPNQRYF   FILE((CUSMAS PREVYEAR)) ...etc...
```

Figure 1.9: Specifying a multi-member file to the OVRDBF and OPNQRYF commands.

If a file is already open, you'll get a message such as "CPF4174 (OPNID(XXXXX) for file YYYYY already exists.)." It is a good idea to code a CLOF command, followed by a MONMSG command for CPF4520 (No file open with identifier &4.) at the beginning of programs, especially interactive programs, to prevent this error from halting a program. Figure 1.10 shows an example of this.

```
CLOF        OPNID(CUSMAS)
MONMSG      MSGID(CPF4520)

OVRDBF      FILE(CUSMAS) SHARE(*YES)
OPNQRYF     FILE((CUSMAS)) etc.
CALL        PGM(HLLPGM)
DLTOVR      FILE(CUSMAS)
CLOF        OPNID(CUSMAS)
```

Figure 1.10: Example of checking for an open file before issuing the OVRDBF command.

HIGH-LEVEL LANGUAGE REQUIREMENTS

The open data path built by OPNQRYF is usually read by a high-level language program (i.e., a program written in a language such as RPG or COBOL). The program may also be read by a CL program or by the Copy From Query File (CPYFRMQRYF) command.

Throughout this book, the term *high-level language program* is used to refer to the process that reads the queried data. The term is used only to distinguish it from the CL program that calls it. Keep in mind that "high-level language program" also can mean a CL program or the CPYFRMQRYF command.

Because BASIC won't share an existing open data path, BASIC programs can't be used with OPNQRYF. Programs working under OPNQRYF are generally simpler than those that don't use OPNQRYF because they usually don't have to select records. Also, some calculations can be carried out by the OPNQRYF command.

The file name in the high-level language program (beginning in column 7 of the RPG F-specification) must match the FORMAT parameter of the OPNQRYF command. For example, the OPNQRYF command shown in Figure 1.11 requires the RPG IV file specification shown in Figure 1.12.

```
OPNQRYF     FILE((ARMAST)) FORMAT(ARWORK) +
            QRYSLT('CODE *EQ 1') KEYFLD((CUSNAM))
```

Figure 1.11: The OVRDBF command specifying format ARWORK.

```
FARWORK IP      E       K DISK
```

Figure 1.12: The RPG IV file specification for format ARWORK.

If there is only one entry in the FILE parameter, the FORMAT entry defaults to that entry as shown in Figure 1.13. F-specifications are shown in Figure 1.14.

```
OPNQRYF  FILE  ((ORDERS))  KEYFLD(ORDDT)
```

Figure 1.13: The OPNQRYF specification for single-format file ORDERS.

```
FORDERS     IP  E          K DISK
```

Figure 1.14: The RPG IV file specification for single-format file ORDERS.

The FORMAT parameter is discussed in greater detail in chapters 4 and 5. For now, examples that don't require the FORMAT parameter are used.

The high-level language program needs a key entry only when the query file is to be accessed randomly by key. In RPG, a K in the record address type entry of the F-spec is sufficient for externally described files. If the high-level language program is reading the file sequentially, the key entry is not necessary. If the OPNQRYF command (Figure 1.15) is building a keyed open data path, but the high-level language program is reading by arrival sequence, you will get an error message in the job log that you can ignore.

```
PGM           /* CUS100C - class 4 customer listing */
OVRDBF        FILE(CUSMAS) SHARE(*YES)
OPNQRYF       FILE((CUSMAS)) QRYSLT('class=4')
                KEYFLD(CUSZIP)
CALL          PGM(CUS100R)
CLOF          OPNID(CUSMAS)
DLTOVR        FILE(CUSMAS)
ENDPGM
```

Figure 1.15: The CL program where OPNQRYF command orders the file.

If CUS100R is an RPG IV program, it needs a file definition specification like the one shown in Figure 1.16.

```
FCUSMAS    IP   E          DISK
```

Figure 1.16: The RPG IV F-specification to process the file previously ordered by OPNQRYF.

Mentioning that a program runs under the control of OPNQRYF in your high-level language source code is a good idea. Although this documentation is not a requirement, it could save users a lot of time trying to determine how the job produces the results it does.

SUMMARY

The preceding brief introduction is an overview of what OPNQRYF is and how it works. Don't worry if you don't completely understand everything presented in this chapter. The examples throughout the book reinforce what is presented. By working with OPNQRYF, you will find that everything covered in this chapter quickly becomes second nature.

You should master OPNQRYF if for no other reason than that it doesn't cost you any extra money. It's not like SQL/400, AS/400 Query, or any of the third-party query products. If you have OS/400, you have OPNQRYF.

Keep in mind other things you have learned in the past: how to ride a bicycle; how to drive a car; how to write computer programs. You had some difficulty at first, but you hung in there, and now you wonder why you ever thought those tasks were difficult. Your experience with OPNQRYF probably will be the same way. And just as you mastered those challenges, you will master OPNQRYF.

2

❖ The KEYFLD Parameter

The Key Field (KEYFLD) parameter causes OPNQRYF to create the open data path in an ordered sequence. KEYFLD has two uses: it provides a method for sorting, and it allows random processing by key over a query file. KEYFLD's default value, *NONE, means that any sequence of records is acceptable. The system—in an attempt to choose the best way to sequence the data—then considers such factors as the linkages needed to join files and the number of records in each file. As these factors change, the system may change the way it accesses the data. Therefore, when no key field is specified, the same OPNQRYF command may present the returned data in different sequences at different times.

If only one file name is listed in the FILE parameter, you can use the special value *FILE. This value causes OPNQRYF to sequence the data according to the access path of the file.

VALID VALUES

The KEYFLD parameter may also contain a list of up to 50 field names to be used to build the access path. Each field name may be followed with either *ASCEND or *DESCEND to specify a sort sequence. Because *ASCEND is the default, it may be omitted. Another special value, *ABSVAL, causes a numeric field to be sorted by its absolute value. *ABSVAL is allowed for character fields, but is ignored. The commands shown in Figure 2.1 sort the customer master file (CUSMAS) in ascending order by customer number (CUSNO).

```
      OPNQRYF    FILE((CUSMAS)) KEYFLD((CUSNO))
  or  OPNQRYF    FILE((CUSMAS)) KEYFLD((CUSNO *ASCEND))
```

Figure 2.1: OPNQRYF command to sort file CUSMAS in ascending CUSNO sequence.

EXAMPLE 1

YTDSLS (year-to-date sales) is a field in the SLSHIST (sales history) file. Each record contains data for one customer. Customers are to be sorted in descending order according to the dollar amount sold to them so far this year. In other words, the customer who bought the most appears first in the report. If two or more customers have purchased the same amount of merchandise, they are to be sorted in ascending order according to the credit code (CRCODE) assigned to them. Figure 2.2 shows the OPNQRYF command to accomplish this.

```
  OPNQRYF     FILE((SLSHIST)) +
                KEYFLD((YTDSLS *DESCEND) (CRCODE))
```

Figure 2.2: The OPNQRYF command to sort file SLSHIST in ascending CRCODE sequence within descending YTDSLS sequence.

SLSDIF (Sales difference) is a field that is calculated by subtracting last year's year-to-date sales from the current year's year-to-date sales. In the example shown in Figure 2.3, you will find which customers have had the greatest impact on business. The *ABSVAL keyword is added because a customer who bought $2 million less in merchandise this year has as great an impact as one who bought $2 million dollars more.

```
  OPNQRYF     FILE((SLSHIST)) +
                KEYFLD((SLSDIF *DESCEND *ABSVAL))
```

Figure 2.3: The OPNQRYF command to sequence file SLSHIST on absolute value of SLSDIF.

VARIABLE KEY FIELD NAME

In the preceding examples, the key field names are hard-coded in the KEYFLD parameter. You can add flexibility to your OPNQRYF jobs by placing field names in CL program variables and using those CL variables in the KEYFLD parameter. Be sure that the values in the CL variables are valid field names and that none of them are blank.

EXAMPLE 1

Suppose you have an RPG program, CUSLIS, a typical read-a-record, print-a-line report program that reads the customer master file and prints a listing. You can allow the user to choose a sort sequence at runtime by using a variable key field, as the code in Figure 2.4 shows.

```
/* List customer master file */
/* Parameters                                      */
/*     &SORTSEQ   - sort sequence                  */
/*         A        sort on customer number        */
/*         B        sort on customer name          */
   PGM          PARM(&SORTSEQ)

   DCL          VAR(&SORTSEQ) TYPE(*CHAR) LEN( 1)
   DCL          VAR(&SORTFLD) TYPE(*CHAR) LEN(10)

   CHGVAR       VAR(&SORTFLD) VALUE(CUSNO) /* default */
   IF (&SORTSEQ *EQ 'B') +
        THEN(CHGVAR  VAR(&SORTFLD) VALUE(CUSNAM))

   OVRDBF       FILE(CUSFILE) SHARE(*YES)
   OPNQRYF      FILE((CUSFILE)) KEYFLD((&SORTFLD))
   CALL         PGM(CUSLIS)
   CLOF         OPNID(CUSFILE)
   DLTOVR       FILE(CUSFILE)
   ENDPGM
```

Figure 2.4: An example of using OPNQRYF to let user choose sequence at runtime.

The CL variable &SORTFLD contains the name of the field to be used to order the data. If the user chooses sequence A, the file will be sorted by customer number (CUSNO). If the user chooses sequence B, the sort field will be CUSNAM (customer name) instead. You could easily add other sort sequences.

EXAMPLE 2

Suppose you need more fields for some sort sequences than for other sort sequences. For example, if you need a "C" sequence in the previous example to sort by state—and within that by sales territory, and within that by postal code—you would need three sort fields (even though sort sequences A and B would need only one sort field).

Note that you cannot declare three variables for sorting and leave the last two blank when you don't need them. A CL variable used in the KEYFLD parameter must have a valid field name. Also note that you cannot put three field names into one CL variable. See Figure 2.5.

```
CHGVAR     VAR(&SORTFLD) VALUE('STATE TERRCD ZIPCD')
OPNQRYF    FILE((CUSFILE)) KEYFLD((&SORTFLD))
```

Figure 2.5: Because a CL variable can contain only one sort field, this example won't run.

You can handle this problem in at least three ways. The first two require that you define three key field variables like the code shown in Figure 2.6.

```
DCL    VAR(&SORTFLD1) TYPE(*CHAR) LEN(10)
DCL    VAR(&SORTFLD2) TYPE(*CHAR) LEN(10)
DCL    VAR(&SORTFLD3) TYPE(*CHAR) LEN(10)
```

Figure 2.6: Defining three variables for later use in sorting.

The first method is to fill the unneeded CL variables with any field name. See Figure 2.7.

```
/* All sort fields default to customer number */
    CHGVAR     VAR(&SORTFLD1) VALUE(CUSNO)
    CHGVAR     VAR(&SORTFLD2) VALUE(CUSNO)
    CHGVAR     VAR(&SORTFLD3) VALUE(CUSNO)
/* Change one or more sort fields as required */
    IF COND(&SORTSEQ *EQ 'B') +
        THEN(CHGVAR  VAR(&SORTFLD1) VALUE(CUSNAM))
    IF COND(&SORTSEQ *EQ 'C') THEN(DO)
        CHGVAR  VAR(&SORTFLD1) VALUE(STATE)
        CHGVAR  VAR(&SORTFLD2) VALUE(TERRCD)
        CHGVAR  VAR(&SORTFLD3) VALUE(ZIPCD)
    ENDDO
```

Figure 2.7: Filling unneeded variables with "dummy" values.

For sequence A, the data is keyed on CUSNO, CUSNO, and CUSNO. For sequence B, the key
is CUSNAM, CUSNO, and CUSNO. This method is 99.9 percent guaranteed to cause the system to build an access path, which can hurt performance. If the file is small, however,
you can get away with it.

The second method is to execute multiple OPNQRYF commands. You can hard code or soft
code the key fields as shown in the two examples in Figure 2.8.

```
/* Hard-coded */
    OVRDBF      FILE(CUSFILE) SHARE(*YES)
    IF (&SORTSEQ *EQ 'B') +
        THEN(OPNQRYF  FILE((CUSFILE)) KEYFLD((CUSNAM)))
    ELSE IF (&SORTSEQ *EQ 'C') +
            THEN(OPNQRYF  FILE((CUSFILE)) +
                            KEYFLD((STATE) (TERRCD) (ZIPCD)))
        ELSE OPNQRYF  FILE((CUSFILE)) KEYFLD((CUSNO))

/* Soft-coded */
    IF (&SORTSEQ *EQ 'A') +
        THEN(CHGVAR  VAR(&SORTFLD1) VALUE(CUSNO))
    IF (&SORTSEQ *EQ 'B') +
        THEN(CHGVAR  VAR(&SORTFLD1) VALUE(CUSNAM))
    IF (&SORTSEQ *EQ 'C') THEN(DO)
        CHGVAR  VAR(&SORTFLD1) VALUE(STATE)
        CHGVAR  VAR(&SORTFLD2) VALUE(TERRCD)
        CHGVAR  VAR(&SORTFLD3) VALUE(CUSNO)
    ENDDO
    .
    .
    .
    OVRDBF      FILE(CUSFILE) SHARE(*YES)
    IF (&SORTSEQ *EQ 'A' *OR &SORTSEQ *EQ 'B') +
        THEN(OPNQRYF  FILE((CUSFILE)) +
                        KEYFLD((&SORTFLD1)))
    IF (&SORTSEQ *EQ 'C') +
        THEN(OPNQRYF  FILE((CUSFILE)) +
                        KEYFLD((&SORTFLD1) (&SORTFLD2) (&SORTFLD3)))
    CALL        PGM(CUSLIS)
    CLOF        OPNID(CUSFILE)
    DLTOVR      FILE(CUSFILE)
```

Figure 2.8: Handling different numbers of variables with separate, conditioned OPNQRYF commands.

The third option is to build the OPNQRYF command in a CL variable and execute it by calling QCMDEXC. Figure 2.9 shows the same example using this method.

```
DCL      VAR(&SORTSEQ) TYPE(*CHAR) LEN(1)
DCL      VAR(&OPNQRYF) TYPE(*CHAR) LEN(2000)
DCL      VAR(&KEYFLD)  TYPE(*CHAR) LEN(256)

OVRDBF  FILE(CUSFILE) SHARE(*YES)
IF (&SORTSEQ *EQ 'B') +
   THEN(CHGVAR VAR(&KEYFLD) VALUE('(CUSNAM)'))
ELSE IF (&SORTSEQ *EQ 'C') +
   THEN(CHGVAR VAR(&KEYFLD) VALUE('(STATE) (TERRCD) (ZIPCD)'))
ELSE CHGVAR VAR(&KEYFLD) VALUE('(CUSNO)')

CHGVAR     VAR(&OPNQRYF) +
              VALUE('OPNQRYF FILE(CUSFILE) KEYFLD(' *CAT +
                  &KEYFLD *CAT +
                  ')')
CALL     PGM(QCMDEXC) PARM(&OPNQRYF 2000) /* <== executes OPNQRYF */
CALL     PGM(CUSLIS)
CLOF     OPNID(CUSFILE)
DLTOVR   FILE(CUSFILE)
```

Figure 2.9: Handling different numbers of variables by using QCMDEXC

Depending on the value of &SORTSEQ, variable &KEYFLD will contain one or more keys. Variable &OPNQRYF contains the entire OPNQRYF command as a character string. The call to QCMDEXC executes the OPNQRYF command.

PROCESSING

If the high-level language program reads the file sequentially and the KEYFLD has a value other than *NONE, OPNQRYF will read the query file by key—even if the high-level language program has no key entry. The system will log message CPF4123 to the job log ("Open options ignored for shared open of member &3."). You can ignore this message.

If a program accesses an OPNQRYF file randomly by key, it must define the file as a keyed file. In RPG, for example, you must code a K in the record address type entry of the file specification.

ACCESSING AN OPNQRYF FILE RANDOMLY

OPNQRYF files usually are accessed sequentially but also may be used for random access. You will probably find that most situations calling for random access require a permanent logical file. Operators that set a starting point—such as the RPG op codes SETLL and SETGT—are random-access operations, as are random reads such as CHAIN.

Suppose you want to restrict a user to access customers located only in Mississippi. You could build a logical file to select only Mississippi customers or you could use OPNQRYF. The RPG program would be written as if it had access to the entire customer master file, as shown in Figure 2.10.

```
FCUSFILE   IF  E           K DISK
```

Figure 2.10: RPG IV code to randomly process file CUSTFILE through OPNQRYF.

The code shown in Figure 2.11 causes OPNQRYF to select the desired records at runtime.

```
OVRDBF     FILE(CUSFILE) SHARE(*YES)

OPNQRYF    FILE((CUSFILE)) +
             QRYSLT('STATE = ''MS''') +
             KEYFLD(*FILE)
CALL       PGM(C2X2RG) PARM(&CUS1 &CUS2 &CUS3)
CLOF       OPNID(CUSFILE)
DLTOVR     FILE(CUSFILE)
```

Figure 2.11: OPNQRYF allows random processing of file CUSFILE.

Input operations to customers outside of Mississippi, even though those customers were really on file, would fail.

You cannot randomly access an OPNQRYF file if you are doing unique key or group processing.

SPECIAL SORTING PROBLEMS

One of the classic sorting problems is sorting with an alternative collating sequence (for example, sorting mixed-case character data in alphabetical order). A second common problem is sorting on a date field in MMDDYY or DDMMYY format. OPNQRYF can handle these problems, but not with the parameters covered so far. These sorting problems are discussed in chapter 4.

QUALIFIED FIELD NAMES

A key field may be qualified with the name or number of the file it is taken from or with the special value *MAPFLD, which means that the field is defined in the MAPFLD parameter.

Avoid qualification. In short, qualification is not usually needed and just clutters up the OPNQRYF command. Qualification is rarely, if ever, needed because the only fields eligible for the KEYFLD parameter are those defined in the record format specified by the FORMAT parameter. If there is ambiguity because two or more files have fields of the same name, that ambiguity must be resolved in the MAPFLD parameter.

PERFORMANCE CONSIDERATIONS

OPNQRYF uses existing access paths when possible. If no access path matches the KEYFLD parameter, the system may build one. Depending on which fields are used as key fields, the same OPNQRYF command may have very different runtimes. When the key is over a field (or fields) for which there is an existing access path, runtime is excellent. But, when the key field is one for which there is no existing access path, the job takes longer to run.

To make your jobs run faster, you should consider creating extra logical files over fields used by OPNQRYF jobs, even if those logicals are never used by high-level language programs. For small files (a few thousand records or less), this speed increase is not crucial. Nevertheless, as the size of a file increases, the value of these extra logicals also increases. Another way you can try to speed up an OPNQRYF command that uses the KEYFLD parameter is to specify ALWCPYDTA(*OPTIMIZE), which allows the system to use a sort routine.

RESTRICTIONS

The KEYFLD parameter has some easy-to-work-with restrictions.

❖ You can have a maximum of 50 key fields. This number should be far more than you need for any application.

❖ Each key field must be passed to the high-level language program through the file format named in the FORMAT parameter. This limitation is not a problem because, if your high-level language program doesn't need the field, the program doesn't have to do anything with the field.

❖ The sum of the lengths of all key fields cannot exceed 10,000 bytes. Again, that number should be enough. If not, consider sorting on the left-most portion of the character fields. If customer name is 35 bytes, you might be able to sort on the first 20. (You will have to use the MAPFLD parameter, discussed in chapter 4, to do this.)

SUMMARY

The KEYFLD parameter produces an ordered queried file. Using this parameter, OPNQRYF sorts and also allows a queried file to be accessed randomly. Random processing isn't allowed for unique key or group processing.

Key fields may be built in ascending or descending order. Numeric fields may be ordered by absolute value. Key field entries may be constant or variable. Variables provide a greater degree of flexibility because the actual field name can be specified at runtime.

If an OPNQRYF has a KEYFLD entry other than *NONE and the high-level language program is reading the file sequentially, the high-level language program will read the file, in order of the key fields, even if the program doesn't specify that the file is to be read by key.

OPNQRYF uses existing access paths when possible. Performance of an OPNQRYF query can be improved by creating a logical file with the access path needed by the query. Specifying ALWCPYDTA(*OPTIMIZE) also can speed up a query.

3

❖ Record Selection

The Query Select (QRYSLT) parameter of the OPNQRYF command determines which records the high-level language program is allowed to read. QRYSLT is to the OPNQRYF command what select and omit specifications are to logical files. The default value, *ALL, lets the underlying high-level language program read the entire file. A high-level language program running under OPNQRYF doesn't usually need to select records. It can be written as if it will process the entire file. OPNQRYF can almost always select records more efficiently than a high-level language program can.

THE BASICS

QRYSLT requires a character string that contains a logical expression. A logical expression is one that is either true or false. The expression 'CUSTNO = 20260' is a logical expression, because the customer number field of any given record either has the value 20260 or it does not. OPNQRYF interprets the expression at runtime to select records. Each record is checked against the expression. The records that prove to be true are passed to the high-level language program.

The expression may be a literal, a CL variable, or an expression comprised of literals or variables combined with concatenation operators (*CAT, *TCAT, *BCAT). The expression may contain field names from the queried data files, operators, parentheses, built-in functions, and literals. Uppercase and lowercase letters are treated equally except when they are part of a character literal.

USING LITERALS

Character, hexadecimal, date, time, and time stamp literals must be surrounded by quotation marks or apostrophes. Numeric literals, including duration literals, must not be surrounded by delimiters. For example, CUSNO = 20360 tests a numeric database field for the numeric value 20360. But CUSTYP = "A" or CUSTYP = 'A' tests the character database field CUSTYP for the single character A.

If the QRYSLT expression is a CL literal, it must be surrounded by apostrophes, and any apostrophes within the expression must be doubled. For example, with QRYSLT('CUSTYP = "A"') , the first apostrophe begins the QRYSLT expression. The next two apostrophes, (the ones preceding the letter A) begin the literal A. The two apostrophes that immediately follow the letter A end the literal. Finally, the last apostrophe ends the QRYSLT expression.

This punctuation is not specific to OPNQRYF. It is true of all CL command parameters that accept character strings. If you want to change print text to JOE'S OFFICE, you might code an override like the one shown in Figure 3.1.

```
OVRPRTF FILE(QSYSPRT) PRTTXT('JOE''S OFFICE')
```

Figure 3.1: Proper specification for an embedded apostrophe.

Only one apostrophe would print between the E and S. In the same way, OPNQRYF would interpret QRYSLT('CUSTYP = "A"') as CUSTYP = 'A'. If you prefer, you may use quotation marks instead of doubled apostrophes as shown in Figure 3.2.

```
QRYSLT('CUSTYP = "A"')
```

Figure 3.2: Alternative use of quotation marks to specify an embedded apostrophe.

OPERATORS

The QRYSLT parameter supports relational operators, logical operators, arithmetic operators, and string operators. Many operators have two forms: a symbol, (=, >, &) and a predefined value (*eq, *gt, *and). The predefined values have to be separated from their operands by spaces, but the symbolic forms do not.

RELATIONAL OPERATORS

Relational operators test the relationship between two values. Table 3.1 shows the seven relational operators.

Operator	Description
*EQ or =	equal to
*NE or –,=	not equal to
*LT or <	less than
*GT or >	greater than
*LE or <= or *NG or " ,>	less than or equal to, not greater than
*GE or >= or *NL or " ,<	greater than or equal to, not less than
*CT	contains

TABLE 3.1: Valid Relational Operators.

The following examples illustrate how relational operators are used to select records.

Example 1

The CUSNO (customer number) field of each record is compared to the value 20270 in Figure 3.3. Only records for customer 20270 will be read by the high-level language program.

```
   OPNQRYF     FILE((SLSHIST)) QRYSLT('CUSNO=20270')
or OPNQRYF     FILE((SLSHIST)) QRYSLT('CUSNO = 20270')
or OPNQRYF     FILE((SLSHIST)) QRYSLT('CUSNO *EQ 20270')
```

Figure 3.3: Three valid forms of selecting CUSNO equal to 20270.

Example 2

Any of the examples shown in Figure 3.4 causes records with the value NH to be omitted. Customers who have a state code as any other value, including Nh, nh, and nH, are selected for retrieval.

```
     OPNQRYF    FILE((CUSMAS)) QRYSLT('state *ne "NH"')
or OPNQRYF    FILE((CUSMAS)) QRYSLT('STATE "= "NH"')
or OPNQRYF    FILE((CUSMAS)) QRYSLT('State *NE ''NH''')
```

Figure 3.4: Three valid forms of selecting STATE equal to NH.

The third variation of the OPNQRYF command uses doubled apostrophes around the literal NH. Because the QRYSLT expression is a literal, OS/400 requires that any apostrophes within the expression be doubled just as you would have to do in an RPG literal that contains an apostrophe.

Example 3

The OPNQRYF shown in Figure 3.5 selects customers whose current year-to-date sales exceed the previous year-to-date sales. Note that CURYTD and PRVYTD are not CL variables, but fields in the queried data file named SLSHIST.

```
OPNQRYF    FILE((SLSHIST)) +
             KEYFLD((CURYTD *DESCEND)) +
             QRYSLT('curytd *gt prvytd')
```

Figure 3.5: Example of selection based on comparison of two fields in the data file SLSHIST.

Example 4

The code shown in Figure 3.6 scans the customer name field of each record to see if it contains the five-character substring SMITH. Records for "SMITH INDUSTRIES" and "SILVER-SMITH SUPPLY" will be retrieved. Records for "James A. Whitesmith" and "Robert Smitherman" will be ignored because the scan is case sensitive.

```
    OPNQRYF     FILE((CUSMAS)) QRYSLT('CUSNAM *CT "SMITH"')
 or OPNQRYF     FILE((CUSMAS)) QRYSLT('CUSNAM *CT ''SMITH''')
```

Figure 3.6: Example of selection using the ·CT operator.

Example 5

RPG program OS945 defines file CUSTOMER as an input full-procedural file, and accesses it with the CHAIN operation. If you want records with the value D in field DELCDE (delete code) to be treated as if they don't exist (i.e., as if the CHAIN failed), you can tell OPNQRYF to ignore those records with the code shown in Figure 3.7.

```
OVRDBF FILE(CUSTOMER) SHARE(*YES)
OPNQRYF    FILE((CUSTOMER)) +
           QRYSLT('DELCDE *NE "D"') +
           KEYFLD(*FILE)
CALL   PGM(OS945)
CLOF   OPNID(CUSTOMER)
DLTOVR FILE(CUSTOMER)
```

Figure 3.7: An example of excluding records based on a given value.

LOGICAL OPERATORS

Logical operators negate or combine conditions. You might occasionally hear logical operators referred to as Boolean operators. As listed in Table 3.2, there are four logical operators.

Operator	Description
Table 3.2: Valid Logical Operators.	
*NOT or "	True if condition is false
*AND or &	True if both conditions are true
*OR or ‡	True if either condition is true
*XOR or &&	True if only one of the two conditions is true False if both conditions are true. False if both conditions are false.

The following are a few examples of logical operators at work.

Example 1

The OPNQRYF examples in Figure 3.8 show two methods for omitting records. Both omit records for customer 20270—one uses *NOT and *EQ; the other uses *NE.

```
     OPNQRYF     FILE((SLSHIST)) +
                 QRYSLT('*NOT (CUSNO *EQ 20270)')
  or
     OPNQRYF     FILE((SLSHIST)) QRYSLT('CUSNO *NE 20270')
```

Figure 3.8: Two examples of omitting records based on the value in a data field.

Example 2

In the example shown in Figure 3.9, a customer record must meet two criteria to be selected for retrieval. The customer class field must have the value 4 and the customer's credit limit must be at least $10,000.

```
  DCL        VAR(&QRYSLT) TYPE(*CHAR) LEN(128)
  CHGVAR     VAR(&QRYSLT) +
             VALUE('CUSCLS = 4 & CRDLMT >= 10000')
  OPNQRYF    FILE((CUSMAS)) QRYSLT(&QRYSLT)
```

Figure 3.9: Setting up multiple selection criteria within a variable.

Example 3

As shown in Figure 3.10, a customer record must meet at least one of two criteria to be selected for retrieval. All customers with a class code of 4 will be selected, regardless of credit limit. All customers with a credit limit of at least $10,000 will be selected, regardless of class code.

```
  OPNQRYF     FILE((CUSMAS)) +
              QRYSLT('CUSCLS *EQ 4 *OR CRDLMT *GE 10000')
```

*Figure 3.10: Using *OR within a QRYSLT expression.*

Any single record is read only once (assuming the high-level language program reads the query file sequentially). Class 4 customers with a credit limit of $10,000 or more won't be read (or selected) twice just because they happen to meet each criterion.

Example 4

The example shown in Figure 3.11 is the opposite of the previous query. Class 4 customers are omitted. Customers with credit limits of $10,000 or more also are omitted. All others are selected.

```
   OPNQRYF      FILE((CUSMAS)) +
                QRYSLT('CUSCLS *NE 4 *AND CRDLMT *LT 10000')
or OPNQRYF      FILE((CUSMAS)) +
                QRYSLT('*NOT (CUSCLS *EQ 4 *OR +
                      CRDLMT *GE 10000)')
```

Figure 3.11: Using *NOT to negate an entire QRYSLT expression.

Example 5

ORDCMT is a file that contains comments about a sales order. CMT1, CMT2, and CMT3 are 25-byte comment fields. The expression shown in Figure 3.12 selects records where the word URGENT is found in any of the three comment fields. This presumes that users who enter these comments treat them as three distinct fields (and don't split words across them).

```
OPNQRYF      FILE((ORDCMT)) +
             QRYSLT('CMT1 *ct "URGENT" | +
                   CMT2 *ct "URGENT" | +
                   CMT3 *ct "URGENT"')
```

Figure 3.12: Checking for a value within multiple fields.

Example 6

Although you would like certain suppliers to participate in the just-in-time and electronic-data-interchange programs, some are only participating in one of them. The query shown in Figure 3.13 selects those suppliers.

```
OPNQRYF FILE((SUPPLIER))+
        QRYSLT('EDI="Y" *XOR JIT="Y"')
```

*Figure 3.13: An example of using *XOR in a QRYSLT expression.*

Note that suppliers who participate in both programs aren't selected and, in addition, note that suppliers who participate in neither program also aren't selected.

ARITHMETIC OPERATORS

The arithmetic (pronounced a-rith-MET-ic) operators may only be used with numeric operands. The plus (+) and minus (–) operators may be used in two ways. They are used:

❖ In a unary way to sign a single value.

❖ In a binary way; they carry out arithmetic (pronounced a-RITH-me-tic) between two values.

The other operators are always used between two values. The arithmetic operators are listed in Table 3.3.

Table 3.3: Valid Arithmetic Operators.	
Operator	**Description**
+	Positive, addition
–	Negative, subtraction
*	Multiplication
**	Exponentiation
/	Division
//	Remainder

Because the slash character (/) is used to qualify names, the division and remainder operators must be preceded by at least one blank.

Example 1

CURYTD contains year-to-date sales to a customer in dollars. PYSOLD is the total sales for the entire previous year. The expression shown in Figure 3.14 selects customers who have bought at least $1 million worth of merchandise since January 1 of the previous year.

```
OPNQRYF     FILE((SLSHIST)) +
              QRYSLT('CURYTD + PYSOLD > 1000000')
```

Figure 3.14: Example of performing addition within a QRYSLT expression.

Example 2

SLDATE is a six-digit numeric variable that contains a date in month-day-year format. Dividing SLDATE by 100 gives a remainder equal to the year. The expression shown in Figure 3.15 selects records for the year 1987.

```
OPNQRYF     FILE((SLSHIST)) QRYSLT('SLDATE // 100 = 87')
```

Figure 3.15: Example of a remainder operation in a QRYSLT expression.

STRING OPERATORS

The only string operators supported by OPNQRYF are the concatenation operators. Table 3.4 lists the valid string operators.

Table 3.4: Valid String Operators.	
Concatenation	*CAT or ||
Concatenation, trailing blanks trimmed	*TCAT or <|
Concatenation, trailing blanks trimmed; one blank inserted	*BCAT or >|

Figure 3.16 shows an example of a string operation. ORDCMT is a file that contains comments about a sales order. CMT1, CMT2, and CMT3 are 25-byte comment fields. Presume that the operators who key in these comments treat the three fields as one long comment field. Therefore, the last two characters of CMT1 may be "UR" and the first four characters of CMT2 may be "GENT". This expression will concatenate the three fields into one before it starts the scan. It will find all occurrences—even when the word is divided across two comment fields—of URGENT.

```
OPNQRYF     FILE((ORDCMT)) +
              QRYSLT('CMT1 || CMT2 || CMT3 *CT "URGENT"')
```

Figure 3.16: Example of using concatenation within a QRYSLT expression.

BUILT-IN FUNCTIONS

A function is a process that works with any number of values to yield some other value. Functions are used to define a derived field. Names of AS/400 built-in functions begin with a percent (%) mark.

The values supplied to functions are called *arguments*. Some functions require more arguments than others. The %COUNT FUNCTION, for example, takes no arguments. Many functions, such as %ABSVAL (absolute value), take one argument. Some functions, such as %RANGE, require two arguments. Still others, such as %VALUES, accept a list of values.

The arguments are placed in parentheses immediately following the function name. Arguments are separated from one another by spaces. Table 3.5 lists a few examples of functions. A function may be used wherever a field or constant may be used.

Table 3.5: Examples of Built-in Functions.		
Expression	**Function**	**Arguments**
%COUNT	%COUNT	none
%SIN(ANGLE)	%SIN	ANGLE
%RANGE(BDATE EDATE)	%RANGE	BDATE; EDATE
%VALUES(3 4 7 10 12)	%VALUES	3, 4, 7, 10, 12

COMMONLY USED FUNCTIONS

A few of the functions are discussed in this chapter and others are investigated further in chapter 4. Appendix C contains a complete list of functions. For more detail, see the discussion of OPNQRYF in the *CL Reference* manual.

%SUBSTRING

The substring function, %SST or %SUBSTRING, returns a portion of a character variable. It requires three arguments:

❖ A character variable.

❖ A starting position.

❖ A length.

The expression %SST(CITY 5 7) means the seven-character portion of field CITY, starting with position 5. If CITY has the value SAN FRANCISCO, then %SST(CITY 5 7) is FRANCIS.

Figure 3.17 shows an example where INVNBR (invoice number) is a character field in the invoice archive file. The first two characters of INVNBR are the last two digits of the year the invoice was issued. Calling the program with a parameter value of '90' gives variable

```
PGM          PARM(&INVPFX)

DCL          VAR(&INVPFX) TYPE(*CHAR) LEN(  2)
DCL          VAR(&QRYSLT) TYPE(*CHAR) LEN(512)

CHGVAR       VAR(&QRYSLT) +
               VALUE('%SST(INVNBR 1 2) *EQ "' +
                 *CAT &INVPFX *CAT '"')

OVRDBF       FILE(INVARC) SHARE(*YES)
OPNQRYF      FILE((INVARC)) QRYSLT(&QRYSLT)
CALL         PGM(ARCPGM01)
CLOF         OPNID(INVARC)
DLTOVR       FILE(INVARC)

ENDPGM
```

Figure 3.17: Example of using the %SST built-in function to build a variable for the QRYSLT keyword.

&QRYSLT the value '%SST(INVNBR 1 2) *EQ "90"'. The records where the first two characters of INVNBR are "90" are selected for retrieval.

%XLATE

The %XLATE (translate) function takes two arguments—a character value and a table name—and yields a translated value. The example in Figure 3.18 shows the often-used table QSYSTRNTBL that converts lowercase letters to uppercase and leaves non-alphabetic values unchanged.

```
OPNQRYF    FILE((CUSMAS)) +
             QRYSLT('%XLATE(CUSNAM QSYSTRNTBL) +
               *CT "SMITH"')
```

Figure 3.18: Example of using the XLATE built-in function to translate lowercase to uppercase prior to checking for a value.

If a customer's name is "Smith & Jones, Inc.," the %XLATE function shown in Figure 3.18 returns "SMITH & JONES, INC.," which will then be scanned for the substring "SMITH." This query select expression finds records containing "SMITH," "smith," or "Smith," or even improbable combinations like "sMITH" and "sMiTh."

To find the table objects on your system, use the Work with Object (WRKOBJ) command to look for objects of type *TBL. You may use the Create Table (CRTTBL) command to create your own tables.

%MAX and %MIN

The %MAX (maximum) function returns the largest of a list of values. A similar function, %MIN (minimum), returns the smallest value of the list. Figure 3.19 shows an example of the %MAX function.

```
CHGVAR     VAR(&QRYSLT) +
             VALUE('%MAX(SLSYTD PYSOLD SLS2YR SLS3YR +
               SLS4YR SLS5YR) *NL 1000000')
OPNQRYF    FILE((SLSHIST)) KEYFLD((CUSNO)) +
             QRYSLT(&QRYSLT)
```

Figure 3.19: Example of using the %MAX function to determine a value for the QRYSLT keyword.

SLSYTD is the year-to-date dollar amount of sales to a customer for the current year. PYSOLD is the amount of sales for the prior year. Fields SLS2YR, SLS3YR, SLS4YR and SLS5YR contain the amount sold to the customer two, three, four, and five years ago.

This example looks for all customers that have been sold at least $1 million in merchandise during the current year or during any year over the past five years.

SPECIAL FUNCTIONS FOR EQUAL CONDITIONS

Three built-in functions, %RANGE, %VALUES, and %WLDCRD (wild card), may be used only as the right-hand operands of an equal condition. They also are restricted in that they may be used only in the QRYSLT and GRPSLT (group select) parameters.

To negate these functions, use the logical not operator (*NOT) rather than the not-equal relational operator (*NE). Both the correct and incorrect forms are shown in Figure 3.20.

```
Wrong: QRYSLT('TYPE *NE %VALUES (4 5 7))')
Right: QRYSLT('*NOT(TYPE *EQ %VALUES (4 5 7))')
```

Figure 3.20: Examples of the right and the wrong way to negate an expression using the %VALUES function.

%RANGE

The %RANGE function takes two arguments: a minimum value and a maximum value. The equality is true if the left-hand value is greater than or equal to the first argument and less than or equal to the second one. The equality always proves false if the first argument is greater than the second. Figure 3.21 shows an example.

```
OPNQRYF    FILE((SLSHIST) +
           QRYSLT('SLDATE *EQ %RANGE(910101 910630)')
```

Figure 3.21: An example of the %RANGE built-in function.

SLDATE is a numeric field that contains a date in year-month-day format. This condition proves true for all dates in the first six months of 1991 and is equivalent to 'SLDATE *GE 910101 *AND SLDATE *LE 910630'.

%VALUES

The %VALUES function accepts a list of literal values. The field on the left-hand side of the equality is tested against the list in the values parameter. If the field equals any one of the values in the list, the equality proves true. Figure 3.22 shows an example.

```
OPNQRYF     FILE((SLSHIST) +
              QRYSLT('CUSNO = %VALUES(20260 20270 20315)')
```

Figure 3.22: An example of the %VALUES built-in function.

Records for customers 20260, 20270 and 20315 are selected. The equivalent compound condition is shown in Figure 3.23.

```
'CUSNO *EQ 20260 *OR CUSNO +
  *EQ 20270 *OR CUSNO *EQ 20315'
```

Figure 3.23: The equivalent compound condition for customers 20260, 20270, and 20315.

%WLDCRD

The %WLDCRD (wild card) function allows more flexible scanning of character strings. The left-hand side of the relational condition is the name of the field to be scanned. The function itself has two arguments: the search pattern and the list of wild characters.

The first argument is a character string that consists of search characters and wild characters. Any character in the string that is not a wild character must be matched in the searched field.

The second argument contains the two wild characters. The first is the wild character that matches a single character. The second is the wild character that matches zero or more characters. This argument has a default value of "_*". Figure 3.24 shows an example.

```
OPNQRYF     FILE((ITEMMAS)) +
              QRYSLT('ITMDSC *EQ %WLDCRD("JJ*")
```

Figure 3.24: An example of the %WLDCRD built-in function using.*

OPNQRYF searches the item description field to decide which item master records are to be read by the high-level language program. The first two characters both must be J. The asterisk says that zero or more characters may follow the Js. The only records selected for retrieval are those with a description that begins with the letters "JJ."

The underscore shown in Figure 3.25 represents one character. Therefore, the first character of the description can be anything. The next two characters must be "HT." Because the asterisk represents zero or more characters, there may be zero or more characters between "HT" and "719," and there may be zero or more characters after "719."

```
OPNQRYF      FILE((ITEMMAS)) +
                QRYSLT('ITMDSC *EQ %WLDCRD("_HT*719*")')
```

Figure 3.25: Example of %WLDCRD built-in function using * and _.

As a result, the following item descriptions in the left column in Table 3.6 are acceptable and those on the right are not acceptable.

Table 3.6: Results of QRYSLT Shown in Figure 3.25.		
Selected	**Rejected**	**(Reason)**
JHT719	HT719	(no character preceding HT)
HHT 719	HHL 719	(third character is not T)
HHTT-3A-R-7190A	JHT	(719 not found in string)
HT-9719-4		

Figure 3.26 shows an example of a more complex %WLDCRD expression.

As you can see in the second argument in this example, the wild characters are "_" for a single character and "&" for zero or more characters. Because one of the characters is used to scan for is an asterisk, the asterisk cannot be used as a wild character.

```
OPNQRYF      FILE((ITEMMAS)) +
             QRYSLT('ITMDSC = %WLDCRD("&4_O*&" "_&")')
```

*Figure 3.26: An example of the %WLDCRD built-in function using * and _ and %.*

The first & (ampersand) matches zero or more characters. These characters must be followed by a '4", any character, a zero, an asterisk, and zero or more characters. Therefore, '440*" and 'TR9-4MO*X" both satisfy the condition. Remember that you cannot use a character you are looking for as a wild character.

Performance Considerations for Wildcard Selection

When you use a wildcard test along with one or more other tests, don't put the wildcard first. Figure 3.27 shows the alternative and the preferred notation.

```
Not this: QRYSLT('NAME=%WLDCARD("T*") & CLASS=4')
but this: QRYSLT('CLASS=4 & NAME=%WLDCRD("T*")')
```

Figure 3.27: Alternative and preferred notation for %WLDCRD with other selection tests.

If you put the wildcard last, the system may be able to speed up the data retrieval if there is an access path over the field in the first test (in this case, the CLASS field). The system won't be able to use an access path for a wild card search.

SPECIAL FUNCTIONS FOR NULL-CAPABLE FIELDS

With the introduction of null-capable fields, IBM added two built-in functions, (%NULL and %NONNULL) to work with null values in fields.

%NULL

Although %NULL is a function, it works like a predefined constant with the null value. It is valid only as the right-hand argument in an equal or not-equal relational condition and may be compared to any data type (as shown in Figure 3.28).

The only records selected by OPNQRYF are those where field JOCODE has the null value. Currently, not all AS/400 high-level languages support null values. RPG IV supports

```
OPNQRYF FILE((EMPMAS)) QRYSLT('JOCODE *EQ %NULL')
```

Figure 3.28: An example of the %NULL built-in function.

them and so does RPG III, but in a limited way. When an RPG III program (compiled with the ALWNULL(*YES) option) reads a field with a null value, it substitutes the default value for the field. While RPG III can read null values, it cannot distinguish them from default values.

Suppose file EMPMAS has a null-capable field, DACODE, with a default value of 'NOTHING' as shown in the DDS code in Figure 3.29.

```
A       DACODE      10      ALWNULL
A                           DFT('NOTHING')
```

Figure 3.29: DDS for a null-capable field with default value of 'NOTHING'.

Six records are in the file, with the following values for DACODE:

- ❖ Null.
- ❖ Null.
- ❖ GOOD.
- ❖ OK.
- ❖ Blank.
- ❖ NOTHING.

Figure 3.30 shows the RPG III code that compares field DACODE to the literal 'NOTHING' and prints the records where the comparison is successful.

```
C       DACODE      IFEQ 'NOTHING'
C                   EXCPTDTL
C                   ENDIF
```

Figure 3.30: RPG III code to select records for printing where DACODE is equal to 'NOTHING'.

The result is that the program prints records 1, 2, and 6 because the default value, NOTHING, is substituted into the records with the null value. But the OPNQRYF command (Figure 3.31) is used to select records where DACODE has the value 'NOTHING' and selects only record 6.

```
OPNQRYF     FILE((EMPMAS)) QRYSLT('DACODE=''NOTHING''')
```

Figure 3.31: Opnqryf selection of 'NOTHING' does not get null values.

If you want to include or omit records with the null value in a field, you must use RPG IV or let OPNQRYF or SQL do the record selection. RPG III cannot accurately interpret null values and other high-level languages cannot process null values at all.

%NONNULL

The %NONNULL function requires a list of arguments. If all the arguments are null, %NON-NULL returns the null value. Otherwise, it returns the first non-null value in the list. The OPNQRYF command in Figure 3.32 selects only those records in which the three type fields are all null.

```
OPNQRYF FILE((CUSMAST))+
        QRYSLT('%NONNULL(TYPE1 TYPE2 TYPE3) *EQ %NULL')
```

Figure 3.32: An example of the %NONNULL function.

The example shown in Figure 3.33 causes all customers with a SALESREP number less than 400 to be selected. If SALESREP is null, it is treated as if it has a value of zero.

```
OPNQRYF FILE((CUSMAST))+
        QRYSLT('%NONNULL(SLSREP 0)<400')
```

Figure 3.33: An example using the %NONNULL function.

SYNTAX CONSIDERATIONS

Most functions can be nested one within another. They are resolved in innermost to outermost order. The first argument of the translate function shown in Figure 3.34 is a sub-

```
OPNQRYF       FILE((CLIENTS)) KEYFLD((CLASS *DESCEND)) +
              QRYSLT('%XLATE(%SST(FNAME 1 2) +
                 QSYSTRNTBL) *EQ "JO"')
```

Figure 3.34: An example of a nested %XLATE function.

string function. The substring must be extracted before the translation can take place. The test for equality occurs last.

Some values of FNAME that would make this equality true are listed in Table 3.7.

Table 3.7: Results of QRYSLT in Figure 3.35.			
Selected FNAME Values			
Joel	JOE	Josephus	jo
John	Jose	jOCK	joe

PRIORITY OF OPERATORS

When two or more operators appear in an expression, OPNQRYF doesn't treat them equally, but resolves some operations before others. Table 3.8 lists the priority of evaluation.

Operators of the same priority are evaluated in left-to-right order. The order of evaluation may be changed by grouping relationships with parentheses.

In Figure 3.35, the system first evaluates 'CUSNO *EQ 20260' and derives an answer of true or false. Next, it evaluates 'CUSCL *NE "A"' and derives another true or false. Finally, it evaluates the *AND, which proves true if both relational conditions are true.

If CUSNO has the value 20270 and CUSCL the value "B", the system goes through the steps listed in Table 3.9 to determine whether the expression is true or false.

Figure 3.36 shows another expression with multiple operations.

The addition is carried out first. The three relational conditions are then evaluated. Next the *AND is resolved. Finally, the *OR is evaluated. If the values of YTDSLS, PYSLS and

Table 3.8: Priority of Evaluation in Expressions.	
Priority	**Operators**
1	+ (positive), – (negative), *NOT, "
2	**
3	*, /, //
4	+ (addition), – (subtraction)
5	*CAT, ‖, *TCAT, <‖, *BCAT, >‖
6	*EQ, *NE, *GT, *LT, *GE, *LE, *NG, *NL, =, " = ,>, <. >=, <=," >, " <, *ct
7	*AND, &
8	*OR, ‖, *XOR, &&

```
QRYSLT('CUSNO *EQ 20260 *AND CUSCL *NE "A"')
```

Figure 3.35: An example of an expression with multiple operations.

Table 3.9: Results of Qryslt Shown in Figure 3.36.		
CUSNO *EQ 20260	***AND**	**CUSCL *NE "A"**
20270 *EQ 20260	*AND	"B" *NE "A"
False	*AND	"B" *NE "A"
False	*AND	True
	False	

```
QRYSLT('YTDSLS *GE 10000 *OR YTDSLS + PYSLS *GT 25000 +
       *AND CLASS *EQ "B"')
```

Figure 3.36: An example of a more complex multiple-operation expression.

CLASS are 900, 24500, and "B" respectively, the system carries out the logic listed in Table 3.10.

Table 3.10: Steps to Determine Results of QRYSLT in Figure 3.38.						
YTDSLS *GE 10000	*OR	YTDSLS + PYSLS	*GT	25000	*AND	CLASS * EQ "B"
900 *GE 10000	*OR	900 + 24500	*GT	25000	*AND	"B" *EQ "B"
900 *GE 10000	*OR	25400	*GT	25000	*AND	"B" *EQ "B"
False	*OR	25400	*GT	25000	*AND	"B" *EQ "B"
False	*OR		True		*AND	"B" *EQ "B"
False	*OR		True		*AND	True
False	*OR				True	
	True					

As shown in Figure 3.37, the addition still has the highest priority, followed by the relational conditions. The parentheses have been added to force the system to resolve the *OR before the *AND.

```
QRYSLT('YTDSLS *GE 10000 *OR YTDSLS +
       PYSLS *GT 25000) *AND CLASS *EQ "B"')
```

Figure 3.37: An example of a multiple-operation expression that uses parenthesis.

Presuming the same values of YTDSLS, PYSLS, and CLASS as Example 2, the system carries out the logic listed in Table 3.11.

USING CL VARIABLES

You can make record selection more flexible by using CL variables, instead of coded literals, in the QRYSLT parameter. Suppose you have an RPG program that prints a summary

Table 3.11: Steps to Determine Results of Q$_{RYSLT}$ in Figure 3.38.						
YTDSLS *GE 10000	*OR	YTDSLS + PYSLS	*GT	25000	*AND	CLASS *EQ "B"
900 *GE 10000	*OR	900 + 24500	*GT	25000	*AND	"B" *EQ "B"
900 *GE 10000	*OR	25400	*GT	25000	*AND	"B" *EQ "B"
False	*OR	25400	*GT	25000	*AND	"B" *EQ "B"
False	*OR		True		*AND	"B" *EQ "B"
False	*OR		True		*AND	True
False	*OR		True		*AND	True
			True		*AND	True
			True			

of sales orders. If you code QRYSLT('CUSNO = 20260'), the program always runs for customer 20260. You easily can change the QRYSLT parameter to use the value of a CL variable, which a user can change before running the program.

The part of the operating system that evaluates the expression in the QRYSLT parameter knows nothing about CL variables. If the values of CL variables are to be included in the selection, the values themselves, not the CL variables, must be included in the string. Therefore, you cannot code QRYSLT('CUSNO = &CUSTOMER'). When programmers begin to work with OPNQRYF, they frequently make this mistake.

Instead, you must put the value of &CUSTOMER into the QRYSLT string. If the value of &CUSTOMER is 12345, the QRYSLT parameter must have the value 'CUSNO = 12345'. Let's examine the example as shown in Figure 3.38.

Presume that an end user fills in parameter &CUSTOMER with the value 20260. The QRYSLT parameter will resolve to 'CUSNO = 20260', and the only records program HLLPGM will read are those for that single customer. Because the customer number is not hard coded in the QRYSLT parameter, this program can be run for any customer in the database.

Numeric CL variables cannot be used with concatenation operators. When you are including a numeric CL variable in the QRYSLT expression, you must copy the numeric vari-

```
     PGM          PARM(&CUSTOMER)

     DCL          VAR(&CUSTOMER ) TYPE(*DEC)  LEN(5 0)
     DCL          VAR(&CUST_ALPHA) TYPE(*CHAR) LEN(5 )

/* Change the numeric variable to character for concatenation */
     CHGVAR       VAR(&CUST_ALPHA) VALUE(&CUSTOMER)
     OVRDBF       FILE(CUSSUM) SHARE(*YES)
     OPNQRYF      FILE((CUSSUM)) +
                    QRYSLT('CUSNO = ' *CAT &CUST_ALPHA)
     CALL         PGM(HLLPGM)
     CLOF         OPNID(CUSSUM)
     DLTOVR       FILE(CUSSUM)

     ENDPGM
```

Figure 3.38: An example of using variables with OPNQRYF to allow end-user selection.

able into a character variable, which can be concatenated. In this case, &CUSTOMER was copied into &CUST_ALPHA, which was used for the concatenation.

Be sure to concatenate quotation marks or apostrophes around values compared to character, hexadecimal, date, time and time stamp fields. CL requires that an apostrophe embedded in a string be doubled to distinguish it from the apostrophe that ends the string. In other words, if you use apostrophes, be sure to double them. For example, if you want to select records based on character database field CUSCAT (customer category), the previous example will look like the code shown in Figures 3.39 or 3.40.

```
     PGM          PARM(&CATEGORY)

     DCL          VAR(&CATEGORY) TYPE(*CHAR) LEN(3)

     OVRDBF       FILE(CUSSUM) SHARE(*YES)
     OPNQRYF      FILE((CUSSUM)) +
                    QRYSLT('CUSCAT = "' *CAT &CATEGORY *CAT '"')
```

Figure 3.39: An example of using variables with quotation marks.

If you call this program with the parameter value JT1, OPNQRYF interprets the request as CUSCAT = "JT1" or CUSCAT = 'JT1'.

```
OPNQRYF     FILE((CUSSUM)) +
              QRYSLT('CUSCAT = ''' *CAT &CATEGORY *CAT '''')
```

Figure 3.40: An example of using variables with embedded apostrophes.

The quotes or apostrophes are required because CUSCAT, a database field, is a character field. The data type of CL variable &CATEGORY has nothing to do with whether or not quotes/apostrophes must be used.

If it is difficult for you to get the right number of quotes or apostrophes in the right places, here is another method you can try. First, declare a CL variable called &QUOTE and give it the value of a quotation mark or a single apostrophe (as in Figures 3.41 or 3.42).

```
DCL    VAR(&QUOTE) TYPE(*CHAR) LEN(1) VALUE('"')
```

Figure 3.41: Step one in setting up variables with the correct quotes for punctuation.

```
DCL    VAR(&QUOTE) TYPE(*CHAR) LEN(1) VALUE('"')
```

Figure 3.42: An alternative for setting up variables with the correct quotes for punctuation.

Then you can concatenate this variable to both sides of the character CL variable as shown in Figure 3.43.

```
OPNQRYF     FILE((CUSSUM)) +
              QRYSLT('CUSCAT = ' *CAT &QUOTE *CAT +
                     &CATEGORY *CAT &QUOTE)
```

Figure 3.43: Step two in setting up variables with the correct quotes for punctuation.

If &CATEGORY has the value JT1, you will get CUSCAT = "JT1" or CUSCAT = 'JT1'.

USING A QRYSLT VARIABLE

In most of the preceding examples, the expression is coded in the QRYSLT parameter. In a few of the examples, however, a CL variable is declared and is used in the QRYSLT parameter. The two sections of code shown in Figure 3.44 are functionally equivalent.

```
/* 1 */
OPNQRYF        FILE((CUSMAS)) QRYSLT('CUSNO=' *CAT &CUSNO)

/* 2 */
DCL            VAR(&QRYSLT) TYPE(*CHAR) LEN(256)
               VAR(&QRYSLT) VALUE('CUSNO=' *CAT &CUSNO)
OPNQRYF        FILE((CUSMAS)) QRYSLT(&QRYSLT)
```

Figure 3.44: Two methods for defining a QRYSLT expression.

The second approach shown in Figure 3.44 does have some advantages. The main advantage is that you can look at the expression by displaying the variable in debug or looking at a CL program dump. This advantage comes in handy when debugging or when an OPNQRYF command that has been working unexpectedly cancels. Putting QRYSLT expressions in variables is a good practice. For the simple expressions, it doesn't matter; but for complex expressions, it is almost a necessity.

Example 1

There are multiple methods to define the expressions you will use in OPNQRYF. The code shown in Figure 3.45 defines the variables to be used.

```
PGM            PARM(&CUST &FROMITM &TOITM &TERMCODE)

DCL            VAR(&CUST)     TYPE(*DEC)  LEN(5 0)
DCL            VAR(&CUSTA)    TYPE(*CHAR) LEN(5)
DCL            VAR(&FROMITM)  TYPE(*CHAR) LEN(7)
DCL            VAR(&TOITM)    TYPE(*CHAR) LEN(7)
DCL            VAR(&TERMCODE) TYPE(*CHAR) LEN(1)

CHGVAR         VAR(&CUSTA) VALUE(&CUST) +
     /* convert to alpha for concatenation */
```

Figure 3.45: Base code that defines variables.

The two variations of code shown in Figure 3.46 are functionally equivalent.

In either case, the QRYSLT resolves to a value such as is shown in Figure 3.47.

The second approach lets you build the QRYSLT parameter one piece at a time, which usually results in fewer errors. The second version is probably more easily modified because

```
/* 1 */
OPNQRYF       FILE((SLSHIST)) +
                QRYSLT('CUSNO=' *CAT &CUSTA *BCAT '*AND +
                   ITEMNR= %RANGE("' *CAT &FROMITM +
                   *CAT '" "' *CAT &TOITEM *CAT '") +
                   *AND TERMS="' *CAT &TERMCODE *CAT '"')
/* 2 */
DCL           VAR(&QRYSLT)  TYPE(*CHAR)  LEN(256)
CHGVAR        VAR(&QRYSLT) +
                VALUE('CUSNO=' *CAT &CUSTA)
CHGVAR        VAR(&QRYSLT) +
                VALUE(&QRYSLT *BCAT '*AND ITEMNR= %RANGE("' +
                   *CAT &FROMITM *CAT '" "' *CAT &TOITEM +
                   *CAT '")')
CHGVAR        VAR(&QRYSLT) +
                VALUE(&QRYSLT *BCAT '*AND TERMS="' *CAT +
                   &TERMCODE *CAT '"')         ...
OPNQRYF       FILE((SLSHIST)) QRYSLT(&QRYSLT)
```

Figure 3.46: Two methods for defining the QRYSLT expression.

```
CUSNO=11830 *AND ITEMNR=%RANGE("0025369" "0538390") *AND TERMS="K".
```

Figure 3.47: The value of the QRYSLT expression shown in Figure 3.46.

there are fewer parentheses, apostrophes, and quotation marks in each portion of code. In the event the system finds errors in the OPNQRYF command, you can request a CL program dump and look at variable &QRYSLT to view the resolved string.

Example 2

Using a variable query-select parameter also permits you to use or not to use a field for selection. In the previous example, the user specifies a customer number, a range of item numbers, and a terms code. The program can show all records for customer 20270, item numbers A402 through A599, and terms code L, but it can't show all records for customer 20270. With just a little modification, as shown in Figure 3.48, you can let the operator choose only a customer number, only a range of items, only a single terms code, or any combination of the three.

Now users can get more selective reports because there no longer is a requirement to specify all parameter values. Depending on the parameter values, the &QRYSLT variable can take many forms (including the ones shown in Figure 3.49).

```
    PGM         PARM(&CUST &FROMITM &TOITM &TERMCODE)
    DCL         VAR(&CUST)    TYPE(*DEC)  LEN(  5 0)
    DCL         VAR(&CUSTA)   TYPE(*CHAR) LEN(  5 )
    DCL         VAR(&FROMITM) TYPE(*CHAR) LEN(  7 )
    DCL         VAR(&TOITM)   TYPE(*CHAR) LEN(  7 )
    DCL         VAR(&TERMCODE) TYPE(*CHAR) LEN(  1 )
    DCL         VAR(&QRYSLT)  TYPE(*CHAR) LEN(512 )
    DCL         VAR(&CONJ)    TYPE(*CHAR) LEN(  4 )
/* If operator entered a customer number, test field CUSNO */
    IF (&CUST *NE 0) THEN(DO)
        CHGVAR  VAR(&CUSTA)  VALUE(&CUST)
        CHGVAR  VAR(&QRYSLT) VALUE('CUSNO=' *CAT &CUSTA)
        CHGVAR  VAR(&CONJ)   VALUE(*AND)
    ENDDO
/* If operator entered 1 or 2 item numbers, test ITEMNR */
/* If 1 item, check for that item                       */
/* If 2 items, check for the range between the two      */
    IF (&FROMITM *NE ' ') THEN(DO)
        CHGVAR  VAR(&QRYSLT) +
                VALUE(&QRYSLT *BCAT &CONJ *BCAT 'ITEMNR=')
        IF (&TOITM *EQ ' ') THEN(DO) /* single item */
            CHGVAR  VAR(&QRYSLT) +
                VALUE(&QRYSLT *BCAT '"' *CAT +
                    &FROMITM *CAT '"')
        ENDDO
        ELSE DO /* test for range of items */
            CHGVAR  VAR(&QRYSLT) +
                VALUE(&QRYSLT *BCAT '%RANGE("' *CAT +
                    &FROMITM *CAT '" "' *CAT &TOITEM +
                    *CAT '")')
        ENDDO
        CHGVAR  VAR(&CONJ) VALUE(*AND)
    ENDDO
/* If operator entered a terms code, test field TERMS */
    IF (&TERMCODE *NE ' ') THEN(DO)
        CHGVAR  VAR(&QRYSLT) +
            VALUE(&QRYSLT *BCAT &CONJ *BCAT +
                'TERMS="' *CAT &TERMCODE *CAT '"')
        CHGVAR  VAR(&CONJ) VALUE(*AND)
    ENDDO
* If operator did not fill in any parm fields, get all records */
    IF (&QRYSLT *EQ ' ') +
        THEN(CHGVAR  VAR(&QRYSLT) VALUE(*ALL))

    OVRDBF      FILE(SLSHIST) SHARE(*YES)
    OPNQRYF     FILE((SLSHIST)) QRYSLT(&QRYSLT)
    CALL        PGM(HISTPGM)
    CLOF        OPNID(SLSHIST)
    DLTOVR      FILE(SLSHIST)

    ENDPGM
```

Figure 3.48: An example of building an QRYSLT expression to allow users complex selections.

```
'CUSNO=20260'
'ITEMNR= "AD922-1"'
'ITEMNR= %RANGE("AD922-1" "AE433-5")'
'TERMS= "A"'
'ITEMNR= "AD922-1" *AND TERMS= "Z"'
'CUSNO=20260 *AND ITEMNR= %RANGE("GT700-1" "GT700-9")'
'CUSNO=20315 *AND TERMS= "D"'
'CUSNO=20260 *AND ITEMNR= %RANGE("TR800  " "TR99999")
*AND TERMS= "K"'
```

Figure 3.49: Potential values of the QRYSLT expression from the program shown in Figure 3.48.

Note the role of the variable &CONJ (conjunction). This variable allows you to separate multiple conditions, with the *AND operator, and yet not start the query selection expression with the word *AND if a parameter is zero or blank.

If the user doesn't fill in values for any of the parameters, the variable &QRYSLT will be blank after the three IF tests. In this example, this condition is checked and the value *ALL is given to the &QRYSLT variable to keep the OPNQRYF from ending abnormally. The user gets a report of the full contents of the file if the user doesn't limit the file with one or more parameter values. You could continue to add parameters that would give the end users even more flexibility, but the technique would remain the same.

Example 3

Using a variable for the QRYSLT expression also works well with lists. Suppose you have an RPG program that currently reads a file and prints a late-orders report. Let's say that the plant manager "suggests" that the report would be more helpful if the manager could enter a list of anywhere from one to a dozen customer numbers, and only orders for those customers would appear on the report. Also, the manager still wants to be able to run the report for all customers.

You don't need to look for a new employer; this request is easily handled by OPNQRYF. Creating a command that lets the plant manager enter one to 12 customer numbers or the special value *ALL is easy. First, see the command shown in Figure 3.50.

```
CMD       PROMPT('Late orders report')
PARM      KWD(CUST) TYPE(*CHAR) LEN(5) MIN(0) MAX(12)+
          SPCVAL(*ALL) DFT(*ALL)
```

Figure 3.50: The command for a late-orders report.

The CL program accepts the list in a parameter and runs the OPNQRYF command as shown in Figure 3.51.

```
/* This program prints a report for one to twelve customers, +
   or for all customers.                                    */
/* Parameters   +
   &CUSTLIST - a list variable passed from a command        +
               it may contain the special value *ALL, or    +
               a list of 1 to 12 customer numbers           */
         PGM        PARM(&CUSTLIST)
         DCL        VAR(&CUSTLIST) TYPE(*CHAR) LEN(  62  )
         DCL        VAR(&OCCURA)   TYPE(*CHAR) LEN(   2  )
         DCL        VAR(&OCCUR)    TYPE(*DEC)  LEN(   3 0)
         DCL        VAR(&SELECT)   TYPE(*CHAR) LEN( 512  )
         DCL        VAR(&NDX)      TYPE(*DEC)  LEN(   2 0)
         DCL        VAR(&LOOP_CTR) TYPE(*DEC)  LEN(   2 0)
         DCL        VAR(&CUSTNBR)  TYPE(*CHAR) LEN(   5  )
/* Check to see if all customers are desired */
         IF (%SST(&CUSTLIST 1 4) *EQ '*ALL') THEN(DO)
            CHGVAR  VAR(&SELECT) VALUE('*ALL')
            GOTO    RUN_QRY
         ENDDO
/* Process the list of customer numbers */
         CHGVAR     VAR(&OCCURA)    VALUE(%SST(&CUSTLIST 1 2))
         CHGVAR     VAR(&OCCUR)     VALUE(%BIN(&OCCURA))
         CHGVAR     VAR(&NDX)       VALUE(3)
         CHGVAR     VAR(&LOOP_CTR)  VALUE(1)
         CHGVAR     VAR(&SELECT)    VALUE('CUSNBR=%VALUES(')
LOOP_BGN:
         IF (&LOOP_CTR *GT &OCCUR) +
            THEN(GOTO LOOP_END)
         CHGVAR     VAR(&CUSTNBR)   VALUE(%SST(&CUSTLIST &NDX 5)
         CHGVAR     VAR(&SELECT)    VALUE(&SELECT *BCAT &CUSTNBR)
         CHGVAR     VAR(&LOOP_CTR) VALUE(&LOOP_CTR + 1)
         CHGVAR     VAR(&NDX)       VALUE(&NDX + 5)
         GOTO       LOOP_BGN
LOOP_END:
         CHGVAR     &SELECT VALUE(&SELECT *TCAT ')')
RUN_QRY:
         IF (&SELECT *NE '*ALL') THEN(DO)
            OVRDBF   FILE((CUMSTR) SHARE(*YES)
            OPNQRYF  FILE((CUMSTR)) QRYSLT(&SELECT) KEYFLD(*FILE)
         ENDDO
         CALL       PGM(CUSLST)
         IF (&SELECT *NE '*ALL') THEN(DO)
            CLOF    CUMSTR
            DLTOVR  CUMSTR
         ENDDO
         ENDPGM
```

Figure 3.51: A program to feed a list of values to an OPNQRYF command.

MODIFYING A STATIC QRYSLT VARIABLE

If you like to avoid the concatenation operators, you can easily modify a predefined QRYSLT variable. Suppose you are going to have OPNQRYF select a certain customer. You could go ahead and code the QRYSLT variable with a dummy customer number as shown in Figure 3.52.

```
DCL     VAR (%QRYSLT) TYPE(*CHAR) LEN(80) +
          VALUE('CUSNO=11111')
DCL     VAR(%CUSNO)  TYPE(*DEC)   LEN(5 0)
```

Figure 3.52: An example of a dummy customer number in the QRYSLT variable prior to user selection.

Now you can have the program replace the dummy customer number with the one you really want (Figure 3.53).

```
CHGVAR     VAR(%SST(&QRYSLT 7 5)) VALUE(&CUSNO)
OPNQRYF    FILE((CUSMAS)) QRYSLT(&QRYSLT)
```

Figure 3.53: Replacing dummy value with user's selection.

Besides eliminating concatenation operators, this method also eliminates the need for character variables for numeric values. If you used concatenation in this example, you would have to declare another variable in order to carry out the concatenation as shown in Figure 3.54. When modifying a predefined QRYSLT variable, the extra character variable is not needed. This approach has one drawback. If you modify the QRYSLT expression, you might also have to modify the CHGVAR commands.

```
DCL       VAR(&CUSNOCHAR) TYPE(*CHAR) LEN(5)


CHGVAR    VAR(&CUSNOCHAR) VALUE(&CUSNO)
CHGVAR    VAR(&QRYSLT) +
            VALUE('CUSNO=' *CAT &CUSNOCHAR)
```

Figure 3.54: An alternative method to Figures 3.45 and 3.46 using concatenation.

When you substitute character values, be sure to count doubled apostrophes as one character. Figure 3.55 shows the two versions of the declaration for &QRYSLT.

```
/* 1. Using apostrophes */
   DCL     VAR(&QRYSLT) TYPE(*CHAR) LEN(80) VALUE('CUSTT=''XX''')
/* 2. Using quotation marks */
   DCL     VAR(&QRYSLT) TYPE(*CHAR) LEN(80) VALUE('CUSTT="XX"')
```

Figure 3.55: Using doubled apostrophes and quotation marks to declare a variable.

The first version has the value CUSTT='XX' (which is 11 characters). The second version has the value CUSTT="XX" (which is also 11 characters long). If you decide to put the value of &STATE (a two-character variable) into the &QRYSLT string, you have to start where the XS are (in position 9) whether you use apostrophes or quotation marks as string delimiters. See Figure 3.56 for an example.

```
CHGVAR     VAR(%SST(&QRYSLT 9 2)) VALUE(&STATE)
OPNQRYF    FILE((CUSMAS)) QRYSLT(&QRYSLT) +
             KEYFLD((CUSCIT) (CUSNAM)
```

Figure 3.56: Correct placement of the %QRYSLT variable.

RECORD SELECTION IN HLL PROGRAMS

The query processor can usually select records more efficiently than a high-level language program can. As you have seen, some high-level languages cannot accurately select or omit records with null-capable fields. When possible, you should shift the burden of record selection to OPNQRYF and write the high-level language program as if it will process the entire file.

It takes a lot of time to convert high-level language to programs that run under OPNQRYF. However, you can still use OPNQRYF to speed up existing programs without changing high-level language programs. Suppose you have an RPG program that selects customers of type OE. You will have a section of code that looks like Figure 3.57.

If you don't have time to change this program, you can leave it as it is, but run it under OPNQRYF as shown in Figure 3.58.

```
C                 CUSTYP    IFEQ 'OE'
... calcs to process the customer go here
C                           ENDIF
```

Figure 3.57: RPG code to select customers with type "OE".

```
OPNQRYF      ... +
             QRYSLT('CUSTYP=''OE''')
```

Figure 3.58: OPNQRYF QRYSLT to select customers with type "OE" for better performance.

Your RPG program will be doing redundant record selection, but that will be acceptable until you can get around to removing the record selection logic. In the meantime, your job is running faster overall and that is your current concern.

PERFORMANCE CONSIDERATIONS

OPNQRYF sometimes will use an existing access path to help it select records. You may be able to speed up processing by creating another logical file keyed on a field used in a QRYSLT parameter.

More often than not, however, the query optimizer ignores access paths and selects records dynamically. OPNQRYF scans the entire file similar to what the system does when the DYNSLT keyword is used in a logical file.

Sometimes you can circumvent dynamic record selection and improve performance of a batch job by using the value *MINWAIT in the OPTIMIZE parameter of the OPNQRYF command as shown in Figure 3.59.

```
OPNQRYF      FILE((CUSSUM)) +
             QRYSLT('CUSNO = ' *CAT &CUST_ALPHA) +
             OPTIMIZE(*MINWAIT)
```

*Figure 3.59: Using OPTIMIZE(*MINWAIT) to improve the performance of OPNQRYF.*

The best way to see what OPTIMIZE(*MINWAIT) will do in each case is try it out. In many cases, you will see an improvement.

When the system is unable to use an access path, it has no other choice than to read the entire file (including deleted records) to look for records that match the QRYSLT criteria. Use the reorganize physical file member (RGZPFM) command to keep your files free of deleted records.

SUMMARY

The QRYSLT parameter is used to restrict the records to which a high-level language program has access. High-level language programs don't usually have to select records when they run under OPNQRYF. Record selection criteria are specified in a free-format string, which contains a logical expression of fields, literals and operators. For specialized queries, the string may be a hard-coded literal. For flexible queries, the QRYSLT expression should be a CL variable or a combination of concatenated CL variables and string literals.

Character literals must be delimited by quotation marks or apostrophes. Numeric literals have no delimiters.

OPNQRYF supports relational, logical, arithmetic, and string operators. Operators are evaluated in left-to-right order, according to a predefined hierarchy.

Much of the power of OPNQRYF results from built-in functions (predefined routines that use data values to build other data values). Built-in function names begin with a percent sign. OPNQRYF uses dynamic record selection. It will use existing access paths to help it select records when possible. You sometimes can improve performance of an OPNQRYF command by creating an access path it can use. Proper use of the OPTIMIZE parameter is also helpful.

4

❖ Assigning Values to Fields

In its simplest form, OPNQRYF takes values from one database file and passes them to a high-level language program in the same record format. Consider the command shown in Figure 4.1. Because the format parameter has not been coded, it defaults to FORMAT(*FILE), which means the data will be sent to the high-level language program in the format of CUSMAS (the only specified file). Even if a format file were specified, there would be no gain in function because the format file couldn't have any fields not found in CUSMAS.

```
OPNQRYF    FILE((CUSMAS)) KEYFLD((CRDLMT *DESCEND))
```

Figure 4.1: An example of a simple OPNQRYF command.

SYNTAX

Without the Mapped Field (MAPFLD) parameter, Figure 4.1 shows about all OPNQRYF can do. And without a doubt, OPNQRYF would still be a very powerful tool with just these capabilities. But MAPFLD increases the usefulness of OPNQRYF in several ways.

1. It allows the values in a database file to be overridden by values from other fields, from literals, or from expressions.
2. It allows the high-level language program to read fields not defined in any of the files listed in the file parameter.
3. In cases where a field of the same name exists in more than one file, it allows a means of qualifying which file's value is to be used.

THE FORMAT PARAMETER

Before continuing the discussion of mapped fields, the FORMAT parameter should be examined. This parameter tells OPNQRYF how the data should look when the high-level language program reads it. What fields does the high-level language program expect? How big are they? What are their types?

If the FILE parameter has only one entry, the FORMAT parameter is optional. In this case, OPNQRYF will use the record layout of the FILE parameter entry. If the FILE parameter has more than one entry, or if additional fields are to be calculated and passed to the high-level language program, you must code the FORMAT parameter. The data is sent to the high-level language program according to the record layout of the file named here. The file may be qualified and, if it contains more than one record format, the desired record name must be added. Look at the OPNQRYF example shown in Figure 4.2 and the corresponding RPG program fragment shown in Figure 4.3.

```
OVRDBF     FILE(ORDSKED) TOFILE(CUSORD) SHARE(*YES)
OPNQRYF    FILE((CUSORD)) FORMAT(ORDSKED) ... etc.
CALL       PGM(XT90)
CLOF       OPNID(CUSORD)
DLTOVR     FILE(ORDSKED)
... etc.
```

Figure 4.2: Using the FORMAT parameter.

```
FORDSKED   IF   E              K DISK
FORDRPT1   O    E                PRINTER OFLIND(*IN88)
```

Figure 4.3: A fragment of RPG IV program XT90.

The data is stored in file CUSORD, but OPNQRYF reformats the data according to the record layout of file ORDSKED. The high-level language program will read the data from CUSORD, but in the format of ORDSKED. The first (and, in this case, the only) file named in the FILE parameter is the one that must have the shared attribute. For this reason, file ORDSKED is overridden to CUSORD. The format file may be a production file, but most often it is a dummy file that contains no data. When you create a dummy file, specify MBR(*NONE) to free the resources needed for a database file member.

THE MAPFLD PARAMETER

Assigning values to fields is done in the MAPFLD parameter. Each mapped field consists of three parts: a field name, an expression, and a definition. The field name is not a CL variable name but a database field name. It may be a field that is defined in the format file or it may be a field defined within the OPNQRYF command. The field name is not preceded by an ampersand and is not qualified.

The expression is a character string that OPNQRYF interprets at runtime. It contains the operation used to give the field a value. Like the expressions used in the QRYSLT parameter, it may contain literals, special constants (such as *INF and *NEGINF), database and MAPFLD field names (not CL variables), operators and built-in functions (but not %VALUES, %RANGE or %WLDCRD).

A mapped field may not refer to itself in its own expression and it may not refer to a mapped field that is defined later in the command. In the code shown in Figure 4.4, FLDA may not refer to FLDB or FLDC. FLDB may refer to FLDA, but not to FLDC. FLDC may refer to FLDA and FLDB.

```
MAPFLD((FLDA ...) +
       (FLDB ...) +
       (FLDC ...))
```

Figure 4.4: An example of the MAPFLD keyword and parameters.

The expression may be either a string literal or a CL variable and may not exceed 256 characters in length. The two sections of code shown in Figure 4.5 are equivalent.

```
/* Expression in a CL literal */
OPNQRYF    FILE((NOKTL)) ... +
           MAPFLD((FLDA '%MAX(FLDB FLDC)'))

/* Expression in a CL variable */
DCL        VAR(&EXPRA) TYPE(*CHAR) LEN(80)
CHGVAR     VAR(&EXPRA) VALUE('%MAX(FLDB FLDC)')
OPNQRYF    FILE((NOKTL)) ... +
           MAPFLD((FLDA &EXPRA))
```

Figure 4.5: Using a string literal and a CL variable in a MAPFLD parameter.

The definition portion of the mapped field is not usually required. The default value, *CALC, tells OPNQRYF to define the field in one of two ways, depending on whether or not the field is defined in the file specified in the FORMAT parameter. If the field is defined in the format file, OPNQRYF uses that definition. If the field is not defined in the format file, OPNQRYF looks at the expression and infers an appropriate definition.

A coded definition is needed only for fields that aren't defined in the FORMAT file but are used as temporary work fields that define other fields. Even in this case, the definition only needs to be specified if OPNQRYF's inferred definition might not achieve the desired results. The definition has four parts:

- ❖ Data type.
- ❖ Field length.
- ❖ Number of decimal positions.
- ❖ CCSID (coded character set identifier).

The data types most often used in data processing environments are *CHAR (character), *DEC (packed decimal) and *ZONED (zoned decimal). Four numeric types are usually associated with scientific and mathematical programming:

- ❖ *BIN2 (two-byte binary integer).
- ❖ *BIN4 (four-byte binary integer).
- ❖ *FLT4 (single-precision floating point real).
- ❖ *FLT8 (double-precision floating point real).

If the field length and decimal positions are not coded, OPNQRYF uses the defaults listed in Table 4.1.

The expression shown in Figure 4.6 creates a 15-byte, zoned-decimal variable called RCVDATZ, which has five decimal positions.

If field length is specified for any numeric type, but no decimal entry is given, OPNQRYF assumes that there are zero decimal places. Because *BIN2 and *BIN4 are integer types, the only value permitted for the decimal entry is zero. If a CCSID is used, you must code the decimal positions as *N (no parameter value). The OPNQRYF command shown in Figure 4.7 illustrates some possible mapped fields.

Table 4.1: Defaults for Length and Decimals.		
Type	Length	Decimals
*CHAR	32	—
*VCHAR	32	—
*HEX	32	—
*VHEX	32	—
*ZONED	15	5
*DEC	15	5
*BIN2	5	0
*BIN4	10	0
*FLT4	7	6
*FLT8	15	14
*DATE	14	—
*TIME	8	—
*TIMESTP	26	—

```
MAPFLD((RCVDATZ 'RCVDAT' *ZONED))
```

Figure 4.6: Using MAPFLD to create a 15-byte, zoned-decimal variable.

The data is stored in two database files: CUSORD and CUSMAS. The high-level language program will read the data in the record format of the file ORDWORK. The high-level language program won't read the ORDWORK file itself.

The first two mapped fields illustrate how constant values can be passed to the OPNQRYF file. The numeric field RANK always will have the value zero, and TERR, a character field, always will have the value A16, even if these fields have values in CUSORD or CUSMAS.

```
OPNQRYF    FILE((CUSORD) (CUSMAS)) +
           FORMAT(ORDWORK) +
           KEYFLD((DUEYR) (DUEDAT) (ORDNO)) +
           MAPFLD(+
             (RANK     '0') +
             (TERR     '"A16"') +
             (CUSNO    'CUSORD/CUSNO') +
             (TERR1    '%SST(*MAPFLD/TERR 1 1)') +
             (CUSNAM   '%XLATE(CUSMAS/CUSNAM QSYSTRNTBL)') +
             (QTYSLD   'QTYORD - QTYBKO') +
             (MONSLS   'PYSOLD / 12') +
             (PRJSLS   '%MIN(MONSLS YTDSLS) * 1.65') +
             (DUEDATZ  'DUEDAT' *ZONED 6) +
             (DUEDATCH 'DUEDATZ' *CHAR 6) +
             (DUEYR    '%SST(DUEDATCH 5 2)') +
             (NOTE     &NTEXT) +
             ) +
           JFLD((1/CUSNO 2/CUSNO))
```

Figure 4.7: Examples of mapped fields.

The next field entry is an example of qualification. Field CUSNO (customer number) is found in both CUSORD and CUSMAS. Therefore, OPNQRYF has to be told from which file to take the value. In this case, CUSNO is qualified by file name. It also could be qualified by file position. The expression '1/CUSNO' would tell OPNQRYF to take the value of CUSNO from the first file, CUSORD.

The special value *MAPFLD can be used to qualify fields that are defined in the MAPFLD parameter. TERR1 is the first character in TERR field defined in the MAPFLD parameter.

Fields can be changed by functions before the high-level language program sees them. The CUSNAM (customer name) is a mixed-case field, but the %XLATE function causes the high-level language program to perceive it as all uppercase. And if CUSNAM were a key field, OPNQRYF would order the data as if it were all uppercase.

The next few fields are computed from more complex expressions. The QTYSLD (quantity sold) field is calculated as the quantity ordered minus quantity back-ordered. MONSLS (monthly sales) is a work field used in calculating PRJSLS (projected sales).

Because MONSLS is not defined in the ORDWORK file, OPNQRYF determines a suitable definition. PRJSLS is computed as 165 percent of the lesser of MONSLS and YTDSLS. OPNQRYF calculates mapped fields in the order in which they are defined. Because MONSLS is used in the expression for PRJSLS, it must be defined before PRJSLS can be defined.

The due date (DUEDAT) is a six-byte, packed decimal field in CUSORD that is stored in month-day-year format. The example is to be sorted by due date. However, sorting on DUEDAT as is won't order the records chronologically. One solution is to sort by year and, within that, by date.

In this example, DUEYR (due year) is defined as a two-character, alphanumeric field in the ORDWORK field. To get the year portion of DUEDAT into DUEYR takes several steps. First, the packed field DUEDAT must be converted to a zoned field of the same length. This new zoned field, DUEDATZ, is converted to a character field, DUEDATCH, also of the same length. Additionally, the fifth and sixth characters of DUEDATCH are mapped into DUEYR.

The problem can be solved in several other ways. DUEYR can be defined as a two-digit numeric field and can be calculated as the remainder of DUEDAT divided by 100 ('DUEDAT // 100'). Or DUEDAT could be changed to year-month-day format, in which case the DUEYR field wouldn't be needed (DUEDAT '1/DUEDAT // 100 * 10000 + 1/DUEDAT / 100'). This expression changes DUEDAT from month-day-year format to year-month-day format by carrying out the following steps:

1. Divide DUEDAT (from the first file in the list) by 100 to get the year portion in the remainder. If CUSORD/DUEDAT has the value 102389, the remainder is 89.
2. Multiply the remainder by 10,000 to put the year digits in the first two places. In this example, the result of this step would be 890000.
3. Add to this the result of dividing DUEDAT (from the first file) by 100. To continue the example, the result at this point is 891023.89. The decimal positions get truncated, leaving 891023.

The qualification is necessary. Otherwise, OPNQRYF assumes that DUEDAT is referring to itself. DUEDAT also could have been qualified by filename (CUSORD/DUEDAT).

So they won't be confused with qualification, be sure to leave at least one blank before division and remainder operators.

NOTE is calculated from the expression stored in the CL variable &NTEXT.

MAPFLD TECHNIQUES

You can make OPNQRYF disregard the actual value stored in a database record and replace it with a plugged value.

SUBSTITUTING A VALUE

Suppose two of the fields in file CUSMAS (customer master) are SLSREP (sales representative number) and CRDLMT (credit limit). Figure 4.8 shows the MAPFLD parameters used to override those two fields.

```
OPNQRYF    FILE((CUSMAS)) +
             MAPFLD((SLSREP '0') (CRDLMT +
                '%MAX(SLSYTD PYSOLD SLS2YR) * 1.25'))
CALL       PGM(CUSLIST1)
```

Figure 4.8: Overriding field values with MAPFLD.

Program CUSLIST1 never will see the values of SLSREP and CRDLMT as they are stored in the database. Every record will have a sales rep value of zero, and the credit limit will be 125 percent of the largest yearly sales for the current year and the previous two years. All other field values will be sent to the high-level language program unchanged.

VIRTUAL FIELDS

Virtual fields appear to exist, but they are not really stored in the database. They are not defined in the files from which OPNQRYF takes the data, but are defined in the file specified in the FORMAT parameter. Presume file ORDSUM (order summary) contains the fields listed in Table 4.2.

Table 4.2: ORDSUM Fields.	
ORDNO	Sales order number (key)
CUSNO	Customer number
ORDDT	Order date (yymmdd)
ORDAMT	Amount of order in dollars
ORDCST	Cost of order in dollars

High-level language programs that read this file often calculate a profit field by subtracting ORDCST from ORDAMT. Reports are sorted various ways, including by customer number, by order date, and by descending order amount.

Building reports sorted by these fields is easy. However, if you need a report sorted by profit, you have to do something different. First, define a dummy physical file (Figure 4.9) to serve as a record format. Call it PROFITFL. This dummy file must contain any fields from ORDSUM that will be needed by the high-level language program. The virtual field named PROFIT will be added to them.

```
A                                          REF(DICTIONARY)
A          R ORDSUMR                        TEXT('ORDER SUMMARY FILE')
A            ORDNO     R
A            CUSNO     R
A            ORDDT     R
A            ORDAMT    R
A            ORDCST    R
A            PROFIT    R                    REFFLD(ORDAMT)
A          K ORDNO
```

Figure 4.9: The DDS for the dummy physical file to add PROFIT to the record layout.

Because PROFITFL contains no data, specify MBR(*NONE) when you create the file. This will keep you from accidentally reading the file if you forget to override it. The high-level language program SLS25 (Figure 4.10) is written as if it will read from PROFITFL.

```
FPROFITFL  IP   E            K DISK
FSLS25PRT  O    E              PRINTER OFLIND(*IN88)
```

Figure 4.10: RPG IV code to read the file defined in Figure 4.9.

Make OPNQRYF retrieve the data from ORDSUM by overriding PROFITFL (the dummy file) to ORDSUM (the real file) before you execute the OPNQRYF command as shown in Figure 4.11.

```
PGM
OVRDBF     FILE(PROFITFL) TOFILE(ORDSUM) SHARE(*YES)
OPNQRYF    FILE((ORDSUM)) +
             FORMAT(PROFITFL) +
             KEYFLD((PROFIT *DESC)) +
             MAPFLD((PROFIT 'ORDAMT - ORDCST'))
CALL       PGM(SLS25)
CLOF       OPNID(ORDSUM)
DLTOVR     FILE(PROFITFL)
ENDPGM
```

Figure 4.11: The OPNQRYF example used to create a PROFIT field and sort on it.

Note that the high-level language file specification matches OPNQRYF's FORMAT parameter and the OVRDBF FILE parameter. The data comes from the file specified in the OVRDBF TOFILE parameter and the OPNQRYF FILE parameter.

DATE ARITHMETIC WITH NUMERIC AND CHARACTER FIELDS

The functions provided with the date, time and time stamp data types are powerful, but most people have dates stored in numeric or character fields and cannot drop everything to convert their databases. In the meantime, you can use these date/time functions with your numeric and character date fields.

Consider a shipment-history file that has two dates: the date the customer requested the product (REQDT) and the date it was actually shipped to the customer (SHPDT). Both dates are stored as packed decimal numbers in year-month-day order. The DDS for the file is shown in Figure 4.12.

```
           * SHIPMENT HISTORY FILE

A            R SHIPHISR
A              ITMNO         7
A              CUSNO         5   0
A              QTYSHP        5   0
A              REQDT         8   0
A              SHPDT         8   0
```

Figure 4.12: The DDS to define the shipment history file.

You can write a program to print a report that shows all shipments. In addition, for the late shipments, you can have the program report how many days the shipment was late. Obviously, you cannot subtract REQDT from SHPDT to find out how many days the shipment was late. But you can convert the REQDT and SHPDT to date data and use the %DAYS function. Figure 4.13 shows the format for file SHIPHIS2. It has all the fields, in the shipment history file, plus a field for the number of days between the two dates.

```
* FORMAT FILE FOR OPNQRYF PGM SHIP1, SHIPMENT STATUS REPORT
A                                              REF(SHIPHIST)
A          R SHIPHISR
A            ITMNO     R
A            CUSNO     R
A            QTYSHP    R
A            REQDT     R
A            SHPDT     R
A            DAYSDF         5  0
```

Figure 4.13: The DDS for a new file to contain the DAYS DIFFERENCE field.

A date stored in a numeric field must first be converted to a character field. The numeric fields REQDT and SHPDT are converted to character fields REQDIG and SHPDIG with the %DIGITS function. Substring and concatenation operations are used to convert REQDIG and SHPDIG to REQDT2 and SHPDT2 character fields in date format. The format of these fields must agree with the date format and date separator for the job. In this job, the date format is *MDY and the date separator is "/," which is typical for installations in the United States.

The %DAYS function is used to get the ordinal value of each date. Subtracting the value of request date from the value of the shipment date gives you the number of days between the dates. If the difference is greater than zero, the shipment was late. Figure 4.14 shows the OPNQRYF command to accomplish all this.

Figure 4.15 shows the RPG IV program SHIPR1, which prints the report.

Figure 4.16 shows the DDS for printer file SHIPR1R.

Figure 4.17 shows a typical report generated by the job.

```
/*==============================================================*/
/* Shipment status report                                       */
/*                                                              */
/* To compile:                                                  */
/*                                                              */
/*          CRTCLMOD    MODULE(XXX/SHIPC1) SRCFILE(XXX/QCLSRC)  */
/*          CRTPGM      PGM(XXX/SHIP1) MODULE(SHIPC1 SHIPR1)    */
/*                                                              */
/*==============================================================*/

PGM
OVRDBF      FILE(SHIPHIS2) TOFILE(SHIPHIST) SHARE(*YES)
OPNQRYF     FILE((SHIPHIST)) +
              FORMAT(SHIPHIS2) +
              KEYFLD((REQDT)) +
              MAPFLD((REQDIG '%DIGITS(REQDT)') +
                  (REQDT2 '%SST(REQDIG 5 2) *CAT "/" *CAT +
                      %SST(REQDIG 7 2) *CAT "/" *CAT +
                      %SST(REQDIG 3 2)') +
                  (SHPDIG '%DIGITS(SHPDT)') +
                  (SHPDT2 '%SST(SHPDIG 5 2) *CAT "/" *CAT +
                      %SST(SHPDIG 7 2) *CAT "/" *CAT +
                      %SST(SHPDIG 3 2)') +
                  (DAYSDF '%DAYS(SHPDT2) - %DAYS(REQDT2)'))
CALLPRC     PRC(SHIPR1)
CLOF        OPNID(SHIPHIST)
DLTOVR      FILE(SHIPHIS2)
ENDPGM
```

Figure 4.14: Using OPNQRYF to calculate the difference between two dates.

```
*==============================================================
* Shipment status repor
* History of shipments, emphasizing late shipments
*
* This program MUST run under OPNQRYF.
*
* To compile:
*
*      CRTRPGMOD   MODULE(XXX/SHIPR1) SRCFILE(XXX/QRPGLESRC)
*
*==============================================================
```

Figure 4.15: An RPG IV program for printing a shipment-status report from OPNQRYF.

```
FShipHis2  if   e              disk
FShiprlr   o    e              printer oflind(*in88)
D cvtDate            pr        6p 0
D   fromdate                   8p 0

C                    write     hdr

C                    read      ShipHisR

C                    dow       not %eof

C                    eval      p#ReqDt = cvtDate(ReqDt)
C                    eval      p#ShpDt = cvtDate(ShpDt)

C                    eval      shipct = shipct + 1
C
C                    if        daysdf > *zero
C                    eval      daysLate = daysdf
C                    eval      status = 'late'
C                    eval      latect = latect + 1
C                    else
C                    eval      status = *blanks
C                    eval      daysLate = *zero
C                    endif

C                    if        *in88
C                    write     hdr
C                    move      *off            *in88
C                    endif

C                    write     dtl
C                    read      ShipHisR
C                    enddo

C                    write     footer
C                    eval      *inLR = *on
  ***********
  * cvtDate: convert an 8-digit date in yyyymmdd format to mmddyy
  ***********

P cvtDate            b
D                    pi        6p 0
D   fromDate                   8p 0
```

Figure 4.15: An RPG IV program for printing a shipment-status report from OPNQRYF. (Continued)

```
D  toDate            s              6p 0
D  MonthDay          s              4
D  Year4             ds             4
D    Year2                    3     4

C                        move      fromDate      MonthDay
C                        movel     fromDate      Year4
C                        movel     MonthDay      toDate
C                        move      Year2         toDate
C                        return    toDate

P                        e
```

*Figure 4.15: An RPG IV program for printing a shipment-status report from OPNQRYF.
(Continued)*

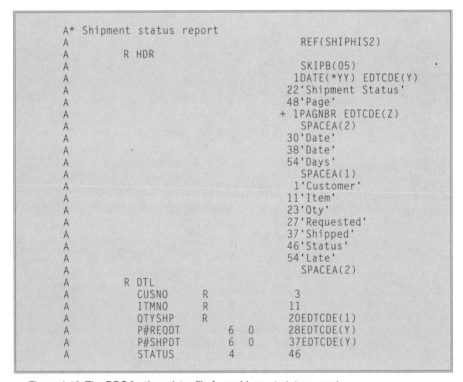

```
A* Shipment status report
A                                           REF(SHIPHIS2)
A            R HDR
A                                           SKIPB(05)
A                                          1DATE(*YY) EDTCDE(Y)
A                                          22'Shipment Status'
A                                          48'Page'
A                                        + 1PAGNBR EDTCDE(Z)
A                                           SPACEA(2)
A                                          30'Date'
A                                          38'Date'
A                                          54'Days'
A                                           SPACEA(1)
A                                           1'Customer'
A                                          11'Item'
A                                          23'Qty'
A                                          27'Requested'
A                                          37'Shipped'
A                                          46'Status'
A                                          54'Late'
A                                           SPACEA(2)
A            R DTL
A              CUSNO     R               3
A              ITMNO     R              11
A              QTYSHP    R              20EDTCDE(1)
A              P#REQDT        6  0      28EDTCDE(Y)
A              P#SHPDT        6  0      37EDTCDE(Y)
A              STATUS         4         46
```

Figure 4.16: The DDS for the printer file for a shipment-status report.

```
A                    DAYSLATE   R                    52REFFLD(DAYSDF)
A                                                    EDTCDE(2)
A                                                    SPACEA(1)
A          R FOOTER
A                                                    SPACEB(1)
A                                                    1'** End of Report **'
A                    LATECT         4   0         +  2EDTCDE(1)
A                                                 +  1'of'
A                    SHIPCT         4   0         +  1EDTCDE(1)
A                                                 +  1'shipments were late.'
```

Figure 4.16: The DDS for the printer file for a shipment-status report. (Continued)

```
3/05/2000                Shipment Status                Page    1

                                 Date    Date                   Days
Customer   Item           Qty Requested Shipped  Status   Late

   06789   EF-1212        100   7/24/99  2/18/00 late      209
   01234   AB-4567         12   1/05/00  1/05/00
   02345   CD-4667        250   1/07/00  1/11/00 late        4
   03456   CD-4667         50   1/07/00 11/15/99
   05678   DE-5678        100   1/07/00  1/05/00
   01234   CD-4667         18   2/25/00  3/01/00 late        5

** End of Report **      3 of      6 shipments were late.
```

Figure 4.17: Sample shipment status report.

The technique used here with dates also could be used for time and time stamp data stored in character and numeric fields. This method is not the only way to do date arithmetic with numeric and character date fields. Another method is examined in the section on joining. For more information on joining, see chapter 5.

MAKING ONE FILE LOOK LIKE ANOTHER FILE

An interesting and potentially useful technique is to make one file appear to be described like another file.

Suppose the company you work for has three plants that are referred to as Plant A, Plant B, and Plant C. You use the same software for all plants, but you maintain a separate set of files, job descriptions, and data areas for each plant in libraries ALIB, BLIB, and CLIB.

When the company decides to buy a commercial manufacturing package, Plant B is the first plant converted to the new software. The president of the company has a favorite report, called RAXR1, that includes inventory costs. You must continue to furnish the president with this report, but now you have to make it read files from two systems.

RAXR1 gets its costs by reading file COSTFL randomly by key as shown in Figure 4.18.

A logical file over the item master file, COSTFL has the fields listed in Table 4.3.

```
FCOSTFL      IF   E             K DISK
...
C       ITMKEY           CHAIN       COSTFL                              78
...
```

Figure 4.18: The RPG IV code for reading the COSTFL file randomly by key.

Table 4.3: Layout of Logical File COSTFL.				
Name	**Data Type**	**Length**	**Decimals**	**Description**
ITEM	character	5		item number
MATCST	packed	7	2	total material cost
LABCST	packed	7	2	total labor cost
BURCST	packed	7	2	total burden cost

Costs for Plant A are in file ALIB/COSTFL. Costs for Plant C are in CLIB/COSTFL. But costs for Plant B are in file BLIB/INVCOST, which is part of the new package. The INVCOST file looks like Table 4.4.

With OPNQRYF, you can make INVCOST look like COSTFL.

Table 4.4: Layout of File INVCOST.				
Name	**Data Type**	**Length**	**Decimals**	**Description**
ITMNBR	Character	8		Item number
MATTL	Packed	8	2	Material cost this level
MATLL	Packed	8	2	Material cost lower level
LBRTL	Packed	8	2	Labor cost this level
LBRLL	Packed	8	2	Labor cost lower level
BDNTL	Packed	8	2	Burden cost this level
BDNLL	Packed	8	2	Burden cost lower level

You don't need DDS for this dynamic file because the DDS for COSTFL is already in existence. You need a CL program that can run in both the old and new environments and a data area that tells which way the program should run.

Create data areas called RAXC1OPT in ALIB, BLIB and CLIB. In ALIB and CLIB, you give it the value OLD. In BLIB, the value is NEW. As the other plants are converted to the new software, the values of their data areas will be changed. Then write the CL program shown in Figure 4.19.

When this program runs, it retrieves the value of data area RAXC1OPT to see if it will get the costs from the old cost file or the new cost file. If it works with the old file, it will read the COSTFL for that plant. If the program is to read the new file, it will use OPNQRYF to build a temporary file that looks like COSTFL, but has data from the new file.

If program RAXR1 issues a random read (such as an RPG CHAIN operation) for item A904T to COSTFL, and the INVCOST file record for A904T has the detail values listed in Table 4.5, the program instead sees the summary figures listed on the right in Table 4.5.

Another way you could handle this situation is to create a physical file called COSTFL in BLIB and store the costs from INVCOST in it. Then you would have to make sure you updated COSTFL every time INVCOST changed. Yet another way is to include both cost files

```
PGM
DCL        VAR(&OPTION) TYPE(*CHAR) LEN(3)
RTVDTAARA DTAARA(RAXC1OPT) RTNVAR(&OPTION)
IF (&OPTION *EQ NEW) THEN(DO)
    OPNQRYF FILE((INVCOST)) FORMAT(COSTFL) +
            KEYFLD((ITEM)) +
            MAPFLD((ITEM    'ITMNBR') +
                  (MATCST 'MATTL + MATLL') +
                  (LABCST 'LBRTL + LBRLL') +
                  (BURCST 'BDNTL + BDNLL'))
    OVRDBF  FILE(COSTFL) TOFILE(INVCOST) SHARE(*YES)
ENDDO
CALL       PGM(RAXR1)
IF (&OPTION *EQ NEW) THEN(DO)
    CLOF    OPNID(INVCOST)
    DLTOVR  FILE(COSTFL)
ENDDO
ENDPGM
```

Figure 4.19: Using a data area to define the program environment.

Table 4.5: Field Values for Detail and Summary File.			
INVCOST File Values		**COSTFL File Values**	
ITMNBR	A904T	ITMNBR	A904T
MATTL	5.45		
MATLL	7.05	MATCST	12.50
LBRTL	6.00		
LBRLL	6.00	LABCST	12.00
BDNTL	.00		
BDNLL	1.25	BURCST	1.25

in the RPG program and use the data area to determine which file to open and read. Then there would be no need for OPNQRYF. In any case, at least there is more than one approach from which to choose.

PREVENTING DIVISION BY ZERO

Suppose you need to calculate a profit margin by dividing the profit by the order amount. The code shown in Figure 4.20 would work if no record had a zero value for ORDAMT.

```
OPNQRYF    FILE((ORDSUM)) FORMAT(WORK234) +
              MAPFLD((PROFIT 'ORDAMT - ORDCST') +
                 (PFTMGN 'PROFIT / ORDAMT'))
```

Figure 4.20: OPNQRYF with no check for a zero divisor.

One way to avoid division by zero is to leave out the records that would cause it (Figure 4.21). The system usually calculates mapped fields before it evaluates the QRYSLT clause, but in cases that involve potential mapping errors, the logic is altered somewhat.

```
OPNQRYF    ... +
              QRYSLT('ORDAMT *NE 0') +
              MAPFLD((PROFIT 'ORDAMT - ORDCST') +
                 (PFTMGN 'PROFIT / ORDAMT'))
```

Figure 4.21: Omitting a record with zero value to prevent dividing by zero.

If you want the zero records included in the query, then you have to do something to prevent division by zero. This technique is based on two simple rules of math:

❖ Any number (except for 0) divided by itself is 1.

❖ Any number multiplied by 1 is equal to itself.

The first step, then, is to transform the expression dividend/divisor as shown in Figures 4.22A, 4.22B, and 4.22C.

```
dividend
--------
divisor
```

Figure 4.22A: The first step in transforming the expression dividend/divisor.

```
dividend   divisor                    dividend x divisor
--------  x --------        or        --------------------
divisor    divisor                    divisor squared
```

Figure 4.22B: The second step in transforming the expression dividend/divisor.

```
PROFIT    ORDAMT                   PROFIT x ORDAMT
------  x ------       or          ---------------
ORDAMT    ORDAMT                    ORDAMT SQUARED
```

Figure 4.22C: The third step shows the new expression.

The preceding operation forces both dividend and divisor to be zero whenever the divisor is zero. The next step is to change the divisor of the new expression to the maximum of the old divisor squared and a number that is smaller than the smallest possible value of the old divisor squared. In this example, the new expression is shown in Figure 4.23.

```
                PROFIT x ORDAMT
-----------------------------------------------
maximum of (ORDAMT x ORDAMT) and (.00001)
```

Figure 4.23: Changing the divisor of the new expression.

An easy way to determine this number is to code a decimal point, twice as many zeros as there are decimal positions in the divisor, and a one. In this example, ORDAMT has two decimal positions. The small value would be .00001. You need at least four zeros after the decimal because ORDAMT has two decimal positions. You can see the results of this translation in Figures 4.24A and 4.24B. When ORDAMT is not equal to zero, profit margin is calculated as shown in Figure 4.24A.

```
PROFIT x ORDAMT
---------------
ORDAMT x ORDAMT
```

Figure 4.24A: Calculating the profit margin when ORDAMT is not equal to zero.

```
     0
--------
0.00001
```

Figure 4.24B: Calculating the profit margin when ORDAMT is zero.

When ORDAMT is zero, profit margin is calculated as shown in Figure 4.24B, which returns a value of zero.

The revised field definition is shown in Figure 4.25.

```
MAPFLD((PROFIT 'ORDAMT - ORDCST') +
       (PFTMGN '(PROFIT * ORDAMT) / +
       (%MAX((ORDAMT * ORDAMT) .00001)'))
or
MAPFLD((PROFIT 'ORDAMT - ORDCST') +
       (PFTMGN '(PROFIT * ORDAMT) / +
       (%MAX((ORDAMT ** 2) .00001)'))
```

Figure 4.25: Two examples of using MAPFLD to prevent a divide-by-zero error.

VARIABLE CONTROL BREAKS

You can use one high-level language control-break program for different sort sequences by using the MAPFLD parameter. Suppose you are reading a join logical file named HISTJL1, which is described as listed in Table 4.6.

You need a format file with a field (call it BREAK) to contain the value of the break field. If the control break is on a sales representative number, BREAK will contain the sales rep number. If the break is on an invoice number, BREAK will contain the invoice number. The DDS for the format is shown in Figure 4.26.

The high-level language program (see Figures 4.27 and 4.28) checks field BREAK for a change in control-field value.

Parameter BDESC (break description) contains a short description of the break field (such as "SALES REP" or "CUSTOMER"). This way, you can provide more meaningful control-break text, such as "TOTALS FOR SALES REP 300" and "TOTALS FOR CUSTOMER 9382," on the

Table 4.6: Layout of Join Logical File HISTJL1.				
Field Name	**Type**	**Length**	**Decimals**	**Comment**
REPNO	Packed	3	0	Sales rep number
REPNAM	Character	15		Sales rep name
CUSNO	Packed	4	0	Customer number
CUSNAM	Character	20		Customer name
INVNO	Zoned	6	0	Invoice number
INVDAT	Packed	6	0	Invoice date
INVLN	Packed	2	0	Invoice line number
ITMNO	Character	7		Item number
ITMDSC	Character	22		Item description
UNTPR	Packed	5	2	Unit price
QTYSLD	Packed	5	0	Quantity sold

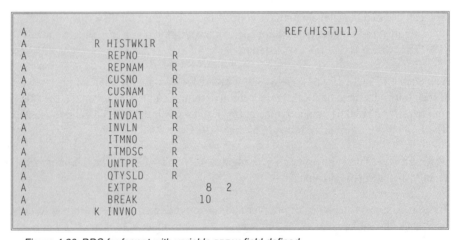

```
A                                          REF(HISTJL1)
A          R HISTWK1R
A            REPNO       R
A            REPNAM      R
A            CUSNO       R
A            CUSNAM      R
A            INVNO       R
A            INVDAT      R
A            INVLN       R
A            ITMNO       R
A            ITMDSC      R
A            UNTPR       R
A            QTYSLD      R
A            EXTPR           8  2
A            BREAK          10
A          K INVNO
```

Figure 4.26: DDS for format with variable BREAK field defined.

```
*  PROGRAM SLS01R-SALES REPORT WITH VARIABLE CTL BREAK
*  This program runs under OPNQRYF
*
*  PARAMETERS
*      BDESC    - Text description of break field
*                 If blank, control totals are not printed
*      PRTDTL   - Print detail lines
*                 0 = NO, produce a summary report
*                 1 = YES, print detail lines
*
*  INDICATORS
*      41 - Print control totals
*      44 - Print detail lines
*
*===============================================================
*  To compile:
*
*      CRTRPGPGM  PGM(XXX/SLS01R) SRCFILE(XXX/QRPGSRC)
*
*===============================================================
FHISTWK1 IP  E          K          DISK
FSLS01P  O   E               88    PRINTER
IHISTWK1R        01
I                                               BREAK L1
I           SDS
I                                      *PROGRAM PGMNAM
I                                      276 2810SYSDAT
I                                      282 2870SYSTIM
C           *ENTRY     PLIST
C                      PARM            BDESC   9
C                      PARM            PRTDTL  1
C*
C    L1                MOVE *ZERO      AMT1
C*
C                      ADD  EXTPR      AMT1
C           *IN44      IFEQ *ON
C                      MOVELINVDAT     ##Y4    4
C                      MOVE ##Y4       ##Y2    2
C                      MOVE INVDAT     ##MD    4
C                      MOVEL##MD       INVDT2  60
C                      MOVE ##Y2       INVDT2
C                      ENDIF
C*
CL1                    ADD  AMT1       AMTR
CL1         BDESC      CAT  BREAK:1    TDESC       P
C***********
C           *INZSR     BEGSR
C*
```

Figure 4.27: An RPG III program to process a BREAK field and force totals.

```
C              BDESC       COMP *BLANKS                        4141
C              PRTDTL      COMP '0'                            4444
C*
C                          ENDSR
OPAGEHDR H            1P
O        OR          88
O                                   *ALL
ODETAILLND           01 44
O                                   *ALL
OBRKFOOT T           L1 41
O                                   *ALL
ORPTFOOT T           LR
O                                   *ALL
```

Figure 4.27: An RPG III program to process a BREAK field and force totals. (Continued)

```
* PROGRAM SLS01R-SALES REPORT WITH VARIABLE CTL BREAK
* This program runs under OPNQRYF
*
* PARAMETERS
*      BDESC    - Text description of break field
*                 If blank, control totals are not printed
*      PRTDTL   - Print detail lines
*                 0 = NO, produce a summary report
*                 1 = YES, print detail lines
*
* INDICATORS
*      41 - Print control totals
*      44 - Print detail lines
*
*===============================================================
* To compile:
*
*      CRTBNDRPG  PGM(XXX/SLS01R) SRCFILE(XXX/QRPGLESRC)
*
*===============================================================

FHistWk1    if   e            k disk
FSls01P     o    e              printer OflInd(*in88)

D BreakDesc        s              9
D PrintDetails     s              1n
D Save1A           s             10    inz(*loval)
D WrkDate          s              D
```

Figure 4.28: An RPG IV program to process a BREAK field and force totals.

```
D                    sds
D       PgmNam               1    10

C       *entry       plist
C                    parm                           BreakDesc
C                    parm                           PrintDetails
C
C                    write        PageHdr
C                    read         HistWk1R
C                    exsr         BgnLvl01
C
C                    dow          not %eof
C                    if           Break <> SavelA
C                    exsr         EndLvl01
C                    exsr         BgnLvl01
C                    endif
C                    if           PrintDetails
C                    exsr         CheckOverFlow
C       *ISO         move         InvDat        WrkDate
C       *MDY         move         WrkDate       InvDt2
C                    write        Detailln
C                    endif
C                    eval         Amt1 = Amt1 + ExtPr
C                    read         HistWk1R
C                    enddo
C                    exsr         EndLvl01
C                    write        RptFoot
C                    eval         *inLR = *on
C********
C       BgnLvl01     BegSR
C                    eval         SavelA = Break
C                    eval         TDesc = %trim(BreakDesc) + ' ' + Break
C                    eval         Amt1 = *zero
C                    EndSR
C********
C       EndLvl01     BegSR
C                    write        BrkFoot
C                    eval         AmtR = AmtR + Amt1
C                    EndSR
C********
C       CheckOverFlow BegSR
C                    if           *in88
C                    write        PageHdr
C                    eval         *in88 = *off
C                    endif
C                    EndSR
```

Figure 4.28: An RPG IV program to process a BREAK field and force totals. (Continued)

printed subtotal line. Because no control break is requested if BDESC is blank, no control totals are printed.

Parameter PRTDTL (print detail lines) is a logical value that gives you the option to print either detail or summary reports. The parameter has nothing to do with the subject of variable control breaks, but is added as a feature that increases the flexibility and usefulness of the program.

BASIC CL LOGIC

Because the CL code needed to run this job might seem a little cumbersome or complicated, here is the basic logic.

1. Assign values to CL variables &BRK and &DESC based on parameter &BRK_FLD.
2. If the control field is a character field, &BRK will contain the name of the control field.
3. If the control field is numeric, &BRK will contain the %DIGITS function with the control field name as its argument.

The code to assign a value to &BRK is shown in Figure 4.29.

```
CHGVAR    VAR(&BRK) VALUE('ITMNO') /* character field */
CHGVAR    VAR(&BRK) VALUE('%DIGITS(CUSNO)') /* numeric field */
```

Figure 4.29: Assigning different values to &BRK.

The %DIGITS function drops the sign and the decimal point, but code numbers—such as customer, vendor, and invoice numbers—are almost always positive integers. Note that &DESC is an abbreviated text description of the control field.

ADDITIONAL BASIC CL LOGIC

Run the OPNQRYF command, shown in Figure 4.30, which maps the control field values into field BREAK.

The only thing lacking is a command to run it all. That is shown in Figure 4.31.

To give you a better idea of how this technique works, Figures 4.32 through 4.35 show a few sample reports produced by this job.

```
/*================================================================*/
/* Program SLS01C - Sales report with variable control break      */
/*                                                                */
/* Parameters                                                     */
/*      &BRK_FLD  = Abbreviation of break field name              */
/*                  REP     - break on sales rep number           */
/*                  CUST    - break on customer number            */
/*                  ITEM    - break on item number                */
/*                  INVOICE - break on invoice number             */
/*      &PRT_DTL  = Print detail lines or not                     */
/*                  '0' - No, produce a summary report            */
/*                  '1' - Yes, print detail lines                 */
/*                                                                */
/*================================================================*/
/* To compile:                                                    */
/*                                                                */
/*          CRTCLPGM   PGM(XXX/SLS01C> SRCFILE(XXX/QCLSRC)        */
/*                                                                */
/*================================================================*/

PGM         PARM(&BRK_FLD &PRT_DTL)

   DCL    VAR(&BRK_FLD) TYPE(*CHAR) LEN( 7)
   DCL    VAR(&PRT_DTL) TYPE(*LGL)
   DCL    VAR(&BRK)     TYPE(*CHAR) LEN(25)
   DCL    VAR(&DESC)    TYPE(*CHAR) LEN( 9)

   DCL    VAR(&ERRBYTES)   TYPE(*CHAR) LEN(4)  VALUE(X'00000000')
   DCL    VAR(&ERROR)      TYPE(*LGL)          VALUE('0')
   DCL    VAR(&MSGKEY)     TYPE(*CHAR) LEN(4)
   DCL    VAR(&MSGTYP)     TYPE(*CHAR) LEN(10) VALUE('*DIAG')
   DCL    VAR(&MSGTYPCTR)  TYPE(*CHAR) LEN(4)  VALUE(X'00000001')
   DCL    VAR(&PGMMSGQ)    TYPE(*CHAR) LEN(10) VALUE('*')
   DCL    VAR(&STKCTR)     TYPE(*CHAR) LEN(4)  VALUE(X'00000001')

   MONMSG      MSGID(CPF0000) EXEC(GOTO CMDLBL(ERRPROC))

/* Set mapped fields for variable control break */

   CHGVAR    VAR(&BRK)  VALUE('" "')
   IF (&BRK_FLD *EQ ' ') +
       THEN(GOTO END_TEST) /* no ctl break wanted */
   IF (&BRK_FLD *EQ REP) THEN(DO)
       CHGVAR  VAR(&BRK ) VALUE('%DIGITS(REPNO)')
       CHGVAR  VAR(&DESC) VALUE('rep')
       GOTO    END_TEST
   ENDDO
   IF (&BRK_FLD *EQ CUST) THEN(DO)
       CHGVAR  VAR(&BRK ) VALUE('%DIGITS(CUSNO)')
       CHGVAR  VAR(&DESC) VALUE('customer')
```

Figure 4.30: A program to run a sales report with variable control breaks.

```
        GOTO     END_TEST
   ENDDO
   IF (&BRK_FLD *EQ ITEM) THEN(DO)
        CHGVAR   VAR(&BRK ) VALUE(ITMNO)
        CHGVAR   VAR(&DESC) VALUE('item')
        GOTO     END_TEST
   ENDDO
   IF (&BRK_FLD *EQ INVOICE) THEN(DO)
        CHGVAR   VAR(&BRK ) VALUE('%DIGITS(INVNO)')
        CHGVAR   VAR(&DESC) VALUE('invoice')
        GOTO     END_TEST
   ENDDO
END_TEST:

   /* Begin processing */

   CLOF      OPNID(HISTJL1)
              MONMSG      MSGID(CPF4520)
   OVRDBF    FILE(HISTWK1) TOFILE(HISTJL1) SHARE(*YES)
   OPNQRYF   FILE((HISTJL1)) +
              FORMAT(HISTWK1) +
              KEYFLD((BREAK) (INVNO) (INVLN)) +
              MAPFLD((BREAK &BRK) +
                    (EXTPR 'QTYSLD * UNTPR'))
   CALL      PGM(SLS01R) PARM(&DESC &PRT_DTL)
   CLOF      OPNID(HISTJL1)
   DLTOVR    FILE(HISTWK1)
   RETURN

/* Error processing routine */

ERRPROC:
   IF        COND(&ERROR) THEN(GOTO CMDLBL(ERRDONE))
   ELSE      CMD(CHGVAR VAR(&ERROR) VALUE('1'))

   /* Move all *DIAG messages to previous program queue */
   CALL      PGM(QMHMOVPM) PARM(&MSGKEY &MSGTYP +
              &MSGTYPCTR  &PGMMSGQ &STKCTR &ERRBYTES)

   /* Resend last *ESCAPE message */
ERRDONE:
   CALL      PGM(QMHRSNEM) PARM(&MSGKEY &ERRBYTES)
   MONMSG    MSGID(CPF0000) EXEC(DO)
     SNDPGMMSG  MSGID(CPF3CF2) MSGF(QCPFMSG) +
                MSGDTA('QMHRSNEM') MSGTYPE(*ESCAPE)
     MONMSG     MSGID(CPF0000)
   ENDDO

ENDPGM
```

Figure 4.30: A program to run a sales report with variable control breaks. (Continued)

```
CMD           PROMPT('Sales history report')
PARM          KWD(BREAK) TYPE(*CHAR) LEN(7) RSTD(*YES) +
                VALUES(REP CUST ITEM INVOICE) +
                PROMPT('Break field')
PARM          KWD(PRTDTL) +
                TYPE(*LGL) RSTD(*YES) DFT(*YES) +
                VALUES('0' '1') +
                SPCVAL((*YES '1') (*NO '0')) +
                CHOICE('*YES, *NO') +
                PROMPT('Print detail lines?')
```

Figure 4.31: Note the command to run a variable-break program.

```
SLS01R                          Sales Report          4/08/98  15:01:57       Page   1

Rep       Customer             Invoice         Item                Qty   Price   Ext
--------- -------------------- --------------- ------------------- ---   -----   -----
111 JONES 7890 DODD'S FURNITURE 100002 4/05/98 1  CD-4667 BROOM      12    5.50    66.00
111 JONES 7890 DODD'S FURNITURE 100002 4/05/98 2  EF-1212 WASTE CAN   3   12.25    36.75
111 JONES 1234 JACK'S HARDWARE  100004 4/06/98 1  DE-5678 DUSTER      1    7.49     7.49
111 JONES 7890 DODD'S FURNITURE 100006 4/07/98 1  AB-4567 MOP         1    4.10     4.10
                                                  Total for rep 111          114.34 *

222 SMITH 3456 CAL'S QUICK STOP 100003 4/06/98 1  AB-4567 MOP        50    4.00   200.00
222 SMITH 3456 CAL'S QUICK STOP 100003 4/06/98 2  EF-1212 WASTE CAN   2   12.00    24.00
                                                  Total for rep 222          224.00 *

333 BROWN 4567 SALLY'S BAKERY   100001 4/05/98 1  AB-4567 MOP         3    4.00    12.00
                                                  Total for rep 333           12.00 *

444 GREEN 3579 JIM'S CAR WASH   100005 4/06/98 1  DE-5678 DUSTER      2    7.49    14.98
444 GREEN 3579 JIM'S CAR WASH   100005 4/06/98 2  EF-1212 WASTE CAN   4   12.00    48.00
444 GREEN 3579 JIM'S CAR WASH   100005 4/06/98 3  AB-4567 MOP         2    3.75     7.50
                                                  Total for rep 444           70.48 *
                                                  Grand totals               420.82 **
```

Figure 4.32: The report output with break(rep).

If the idea of flexible control breaks interests you, refer to appendix B. There you will find a version of this job that supports up to three control fields.

LOGICAL FUNCTIONS

There are four logical functions that work on character and hexadecimal data at the bit level: %AND, %OR, %XOXOR (exclusive or) and %NOT. Most data processing shops will have little or no use for these.

```
SLS01R                    Sales Report              4/08/98  15:01:57    Page   1

Rep       Customer          Invoice          Item              Qty   Price   Ext
--------- ----------------- ---------------- --------------------- ---  -----  -----
1111 JONES 1234 JACK'S HARDWARE  100004 4/06/98 1 DE-5678 DUSTER      1   7.49    7.49
                                          Total for customer 1234            7.49 *

222 SMITH  3456 CAL'S QUICK STOP  100003 4/06/98 1 AB-4567 MOP        50   4.00  200.00
222 SMITH  3456 CAL'S QUICK STOP  100003 4/06/98 2 EF-1212 WASTE CAN   2  12.00   24.00
                                          Total for customer 3456          224.00  *

444 GREEN  3579 JIM'S CAR WASH    100005 4/06/98 1 DE-5678 DUSTER       2   7.49   14.98
444 GREEN  3579 JIM'S CAR WASH    100005 4/06/98 2 EF-1212 WASTE CAN    4  12.00   48.00
444 GREEN  3579 JIM'S CAR WASH    100005 4/06/98 3 AB-4567 MOP          2   3.75    7.50
                                          Total for customer 3579           70.48  *

333 BROWN  4567 SALLY'S BAKERY    100001 4/05/98 1 AB-4567 MOP          3   4.00   12.00
                                          Total for customer 4567           12.00 *

111 JONES  7890 DODD'S FURNITURE  100002 4/05/98 1 CD-4667 BROOM       12   5.50   66.00
111 JONES  7890 DODD'S FURNITURE  100002 4/05/98 2 EF-1212 WASTE CAN    3  12.25   36.75
111 JONES  7890 DODD'S FURNITURE  100006 4/07/98 1 AB-4567 MOP          1   4.10    4.10
                                          Total for customer 7890          106.85 *
                                          Grand totals                     420.82 **
```

Figure 4.33: The report output with BREAK(CUST).

```
SLS01R                    Sales Report              4/08/98  15:07:39    Page   1

Rep       Customer          Invoice          Item              Qty   Price   Ext
--------- ----------------- ---------------- --------------------- ---  -----  -----
                                          Total for rep 111             114.34 *
                                          Total for rep 222             224.00 *
                                          Total for rep 333              12.00 *
                                          Total for rep 444              70.48 *
                                          Grand totals                  420.82 **
```

*Figure 4.34: The report output with BREAK(REP) PRTDTL(*NO).*

```
SLS01R                    Sales Report              4/08/98  15:07:43    Page   1

Rep       Customer          Invoice          Item              Qty   Price   Ext
--------- ----------------- ---------------- --------------------- ---  -----  -----
333 BROWN  4567 SALLY'S BAKERY    100001 4/05/98 1 AB-4567 MOP          3   4.00   12.00
111 JONES  7890 DODD'S FURNITURE  100002 4/05/98 1 CD-4667 BROOM       12   5.50   66.00
111 JONES  7890 DODD'S FURNITURE  100002 4/05/98 2 EF-1212 WASTE CAN    3  12.25   36.75
222 SMITH  3456 CAL'S QUICK STOP  100003 4/06/98 1 AB-4567 MOP         50   4.00  200.00
222 SMITH  3456 CAL'S QUICK STOP  100003 4/06/98 2 EF-1212 WASTE CAN    2  12.00   24.00
111 JONES  1234 JACK'S HARDWARE   100004 4/06/98 1 DE-5678 DUSTER       1   7.49    7.49
444 GREEN  3579 JIM'S CAR WASH    100005 4/06/98 1 DE-5678 DUSTER       2   7.49   14.98
444 GREEN  3579 JIM'S CAR WASH    100005 4/06/98 2 EF-1212 WASTE CAN    4  12.00   48.00
444 GREEN  3579 JIM'S CAR WASH    100005 4/06/98 3 AB-4567 MOP          2   3.75    7.50
111 JONES  7890 DODD'S FURNITURE  100006 4/07/98 1 AB-4567 MOP          1   4.10    4.10
                                          Grand totals                     420.82 **
```

Figure 4.35: The report output with no specified parameters.

The %NOT function reverses the bits in a string. Each bit that is off is turned on, and each one that is on is turned off.

The %AND, %OR and %XOR functions compare two strings. Bits in the resultant string are turned off or on according to the same logic mentioned earlier in the discussion of logical operators. The %AND function turns on a resultant bit if both compared bits are on. The %OR turns on a resultant bit if either compared bit is on. The %XOR turns on a resultant bit if one compared bit is on and the other is off.

One installation had a file that used the individual bits of a field to determine whether or not a certain action had taken place. The programmer needed OPNQRYF to inspect these bits. Specifically, she wanted to select records that met two conditions: (1) the first bit of a certain test byte had to be off; (2) either the fourth or fifth bit (or both bits) had to be on.

The solution was to use the %AND function to test one bit at a time. For example, to test the first bit, she "anded" the test byte with a binary 10000000 (hex 80). The result would then be either binary 00000000 (hex 00) or binary 10000000 (hex 80). She "anded" the fourth bit with binary 00010000 (hex 10), and the fifth bit with binary 00001000 (hex 08).

Figure 4.36 shows part of a CL program that illustrates how the programmer was able to test individual bits and select the records she needed.

```
DCL       VAR(&QRYSLT)TYPE(*CHAR)LEN(256)
CHGVAR    VAR(&QRYSLT) VALUE(TEST0*NEX"00"*AND+
            (TEST3 *NE X"00" *OR TEST4 *NE X"00")')
OVRDBF      FILE(BINDATA)) SHARE(*YES)
OPNQRYF    FILE((BINDATA)) QRYSLT(&QRYSLT)+
          MAPFLD((TESTBYTE '%AND(TESTBYTE X"80')')
              (TEST0 '%AND(TESTBYTE X"80")')+
              (TEST3 '%AND(TESTBYTE X"10")')+
              (TEST4 ' %AND(TESTBYTE x"08")'))
```

Figure 4.36: Testing individual bits for record selection.

TEST0 is all binary zeros if bit 0 is off. The same is true for the other two TESTx fields. If a field is equal to hex 00, the tested bit is off.

OTHER FUNCTIONS

The %STRIP function removes leading and trailing characters from a string. It requires one argument: a character string. Two more arguments are optional. The second argument is the character to be removed from the string. The default value is a space. The second is whether to remove the strip character from the beginning of the string (*LEAD), the end of the string (*TRAIL), or from both beginning and end (*BOTH). The default is *BOTH. Figure 4.37 shows an example of how to remove leading blanks from the item description before passing the data to the HLL program.

```
OPNQRYF ... MAPFLD((ITDESC '%STRIP(1/ITDESC " " *LEAD)'))
```

Figure 4.37: Stripping leading blanks from item description field using %STRIP.

The %USER function returns the ID of the user who is running the job. It takes no arguments. The example in Figure 4.38 shows how to set field UABBR to the first three characters of the user ID.

```
OPNQRYF ... MAPFLD((UABBR '%SST(%USER 1 3)'))
```

Figure 4.38: Retrieving a user ID with %USER.

To find the length of a string, use the %LEN function. For fixed-length fields, the length is always the allocated length of the field. For variable-length fields, %LEN returns the number of characters stored in the field.

OPNQRYF also handles both natural and common logarithms used in some advanced business formulas and trigonometry.

You can find a complete list of the functions in appendix C. For a more thorough discussion of each function, see the *CL Reference* manual.

SUMMARY

The FORMAT parameter tells OPNQRYF how the high-level language program expects the data record to be arranged. This parameter provides high-level language programs with alternate logical views of the database.

A format file is often a physical file that contains no data, but exists only for the benefit of OPNQRYF. Such files need not contain any members.

The MAPFLD parameter serves two main purposes. First, it resolves ambiguity when fields from two or more database files have the same name. Second, it provides a way to calculate or "plug" values into the fields of an OPNQRYF file.

Each mapped field is assigned a value by a free-format expression, which may be a character literal or variable. The expression may contain database field names, literals, built-in functions, and operators. The data type and size may also be defined, if desired, or the system may infer a definition from the expression.

5

❖ Joining Files

Requests for information are sometimes solved by reading data from just one file. But, more often than not, you can answer a request only by combining data from two or more files. In relational database systems, the process of combining data from two or more relations is called *joining*.

OVERVIEW

The AS/400 supports joining through join logical files. In certain cases, it might be better to let OPNQRYF carry out the join instead. For example, suppose you have two files that are used daily, but only need to be joined during end-of-month processing. In such a case, creating a join logical file adds needless overhead to the system because the join logical needs to be maintained throughout the month.

There are also times when the joined data should have key fields from two or more files. OS/400 DDS requires that all key fields in join logical files be from the same file, but OPNQRYF permits key fields from all underlying files.

Another reason for having OPNQRYF join files is that it supports a type of join, called the *exception join*, that is not supported by join logical files.

JOIN PARAMETERS

The following sections examine each one of the join parameters individually. The five parameters affected by join processing are:

- ❖ FILE
- ❖ FORMAT
- ❖ JFLD
- ❖ JDFTVAL
- ❖ JORDER

THE FILE PARAMETER

The FILE parameter must include at least two entries. The first entry is called the *primary join file*. The others are known as *secondary join* files. Figure 5.1 shows a simple example of the FILE parameter where the customer master and order header files are to be joined.

```
OPNQRYF      FILE((CUSMAS) (ORDHDR))  etc.
```

Figure 5.1: A simple example of a FILE parameter.

In the example shown in Figure 5.2, file BYHIST in library ADL is being joined to BYMIN in GMTK. BYMIN has multiple record formats. Only format MIN001 is joined.

```
OPNQRYF      FILE((ADL/BYHIST) (GMTK/BYMIN *FIRST MIN001))  etc.
```

Figure 5.2: An example of joining files.

A logical file with at least two record formats is listed twice. In the example shown in Figure 5.3, the header format is being joined to the detail format. OPNQRYF will use the data in member BATCH5 in both files.

This chapter uses terms such as "the first file" or "the primary join file." Keep in mind that two or more entries in the FILE parameter can refer to the same database file.

```
OPNQRYF FILE((ORDERS BATCH5 ORDHDR) +
                  (ORDERS BATCH5 ORDDTL)) etc.
```

Figure 5.3: An example of a join with multiple record formats.

THE FORMAT PARAMETER

The FORMAT parameter's default value, *FILE, is only valid when one file is listed in the FILE parameter. Therefore, a format name is required when files are being joined. The format file name could be one of the files being joined. Most often, the format file name is the name of a dummy physical file where the record format is used by the high-level language program. Figure 5.4 shows an example that uses the format parameter.

```
OVRDBF FILE(ORDWRK) TOFILE(CUSMAS) SHARE(*YES)
OPNQRYF    FILE((CUSMAS) (ORDHDR)) FORMAT(ORDWRK)
```

Figure 5.4: FORMAT parameter example.

Although the data comes from files CUSMAS and ORDHDR, it is presented to the high-level language program in the format of file ORDWRK. ORDWRK could be an actual production file or it could be a physical file with no members that is created especially for the OPNQRYF command.

In Figure 5.5, BYWORK is a multi-format logical file found in one of the libraries in the library list. The queried data is passed along to the high-level language program in the format of record type BYMON.

```
OVRDBF FILE(BYWORK) TOFILE(ADL/BYHIST) SHARE(*YES)
OPNQRYF    FILE((ADL/BYHIST) (GMTK/BYMIN *FIRST MIN001)) +
               FORMAT(BYWORK BYMON)
```

Figure 5.5: Example of a FILE parameter for a logical file.

Note that the FORMAT parameter shown in Figure 5.6 refers to CUSORD (customer orders), one of the files in the join pair.

```
OVRDBF FILE((CUSORD)) SHARE(*YES)
    OPNQRYF FILE((CUSORD) (CUSMAS)) FORMAT((CUSORD)+
            QRYSLT('STATE= "RI")+
            JFLD((1/CUST 2/CUST))+
            MAPFLD((CUST '1/CUST'))
```

Figure 5.6: Joining multiple files for use with other parameters.

Fields from CUSMAS won't be available to the HLL program, but they are available to the QRYSLT and MAPFLD parameters. In this case, the customer master file is joined in order to test the state code (which isn't in the customer orders file). Only orders for customers in Rhode Island will be selected.

THE JFLD PARAMETER

The Join Field (JFLD) parameter tells which common fields are to be used to bring about the join. For example, the system might match the item number in one file to the item number in another file.

Figure 5.7 adds the JFLD parameter to the previous examples. Records in the customer master file are to be matched to order-header records with the same customer numbers. Because the customer-number field has the same name in both files, the join fields must be qualified—either by file name or by ordinal position in the FILE parameter.

```
OVRDBF      FILE(ORDWRK) TOFILE(CUSMAS) SHARE(*YES)

/* Join fields specified by file name */

OPNQRYF     FILE((CUSMAS) (ORDHDR)) FORMAT(ORDWRK) +
            JFLD((CUSMAS/CUSNO ORDHDR/CUSNO))

/* Join fields specified by file number */

OPNQRYF     FILE((CUSMAS) (ORDHDR)) FORMAT(ORDWRK) +
            JFLD((1/CUSNO 2/CUSNO))
```

Figure 5.7: An example of the JFLD parameter.

As shown in Figure 5.8, ITEM is a field in BYHIST. PARTNR is in BYMIN. The system joins BYHIST records for item 12345, for example, to BYMIN records where PARTNR is 12345. Note that it isn't necessary to qualify the field names here.

```
OVRDBF FILE(BYWORK) TOFILE(ADL/BYHIST) SHARE(*YES)
OPNQRYF    FILE((ADL/BYHIST) (GMTK/BYMIN *FIRST MIN001)) +
           FORMAT(BYWORK BYMON) +
           JFLD((ITEM PARTNR))
```

Figure 5.8: Example of joining records based on a field value.

THE JORDER PARAMETER

The Join Order (JORDER) parameter tells in which order the files are to be joined. The default value for JORDER is *ANY, which gives the system flexibility to try to make the join more efficient. In general, it's best not to code the JORDER parameter. As you acquire proficiency with OPNQRYF, you might find that you can sometimes improve performance by specifying a join order when three or more files are being joined.

RESOLVING AMBIGUITY OF FIELD NAMES

If a field of the FORMAT file is found in one or more input files, OPNQRYF must know which file's value to use. In these cases, you should use the MAPFLD parameter to qualify it. Presume files ORDSKED and CUSMAS are being joined. They have a common field CUSNBR (customer number) which is included in the format file. Figure 5.9 illustrates the necessary code.

```
OVRDBF     FILE(SKEDWORK) TOFILE(ORDSKED) SHARE(*YES)
OPNQRYF    FILE((ORDSKED) (CUSMAS)) FORMAT(SKEDWORK) +
           MAPFLD((CUSNBR '1/CUSNBR')) etc.
```

Figure 5.9: Using MAPFLD to qualify duplicate field names.

JOIN TYPES

OPNQRYF supports three types of joins:

- ❖ Inner join.
- ❖ Left outer join.
- ❖ Exception join.

These three join types are distinguished by what action is taken when records in the primary join file don't match records in the secondary join file. Let's look at how these join types behave. To do so, two files, ORDSKED (order schedule) and CUSMAS (customer master) are used. The layouts and field values are shown in Tables 5.1 and 5.2.

Table 5.1: ORDSKED (Customer Order Schedule).			
ORDNBR	CUSNBR	ITMNBR	ORDQTY
111	C7	I1	5
112	C2	I5	3
113	C1	I7	4
114	C3	I1	3
115	C2	I4	8

Table 5.2: CUSMAS (Customer Master File).	
CUSNBR	CUSNAM
C1	HARDWARE STORE
C2	PET SHOP
C6	RESTAURANT
C7	GROCERY

A dummy physical file will serve as a format for the inner and left outer joins. Create a physical file, SKEDWRK, with the DDS shown in Figure 5.10.

THE INNER JOIN

An inner join builds a record in the resultant table only when matches occur. An inner join of ORDSKED (primary join file) and CUSMAS (secondary join file) over CUSNBR would yield the data shown in Table 5.3.

Order 114 was not placed into the table because there was no match for customer C3 in the CUSMAS file. Because customer C6 had no orders, its customer master record wasn't joined to any ORDSKED records.

```
A                                               REF(ORDSKED)
A           R SKEDWRKR
A             ORDNBR      R
A             CUSNBR      R
A             ITMNBR      R
A             ORDQTY      R
A             CUSNAM      R              REFFLD(CUSNAM CUSMAS)
A           K ORDNBR
```

Figure 5.10: DDS for dummy physical file for inner and left outer joins.

Table 5.3: Results from the Inner Join of ORDSKED and CUSMAS Over CUSNBR.				
ORDNBR	CUSNBR	ITMNBR	ORDQTY	CUSNAM
111	C7	I1	5	GROCERY
112	C2	I5	3	PET SHOP
113	C1	I7	4	HARDWARE STORE
115	C2	I4	8	PET SHOP

OPNQRYF does an inner join when the JDFTVAL (Join with Default Value) parameter has a value of *NO. The join just discussed would be coded as shown in Figure 5.11.

```
OPNQRYF     FILE((ORDSKED) (CUSMAS)) +
            FORMAT(SKEDWRK) +
            JFLD((1/CUSNBR 2/CUSNBR)) +
            JDFTVAL(*NO) +
            MAPFLD((CUSNBR '1/CUSNBR'))
```

Figure 5.11: OPNQRYF example of an inner join.

Because it's an inner join, the order of the files listed in the FILE parameter could be reversed. In inner joins, it really doesn't matter which file is primary and which is secondary. Because *NO is the default value for JDFTVAL, that parameter could be omitted. Thus, another way to code this command is shown in Figure 5.12.

```
OPNQRYF     FILE((CUSMAS) (ORDSKED)) +
            FORMAT(SKEDWRK) +
            JFLD((1/CUSNBR 2/CUSNBR)) +
            MAPFLD((CUSNBR '1/CUSNBR'))
```

Figure 5.12: Alternative coding method for an inner join.

The MAPFLD entry tells OPNQRYF from which file the value of CUSNBR is to be taken.

If any join logical files are used with an OPNQRYF inner join, they must be inner joins themselves. They must not have the JDFTVAL keyword in their DDS.

The Left Outer Join

The inner join example produced an incomplete order schedule because order 114 was omitted. To include that order, you will need a left outer join. Unmatched records in the primary file will be matched with a dummy secondary file record with default values. This example presumes that field CUSNAM in file CUSMAS has a default value of blanks. When the query from the preceding inner join example is used in a left outer join, the query returns the data as shown in Table 5.4.

Table 5.4: Results of the Left Outer Join.				
ORDNBR	CUSNBR	ITMNBR	ORDQTY	CUSNAM
111	C7	I1	5	GROCERY
112	C2	I5	3	PET SHOP
113	C1	I7	4	HARDWARE STORE
114	C3	I1	3	
115	C2	I4	8	PET SHOP

To tell OPNQRYF you want a left outer join, specify JDFTVAL(*YES) , as shown in Figure 5.13.

The order of the files listed in the FILE parameter cannot be reversed. In left outer joins, it does matter which file is primary and which is secondary. If you reverse the order of the files, you get the data shown in Table 5.5 instead.

```
OPNQRYF      FILE((ORDSKED) (CUSMAS)) +
             FORMAT(SKEDWRK) +
             JFLD((1/CUSNBR 2/CUSNBR)) +
             JDFTVAL(*YES) +
             MAPFLD((CUSNBR '1/CUSNBR'))
```

Figure 5.13: An example of OPNQRYF with a left outer join.

Table 5.5: Results When Primary and Secondary Files Are Reversed.				
ORDNBR	CUSNBR	ITMNBR	ORDQTY	CUSNAM
113	C1	I7	4	HARDWARE STORE
112	C2	I5	3	PET SHOP
115	C2	I4	8	PET SHOP
0	C6		0	RESTAURANT
111	C7	I1	5	GROCERY

The results listed in Table 5.5 presumes the default values for fields ORDNBR, ITMNBR, and ORDQTY are zero, blank, and zero respectively.

If any join logical files are used with an OPNQRYF left outer join, they must be left outer joins themselves. They must have the JDFTVAL keyword in their DDS.

THE EXCEPTION JOIN

Sometimes it's necessary to know the records of a file that don't have matching values in another file. For example, you might want to know which orders are for customers who aren't in the customer master file. The AS/400 handles this type of request with the exception join.

An exception join of ORDSKED and CUSMAS returns only one order, as shown in Table 5.6.

To cause an exception join, give the JDFTVAL parameter a value of *ONLYDFT as shown in Figure 5.14.

Table 5.6: Result of Exception Join.				
ORDNBR	**CUSNBR**	**ITMNBR**	**ORDQTY**	**CUSNAM**
114	C3	I1	3	

```
OPNQRYF     FILE((ORDSKED) (CUSMAS)) +
            FORMAT(SKEDWRK) +
            JFLD((1/CUSNBR 2/CUSNBR)) +
            JDFTVAL(*ONLYDFT) +
            MAPFLD((CUSNBR '1/CUSNBR'))
```

Figure 5.14: An example of OPNQRYF *with an exception join.*

Additionally, you might want to know which customers have no orders in the order-schedule file. The code shown in Figure 5.15 accomplishes that.

```
OPNQRYF     FILE((CUSMAS) (ORDSKED)) +
            FORMAT(CUSMAS) +
            JFLD((1/CUSNBR 2/CUSNBR)) +
            JDFTVAL(*ONLYDFT) +
            MAPFLD((CUSNBR '1/CUSNBR'))
```

Figure 5.15: Another example of an exception join.

The command shown in Figure 5.15 gives the results shown in Table 5.7.

Table 5.7: Results of Exception.	
CUSNBR	**CUSNAM**
C6	RESTAURANT

Using the name of the primary join file in the format parameter is common when doing an exception join because the default values from the secondary files usually are not significant. Ambiguous field references usually are mapped to the primary file for the same reason.

Join logical files used with OPNQRYF joins must match in type. Because DDS doesn't support the exception join, join logical files may not be used in OPNQRYF exception joins. Although the inner and left outer joins are common, the exception join is not available on many relational systems.

VARIATIONS

In the preceding examples, files are joined on one common field. But often it is necessary to join on multiple fields.

JOINING ON MORE THAN ONE FIELD

Consider a sales analysis report that reads data from two physical files and passes data to an RPG program according to the format of file SLSWK. See Table 5.8.

Table 5.8: File Formats for Sales Analysis Example.	
SALESSUM (Sales Summary)	
YEAR	Sales Year
CUSNBR	Customer Number
AMTSLD	Amount Sold in Dollars
FORECAST (Sales Forecasts)	
CUSNBR	Customer Number
FORYR	Year
FORAMT	Forecasted Sales in Dollars
SLSWK	
CUSNBR	Customer Number
YEAR	Sales Year
AMTSLD	Total Amount Sold
FORAMT	Forecast Amount

To be meaningful, the records must be joined by two fields—customer number and year—as shown in Figure 5.16.

```
OVRDBF      FILE(SLSWK) TOFILE(SALESSUM) SHARE(*YES)
OPNQRYF     FILE((SALESSUM) (FORECAST)) FORMAT(SLSWK) +
              KEYFLD((AMTSLD *DESC)) +
              JFLD((YEAR FORYR) (1/CUSNBR 2/CUSNBR)) +
              JDFTVAL(*YES) +
              MAPFLD((CUSNBR '1/CUSNBR'))
CALL        PGM(FORECAS1)
CLOF        OPINID(SALESSUM)
DLTOVR      FILE(SLSWK)
```

Figure 5.16: Example of joining records on more than one field.

JOINING A FILE TO ITSELF

A file can be joined to itself in the same way that two different files can be joined to each other. The only difference is that fields from the files must be qualified with file numbers ('1/CUSNO') rather than by file names ('CUST/CUSNO'). Consider the data from an employee master file as listed in Table 5.9.

To find out who makes as much (or more than) a supervisor, you first need a file to provide a data format. Figure 5.17 shows the DDS for the WORKS file.

Now you need a query. See Figure 5.18.

Each record built by OPNQRYF contains data from two EMP records: an employee record and the supervisor's record. Program SALARYRPT sees only the record where the employee's salary is at least as much as his supervisor's. Table 5.10 shows the results of the OPNQRYF.

Obviously, you couldn't qualify by file name (such as EMP/EMPNAM) because the query processor wouldn't have known which EMP record (the employee's or the supervisor's) to use.

UNEQUAL JOINS

In the examples provided so far, files have been joined only on matching values. For example, a customer number of one file must equal a customer number of another file. Table 5.11 lists the six relational operators on which OS/400 allows joining.

Table 5.9: Employee Master File Data.				
EMPNO	EMPNAM	SALARY	SUPERV	. . . and other fields . . .
0076	SMITH	2500	1112	
1112	JONES	2400	1333	
1118	GOMEZ	2200	1333	
1222	BROWN	2200	1118	
1333	GREEN	3000	0000	
1444	WHITE	1900	1118	
1555	BLACK	2000	1112	
1666	GRAY	2000	1112	
0076	SMITH	2500	1112	
1112	JONES	2400	1333	
1118	GOMEZ	2200	1333	
1222	BROWN	2200	1118	
1333	GREEN	3000	0000	
1444	WHITE	1900	1118	
1555	BLACK	2000	1112	
1666	GRAY	2000	1112	

For example, suppose that, at the end of the year, you want to give gifts to customers based on how much they bought. Table 5.12 lists the gifts and how much a customer must have purchased to be eligible for each gift.

A customer may be eligible for more than one gift. For example, a customer with a purchasing value of $1,550.00 could have a choice of a radio, a tennis racket, or a microwave oven. You cannot use an equal join to obtain a list of the gifts for which each

```
A* File WORK8
A          R WORK8R
A* Employee fields
A          EMPNO      R        REFFLD(EMPNO   EMP)
A          EMPNAM     R        REFFLD(EMPNAM EMP)
A          EMPSAL     R        REFFLD(SALARY EMP)
A* Supervisor fields
A          SUPNO      R        REFFLD(EMPNO   EMP)
A          SUPNAM     R        REFFLD(EMPNAM EMP)
A          SUPSAL     R        REFFLD(SALARY EMP)
A          K EMPNO
```

Figure 5.17: The DDS for the file named WORKS.

```
OVRDBF     FILE(WORK8) TOFILE(EMP) SHARE(*YES)
OPNQRYF    FILE((EMP) (EMP)) FORMAT(WORK8) +
           QRYSLT('1/SALARY *GE 2/SALARY') +
           KEYFLD((EMPNO)) +
           JFLD((1/SUPERV 2/EMPNO)) +
           MAPFLD((EMPNO  '1/EMPNO') +
                 (EMPNAM '1/EMPNAM') +
                 (EMPSAL '1/SALARY') +
                 (SUPNO  '1/SUPERV') +
                 (SUPNAM '2/EMPNAM') +
                 (SUPSAL '2/SALARY'))
CALL       PGM(SALARYRPT)
CLOF       OPNID(EMP)
DLTOVR     FILE(WORK8)
```

Figure 5.18: Example of joining a file to itself.

Table 5.10: Results of QRYSLT in Figure 5.18.					
EMPNO	EMPNAM	EMPSAL	SUPNO	SUPNAM	SUPSAL
0076	SMITH	2500	1112	JONES	2400
1222	BROWN	2200	1118	GOMEZ	2200

Table 5.11: Valid Relational Operators for Joins.	
Operator	Description
*EQ	Equal (default)
*NE	Not equal
*GT	Greater than
*GE	Greater than or equal to
*LT	Less than
*LE	Less than or equal to

Table 5.12: Values in GIFTS File.	
MINAMT	GIFT
500.00	RADIO
1,000.00	TENNIS RACKET
1,500.00	MICROWAVE OVEN
2,500.00	TV SET

customer is eligible, because few, if any, customers purchase the exact minimum amount, and only one gift per customer would be returned by the query. You must use some type of unequal join.

To specify an unequal join, code a join operator after the two join fields in a join pair (as shown in Figure 5.19). In this case, sales summary records are joined to gifts where the amount sold to a customer is greater than or equal to the minimum amount eligible for a gift.

Table 5.13 lists the sales summary data and Table 5.14 lists the result of the query.

```
OPNQRYF      FILE((SALESSUM) (GIFTS)) FORMAT(GIFTLST) +
             KEYFLD((CUSNBR)) +
             JFLD((AMTSLD MINAMT *GE))
```

Figure 5.19: An example of an unequal join.

Table 5.13: Sales Summary Data.		
YEAR	**CUSNBR**	**AMTSLD**
1990	C1	329.21
1990	C2	1,827.91
1990	C7	1,000.00

Table 5.14: Results of the Query in Table 5.13.	
CUSNBR	**GIFT**
C2	RADIO
C2	TENNIS RACKET
C2	MICROWAVE OVEN
C7	RADIO
C7	TENNIS RACKET

JOINING ON FIELDS OF DIFFERENT TYPES AND FORMATS

The field pairs in the JFLD parameter don't have to match in size or data type, but numeric fields can be joined only to other numeric fields, and character fields to other character fields. In other words, you can join a five-digit zoned decimal field with zero decimal positions and a seven-digit packed decimal field with one decimal position. OPNQRYF will take care of the mechanics needed to compare the fields. However, you cannot join a four-byte character field and a four-byte zoned decimal field, even when the character field contains valid zoned decimal data.

You can join incompatible fields by redefining one or both of them with the MAPFLD parameter. Date fields present a good way to illustrate this technique. Dates are stored in a variety of ways: as character fields and numeric fields, in year-month-day, month-day-year, day-month-year, and Julian formats. Sometimes all four digits of the year are stored, sometimes only two digits represent the year, and sometimes the last digit of the century prefixes the last two digits of the year. For example, "076" means 20th century, seventy-six, or 1976. Sometimes dates are stored in separate month, day, and year fields.

IBM has added date and time stamp data types. Because many applications don't use these data types, this incompatibility will continue to be a problem. For additional details, see chapter 6.

Two files, FILEA and FILEB, are used to illustrate how to join incompatible dates. Unless otherwise stated, assume that FILEA has a date field called DATEA and FILEB has a date field called DATEB.

When two date fields have the same format (such as month-day-year stored in six digits) and the same data type, joining is no different than joining on the customer number or item number (as in the preceding examples). Suppose that DATEA and DATEB are both six-digit numbers in year-month-day format, and that DATEA is packed while DATEB is zoned. (Note: Remember that any numeric joins to any numeric. Therefore, packed and zoned are equivalent as far as joining is concerned.) Figure 5.20 shows an example.

```
OPNQRYF      FILE((FILEA) (FILEB)) FORMAT(WORK) +
             JFLD((DATEA DATEB))
```

Figure 5.20: Joining files based on date fields.

When the date format is the same, but the data type is different, the numeric variable should be mapped to a character work variable to carry out the join. Consider the case where DATEA is character and DATEB is packed decimal. Both fields store dates as six digits in MMDDYY format. The OPNQRYF command to carry out the join would look like Figure 5.21.

The %DIGITS function puts the digits of DATEB into a character variable. Another method is to map the packed field into a zoned field, which is then mapped into a character field.

```
OPNQRYF    FILE((FILEA) (FILEB)) FORMAT(WORK) +
           JFLD((DATEA WORKB)) +
           MAPFLD((WORKB '%DIGITS(DATEB)'))
```

Figure 5.21: Joining files based on mapped fields.

When two files are to be joined over character-date fields of different formats, one or both of the date fields must be reformatted. The reformatting is usually done through a series of substring and concatenation operations. If dates stored in DATEA are in the format YYYYMMDD (19910926, for example) and those in DATEB are formatted as MMD-DYY (092691, for example), change both dates to YYMMDD format. See Figure 5.22.

```
OPNQRYF    FILE((FILEA) (FILEB)) FORMAT(WORK) +
           JFLD((WORKA WORKB)) +
           MAPFLD((WORKA '%SST(DATEA 3 6)') +
                  (WORKB '%SST(DATEB 5 2) *CAT +
                  %SST(DATEB 1 4)'))
```

Figure 5.22: Another example of joining files based on mapped fields.

There are two methods of joining over numeric fields that contain dates. One method is to convert one field through a series of multiplication and division operations. Presume that DATEA, as shown in Figure 5.23, is in YYMMDD format and DATEB is in MMDDYY format.

```
OPNQRYF    FILE((FILEA) (FILEB)) FORMAT(WORK) +
           JFLD((DATEA WORKB)) +
           MAPFLD((WORKB +
                  'DATEB // 100 * 10000 + DATEB / 100' +
                  *PACKED 6))
```

Figure 5.23: Reformatting numeric fields with arithmetic operations.

If DATEB has the value 092791, then DATEB // 100 is 91, the year. Multiplying that by 10000 gives 910000, which places the year in its proper position. DATEB / 100 is 927.91, which added to 910000 is 910927.91. Because WORKB is given a length of 6, but no decimal positions entry, it is presumed to be a whole number. Therefore, the fractional portion gets truncated.

The other approach (Figure 5.24), converting both date fields to character type, requires a little more code, but it's probably faster because of the relative sluggishness of multiplication and division operations.

```
OPNQRYF    FILE((FILEA) (FILEB)) FORMAT(WORK) +
           JFLD((WORKA WORKB)) +
           MAPFLD((WORKA '%DIGITS(DATEA)') +
               (CB '%DIGITS(DATEB)') +
               (WORKB '%SST(CB 5 2) *CAT '%SST(CB 1 4)'))
```

Figure 5.24: Converting dates to character type.

Sometimes dates are stored as separate year, month, and day fields. Consider a situation where FILEA has a six-digit, packed decimal field called DATEA that contains a date in month-day-year format. In contrast, FILEB has two-byte character fields called YEARB, MONTHB, and DAYB. Figures 5.25 through 5.27 show three ways to carry out the join.

```
OPNQRYF    FILE((FILEA) (FILEB)) FORMAT(WORK) +
           JFLD((YEARA   YEARB) +
               (MONTHA MONTHB) +
               (DAYA      DAYB)) +
           MAPFLD((DATEC  '%DIGITS(DATEA)') +
               (YEARA   '%SST(DATEC 5 2)') +
               (MONTHA  '%SST(DATEC 1 2)') +
               (DAYA    '%SST(DATEC 3 2)'))
```

Figure 5.25: Converting DATEA to three, two-byte character fields.

```
OPNQRYF    FILE((FILEA) (FILEB)) FORMAT(WORK) +
           JFLD((DATEA   WORKB)) +
           MAPFLD((DATE1 'MONTHB *CAT DAYB *CAT YEARB') +
               (WORKB 'DATE1' *ZONED 6))
```

Figure 5.26: Converting YEARB, MONTHB, and DAYB to one numeric field.

JOINING THROUGH AN INTERMEDIARY FILE

Sometimes two files need to be joined, but there is no function to convert one join field to the needed matching value of the other join field. For example, perhaps the company you

```
OPNQRYF     FILE((FILEA) (FILEB)) FORMAT(WORK) +
            JFLD((A B)) +
            MAPFLD((A '%DIGITS(DATEA)') +
                (B 'MONTHB *CAT DAYB *CAT YEARB'))
```

Figure 5.27: Converting DATEA to a character field. Convert YEARB, MONTHB, and DAYB to a character field.

work for is bought by another company, and they insist that you cease to use your existing customer numbers and begin to use corporate customer numbers. In such a case, you have to set up a reference file that consists of two fields—the old customer number and the new customer number—to help join the new customer order schedule to the old history.

This method also can be used to join over dates stored in character or numeric fields (especially Julian dates) to other date types. Imagine a file called DATEFL (date file). Each record has one date stored in several formats. Field MDY is a six-byte numeric variable in month-day-year format. JULIAN is a Julian format field. Other formats, such as year-month-day also have fields. Such a file might look something like the data listed in Table 5.15.

Table 5.15: Example of a File with Multiple Date Formats.		
MDYN	**YMDN**	**JULIAN**
010188	880101	88001
010288	880102	88002
. . .		
123193	931231	93365

If DATEA is stored as month-day-year and DATEB as Julian, you could join the two files with the code shown in Figure 5.28. (Presume all date fields are numeric.)

If DATEA in a certain FILEA record has the value 020291, for example, it will join to a record in DATEFL where MDYN is 020291 and JULIAN is 91033. This DATEFL record will join to any records in FILEB where DATEB is also equal to 91033.

```
OPNQRYF     FILE((FILEA) (DATEFL) (FILEB)) +
            FORMAT(WORK) +
            JFLD((DATEA MDYN) (JULIAN DATEB))
```

Figure 5.28: Example of joining files with numeric dates.

ANOTHER WAY TO DO DATE ARITHMETIC

While considering the subject of date fields, take a look at a method for carrying out date arithmetic by joining to the DATEFL file. This method can be a handy way to get the number of days between two dates (even if the two dates have different formats).

You shouldn't use this technique with the date and time stamp data types introduced in V2R1M1 of OS/400. It should be used with dates stored in character or numeric fields. See chapter 6 for more information on date and time stamp date types.

To do date arithmetic, you have to include another field in the dates file. This field is the number of days since a base date, which can be any date you want to use. In this example, the field is called SINCE, and it will be the number of days since the earliest date in the file. (This number corresponds to the %DAYS function that is used with date and time stamp data types.) You must join to the dates file twice, once on each date.

Returning to the shipment-history applications examples used in chapter 4, suppose you have a file, SHIPHIST, which contains shipment history. Each record has a customer number, item number, quantity shipped, the date the customer requested the merchandise be shipped, and the date the merchandise was actually shipped. Figure 5.29 shows the DDS definition for SHIPHIST.

```
A* SHIPMENT HISTORY FILE
A                                         REF(DICTIONARY)
A          R SHIPHISR
A            ITMNO      R
A            CUSNO      R
A            QTYSHP     5  0
A            REQDT      6  0                TEXT('REQUEST DATE')
A                                          EDTCDE(Y)
A            SHPDT      6  0                TEXT('SHIP DATE')
A                                          EDTCDE(Y)
```

Figure 5.29: DDS definition for file SHIPHIST.

First, you need a format file, SHIPHIS2, to contain these fields plus a field for the number of elapsed days between the two dates. See Figure 5.30.

```
A* FORMAT FILE FOR OPNQRYF JOB SHIPC1 - SHIPMENT STATUS REPORT
                                       REF(SHIPHIST)
A            R SHIPHISR
A              ITMNO      R
A              CUSNO      R
A              QTYSHP     R
A              REQDT      R
A              SHPDT      R
A              DAYSDF            4   0     TEXT('DAYS DIFFERENCE')
A* NUMBER OF DAYS BETWEEN SHPDT AND REQDT
```

Figure 5.30: DDS for intermediate file SHIPHIS2.

Figure 5.31 shows the DDS for file DATEFL.

```
A        R DATEREC              TEXT('DATE FILE)
A          YMDC      6          TEXT('YYMMDD CHARACTER')
A          YMDN      6   0      TEXT('YYMMDD NUMERIC')
A          MDYC      6          TEXT('MMDDYY CHARACTER')
A          MDYN      6   0      TEXT('MMDDYY NUMERIC')
A          JULIAN    5   0      TEXT('JULIAN DATE - YYDDD')
A          SINCE     5   0      TEXT('DAYS SINCE 1ST DATE')
A        K YMDN
```

Figure 5.31: DDS for file DATEFL.

The HLL program that produces the report would be similar to the RPG III and IV programs SHIPR1 and printer file SHIPR1R listed in the chapter 4 discussion of date arithmetic with numeric and character fields. Figure 5.32 shows the CL program that runs the job.

The DATEFL file is listed twice in the FILE parameter because information from two DATEFL records is needed for each SHIPHIST record. You must have the SINCE field that corresponds to the requested ship date and the SINCE field that corresponds to the actual ship date.

OPNQRYF joins a SHIPHIST (shipment history) record to the DATEFL record whose YMDN field matches the request date. The DATEFL fields from this join can be referred to with the file number 2 (as in 2/SINCE). It also joins the same SHIPHIST record to the DATEFL

```
/* SHIPMENT STATUS REPORT */
   PGM
   OVRDBF     FILE(SHIPHIS2) TOFILE(SHIPHIST) SHARE(*YES)
   OPNQRYF    FILE((SHIPHIST) (DATEFL) (DATEFL)) +
                FORMAT(SHIPHIS2) +
                KEYFLD((REQDT)) +
                JFLD((REQDT 2/YMDN) (SHPDT 3/YMDN)) +
                JDFTVAL(*YES) +
                MAPFLD((DAYSDF '3/SINCE - 2/SINCE'))
   CALL       PGM(SHIPR1)
   CLOF       OPNID(SHIPHIST)
   DLTOVR     FILE(SHIPHIS2)
   ENDPGM
```

Figure 5.32: The CL code to run the program to calculate difference between two dates.

record whose YMDN field matches the actual ship date. The fields from this DATEFL record are referred to with the file number 3. See Table 5.16 for an example of OPNQRYF data.

Customer	Item	Qty	Request Date	Since	Ship	Since
7colspan Table 5.16: Sample Data.						
Customer	Item	Qty	Request Date	Since	Ship	Since
6789	EF-1212	100	91/07/24	204	92/02/18	413
1234	AB-4567	12	92/01/05	369	92/01/05	369
2345	CD-4667	250	92/01/07	371	92/01/11	375
3456	CD-4667	50	92/01/07	371	91/11/15	318
5678	DE-5678	100	92/01/07	371	92/01/05	369
1234	CD-4667	18	92/02/25	420	92/03/01	425

OPNQRYF subtracts the SINCE value of the request date from the SINCE value of the actual ship date to get the difference between the two dates in days. If the result is positive, the actual ship date is after the requested date, and the shipment was late.

Suppose a shipment history record has a request date of 920225 and a ship date of 920301. The value of SINCE in the DATEFL record with a YMDN field of 920225 is 420 (if the first date in DATEFL is January 1, 1991). The DATEFL record whose YMDN field is 920301 has a value of 425 in the SINCE field. OPNQRYF subtracts 420 from 425 and determines that the shipment was five days late. The result of this job is a report that looks like the example shown in Figure 5.33.

```
3/07/92              SHIPMENT STATUS              PAGE    1

                           DATE    DATE               DAYS
CUSTOMER  ITEM     QTY  REQUESTED  SHIPPED  STATUS   LATE
   6789   EF-1212  100   91/07/24  92/02/18  LATE     209
   1234   AB-4567   12   92/01/05  92/01/05
   2345   CD-4667  250   92/01/07  92/01/11  LATE       4
   3456   CD-4667   50   92/01/07  91/11/15
   5678   DE-5678  100   92/01/07  92/01/05
   1234   CD-4667   18   92/02/25  92/03/01  LATE       5

** END OF REPORT **      3 OF    6 SHIPMENTS WERE LATE
```

Figure 5.33: Sample output of the Shipment Status Report program.

If DATEFL might be helpful to you, refer to appendix D where you will find a short RPG program that will generate the file for you.

THE CARTESIAN PRODUCT

The Cartesian product of two files is produced when every record of one file is joined to every record of another file. Consider two files:

❖ CUSMAS (customer master file). See Table 5.17.

❖ ITMMAS (item master file). See Table 5.18.

Table 5.17: Customer Master File.	
CUSNBR	**CUSNAM**
C1	HARDWARE STORE
C2	PET SHOP
C6	RESTAURANT
C7	GROCERY

Table 5.18: Item Master File.	
ITMNBR	**ITMDSC**
I1	MOP
I2	BROOM

Table 5.19 shows the Cartesian product of the two files.

Table 5.19: Cartesian Product of Customer Master and Item Master Files.			
CUSNBR	**CUSNAM**	**ITMNBR**	**ITMDSC**
C1	HARDWARE STORE	I1	MOP
C1	HARDWARE STORE	I2	BROOM
C2	PET SHOP	I1	MOP
C2	PET SHOP	I2	BROOM
C6	RESTAURANT	I1	MOP
C6	RESTAURANT	I2	BROOM
C7	GROCERY	I1	MOP
C7	GROCERY	I2	BROOM

To cause OPNQRYF to generate the Cartesian product of two files, omit the join specifications (as in the example shown in Figure 5.34). Don't code the JFLD, JORDER, or JDFTVAL parameters.

The Cartesian product is always a type of inner join. If you need a left outer join or a default join, you must use the JFLD parameter.

```
OPNQRYF      FILE((CUSMAS) (ITMMAS)) FORMAT(CUSITM)
```

Figure 5.34: Using OPNQRYF *to generate the Cartesian product of two files.*

Using a Cartesian Product to Generate Percentage of Total

Now that you know what Cartesian products are, what do you do with them? One way you can use them is to generate percentages on detail lines. To illustrate this technique, look at the sales figures data listed in Table 5.20. Each record contains the total dollar amount sold to a customer in a given year.

Now you can write a program that will show all summary figures for a given year (which is passed in as a parameter), sorted in descending order by AMTSLD (amount sold). That seems easy enough. If you want to print the percentage of total sales on each detail line, it presents a problem because the RPG program won't know what the total sales are until it has read all the records and accumulated AMTSLD. What you need is a way for the RPG program to know what the total sales are before it reads any records.

You can handle this problem in several ways, but this example shows how to do it with a Cartesian product. First, define a file to contain the total sales as shown in Figure 5.35.

Second, define a format file for the report program (Figure 5.36). Each record has a customer number, the sales for that customer, and the total sales for all customers.

Now that each detail record contains the total sales, it will be simple for the RPG program to divide AMTSLD by TOTSLS to determine a percentage.

Obtaining the total sales amount is not difficult. You can write a short RPG program to read the sales figures and build one record in SALESTOT at end of job. You also can do it with OPNQRYF and the Copy From Query File (CPYFRMQRYF) command. Because this technique hasn't been covered yet, don't worry if you don't understand exactly how that works; you will understand it later. The first OPNQRYF command in the program summarizes the total sales into file SALESTOT. Chapters 7 and 9 address summarizing data and the CPYFRMQRYF command.

Once SALESTOT has the total sales figure, you can join it to each record of SALESSUM to build detail records that contain the total sales field. Because the only record of SALESTOT

Table 5.20: File SALESSUM (Sales Summary).		
YEAR	CUSNBR	AMTSLD
1990	11111	25.00
1991	11111	50.00
1989	11111	40.00
1990	22222	30.00
1991	22222	34.00
1991	33333	50.00
1990	44444	25.00
1991	44444	25.00
1988	55555	10.00
1990	55555	15.00
1991	55555	25.00
1988	66666	35.00
1989	66666	40.00
1990	66666	50.00
1991	66666	70.00

```
A* Physical file SALESTOT
A          R SALESTOTR
A            TOTSLS        9   2
```

Figure 5.35: DDS for the file to contain total sales.

```
A* Physical file WORK11
A          R WORK11R
A            CUSNBR     R         REFFLD(CUSNBR SALESSUM)
A            AMTSLD     R         REFFLD(AMTSLD SALESSUM)
A            TOTSLS     R         REFFLD(TOTSLS SALESTOT)
A          K AMTSLD               DESCEND
```

Figure 5.36: DDS for the output file.

is being joined to each record of SALESSUM, you must use a Cartesian product. Figure 5.37 shows the code to print a summary report with percentages on the detail lines:

```
/* Print yearly sales by customer with percentages */
    PGM         PARM(&YEAR)
    DCL         VAR(&YEAR) TYPE(*CHAR) LEN(4)
/* Summarize total sales for selected year into 1 record */
/* in file SALESTOT                                     */
    OPNQRYF     FILE((SALESSUM)) FORMAT(SALESTOT) +
                QRYSLT('YEAR *EQ ' *CAT &YEAR) +
                MAPFLD((TOTSLS '%SUM(AMTSLD)'))
    CPYFRMQRYF  FROMOPNID(SALESSUM) TOFILE(SALESTOT) +
                MBROPT(*REPLACE)
    CLOF        OPNID(SALESSUM)
/* Join total sales to every record of sales summary file */
/* and print report */
    OVRDBF      FILE(WORK11) TOFILE(SALESSUM) SHARE(*YES)
    OPNQRYF     FILE((SALESSUM) (SALESTOT)) FORMAT(WORK11) +
                QRYSLT('YEAR *EQ ' *CAT &YEAR) +
                KEYFLD((AMTSLD *DESC))
    CALL        PGM(SLSRPT767) PARM(&YEAR)
    CLOF        OPNID(SALESSUM)
    DLTOVR      FILE(WORK11)
    ENDPGM
```

Figure 5.37: CL program to print summary report.

Figures 5.38 contains the RPG IV program to calculate the percentages and print the report. Figure 5.39 contains the printer file DDS.

If you call the CL program, passing it a parameter value of 1990, you will get results like those shown in Figure 5.40.

Note that the RPG program doesn't have to accumulate total sales; each detail record already contains that figure.

```
* Program SLSRPT767
* Print sales report by customer, with percentage of total

FWork11    if  e       k disk
FSlsRpt767Po   e         printer OflInd(*in88)

D EntryPlist    pr              ExtPgm('SLSRPT767')
D  PYear                  4
D
D EntryPlist    pi
D  PYear                  4

C                eval     P@year = PYear
C                write    PageHdr
C
C                read     Work11R
C                dow      not %eof
C                if       Totsls = *zero
C                eval     Pct = *zero
C                else
C                eval (h) Pct = 100 * (amtsld / totsls)
C                endif
C                if       *in88
C                write    PageHdr
C                eval     *in88 = *off
C                endif
C                write    Detail01
C                read     Work11R
C                enddo
C
C                write    Total01
C                eval     *inLR = *on
```

Figure 5.38: RPG IV Sales Summary Report program.

JOINING IN THE QRYSLT PARAMETER

As a rule, Cartesian products aren't useful unless they are restricted by the QRYSLT parameter. For example, the Cartesian product of the customer master and order schedule files presented earlier in this chapter would be nonsense unless the records were matched by customer number. See Figure 5.41.

The effect, in this case, would be an inner join on an equal condition (see Figure 5.42).

The preceding is why the use of Cartesian products is sometimes known as joining in the QRYSLT parameter.

```
      * Print sales report by customer, with percentage of total
A                                             REF(WORK11)
A          R PAGEHDR                          SKIPB(05) SPACEA(2)
A                                            1DATE EDTCDE(Y)
A                                           14'Sales Summary for'
A            P@YEAR              4           +1
A                                           43'Page'
A                                           +1PAGNBR EDTCDE(Z)
A                                             SPACEA(2)
A                                           11'Cust'
A                                           24'Amount'
A                                           37'Pct'
A          R DETAIL01                         SPACEA(1)
A            CUSNBR        R                 11
A            AMTSLD        R                 +5EDTCDE(J)
A            PCT                  5 2        +3EDTCDE(M)
A          R TOTAL01                          SPACEB(1)
A                                           13'Total'
A            TOTSLS        R                 21EDTCDE(J)
```

Figure 5.39: Printer file SLSRPT767.

```
8/10/98     Sales Summary for 1998    Page   1

            Cust      Amount     Pct

            66666     50.00     34.48
            22222     30.00     20.69
            11111     25.00     17.24
            44444     25.00     17.24
            55555     15.00     10.34

            Total    145.00
```

Figure 5.40: Sample output from Sales Summary Report program.

```
OPNQRYF     FILE((CUSMAS) (ORDSKED)) +
            FORMAT(SKEDWRK) +
            QRYSLT('1/CUSNBR *EQ 2/CUSNBR') +
            MAPFLD((CUSNBR '1/CUSNBR'))
```

Figure 5.41: Match records by equal customer number.

```
OPNQRYF    FILE((CUSMAS) (ORDSKED)) +
           FORMAT(SKEDWRK) +
           JFLD(1/CUSNBR 2/CUSNBR)) +
           MAPFLD((CUSNBR '1/CUSNBR'))
```

Figure 5.42: Using JFLD to match records by customer number.

WHY JOIN IN THE QRYSLT PARAMETER?

While the QRYSLT parameter offers an alternative method of defining join specifications, it is restricted to inner joins. On the other hand, the JFLD parameter allows left outer and exception joins. Why join in the QRYSLT parameter? One reason is for convenience. Suppose you have a sales detail file that contains, among other things, an item number and a date (as shown in Table 5.21).

Table 5.21: SLSDTL (Sales Detail) File.						
CUSNO	**INVNO**	**INVDAT**	**INVLN**	**ITMNO**	**QTYSLD**	**UNTPR**
111	123445	19901123	1	AB-4567	1	4.00
111	135778	19910305	1	AB-4567	1	4.00
111	247665	19910801	1	AB-4567	1	4.00

Suppose further that you have a costing file that has an item number, a cost, and a range of dates that the cost is in effect (see Table 5.22).

Now suppose you want to join the sales detail file to the item cost file. You have to join on two fields: item number and date. The item number join is easy because it is an exact match, but the date field join is a different matter. The invoice date in the sales detail file must be between the from date (FRMDAT) and through date (THRDAT) fields in the cost file. You can do the join in the JFLD parameter (as shown in Figure 5.43).

If you think the JFLD parameter is a little messy and prefer to use the %RANGE function, as shown in Figure 5.44, you can join in the QRYSLT parameter instead.

Figure 5.45 shows you how you can mix and match the two methods.

Table 5.22: *ITMCOST (Item Cost) File.*			
ITMNO	**FRMDAT**	**THRDAT**	**ITMCST**
AB-4567	0	19901231	2.10
AB-4567	19910101	19910731	2.25
AB-4567	19910801	99999999	2.50
CD-4667	0	19910331	2.00
CD-4667	19910401	19910731	2.25
CD-4667	19910801	99999999	2.50
DE-5678	0	99999999	4.48
EF-1212	19910101	19910321	4.80
EF-1212	19910322	19910717	4.89
EF-1212	19910718	99999999	5.00

```
OPNQRYF     FILE((SLSDTL) (ITMCOST)) +
            FORMAT(HISTWK3) +
            KEYFLD((INVNO)) +
            JFLD((1/ITMNO 2/ITMNO) +
                (INVDAT FRMDAT *GE) +
                (INVDAT THRDAT *LE)) +
            MAPFLD((ITMNO '1/ITMNO'))
```

Figure 5.43: Joining based on a range of dates in the *JFLD* parameter.

```
OPNQRYF     FILE((SLSDTL) (ITMCOST)) FORMAT(HISTWK3) +
            QRYSLT('(1/ITMNO=2/ITMNO) +
                & (INVDAT=%RANGE(FRMDAT THRDAT))') +
            KEYFLD((INVNO)) +
            MAPFLD((ITMNO '1/ITMNO'))
```

Figure 5.44: Joining with *%RANGE* in the *QRYSLT* parameter.

```
OPNQRYF     FILE((SLSDTL) (ITMCOST)) FORMAT(HISTWK3) +
            QRYSLT('INVDAT = %RANGE(FRMDAT THRDAT)') +
            KEYFLD((INVNO)) +
            JFLD((1/ITMNO 2/ITMNO)) +
            MAPFLD((ITMNO '1/ITMNO'))
```

Figure 5.45: Joining using multiple methods.

None of these methods has any performance advantage over the others. You can pick the one you like. In any case, you should get a report that looks like the one shown in Figure 5.46.

```
SLS11R                    SALES REPORT                    11/22/91   PAGE   1

INVOICE           INVOICE    ITEM           UNIT  UNIT  EXTENDED  EXTENDED   PROFIT
NUMBER   CUST     DATE       NUMBER  QTY  PRICE  COST      PRICE      COST  OR LOSS

123445   0111     1990/11/23 AB-4567   1   4.00  2.10       4.00      2.10     1.90
135778   0111     1991/03/05 AB-4567   1   4.00  2.25       4.00      2.25     1.75
247665   0111     1991/08/01 AB-4567   1   4.00  2.50       4.00      2.50     1.50

** END OF REPORT **
```

Figure 5.46: Sample output from the Sales Report program.

Another reason to join using the QRYSLT parameter is that, in a few cases, you cannot join a file with the JFLD parameter. Here is one such case. Suppose you have a file with a repeating group in it. Suppose the "unnormalized" file is an employee master file that contains three skill fields as shown in Table 5.23.

Table 5.23: EMP (Employee Master) File.					
EMPNO	**EMPNAM**	**. . . other irrelevant fields . . .**	**SKILL1**	**SKILL2**	**SKILL3**
0076	SMITH		SPA		
1112	JONES		FRE	SPA	
1118	GOMEZ		GER	FRE	SPA
1222	BROWN				
1333	GREEN			GER	

Table 5.24 shows the skills master file.

Table 5.24: SKILLS (Skills) File.	
SKLCOD	**SKLDSC**
FRE	FRENCH
GER	GERMAN
SPA	SPANISH

For joining purposes, create a dummy physical file called EMPWRK1. See in Figure 5.47.

```
A        R EMPWRK1R
A          EMPNO      R        REFFLD(EMPNO  EMP)
A          EMPNAM     R        REFFLD(EMPNAM EMP)
A          SKLCOD     R        REFFLD(SKLCOD SKILLS)
A          SKLDSC     R        REFFLD(SKLDSC SKILLS)
A        K EMPNO
```

Figure 5.47: DDS for dummy physical file EMOWRK1.

Any of the three skill fields in the EMP file is to join to one field in the SKILLS file. Figure 5.48 shows how you do it.

```
PGM
OVRDBF     FILE(EMPWRK1) TOFILE(EMP) SHARE(*YES)
OPNQRYF    FILE((EMP) (SKILLS)) +
             FORMAT(EMPWRK1) +
             QRYSLT('SKLCOD = SKILL1 *OR +
                     SKLCOD = SKILL2 *OR +
                     SKLCOD = SKILL3') +
             KEYFLD((EMPNO)) +
             OPNID(JOINFILE)
CALL       PGM(SKILLLIST)
CLOF       OPNID(JOINFILE)
DLTOVR     FILE(EMPWRK1)
ENDPGM
```

Figure 5.48: Joining one field in one file to any of three fields in another file.

Table 5.25 shows what you get when you run the job. Each skill field in the employee master file with a matching value in the skills file produces a query record. If you are stuck with a file that is not normalized, you have found a way to process it as if it were normalized.

Table 5.25: Result of Skills Join Shown in Figure 5.48.			
EMPNO	**EMPNAM**	**SKLCOD**	**SKLDSC**
0076	SMITH	SPA	SPANISH
1112	JONES	FRE	FRENCH
1112	JONES	SPA	SPANISH
1118	GOMEZ	FRE	FRENCH
1118	GOMEZ	GER	GERMAN
1118	GOMEZ	SPA	SPANISH
1333	GREEN	GER	GERMAN

JOINING MORE THAN TWO FILES

Almost all of the examples presented in this chapter deal with joining two files. The examples are limited to two files to keep the examples as uncluttered as possible. Joining three or more files is not more difficult; it just requires a little more code.

Now you can modify one of the queries—joining an order schedule file to the customer master to get the customer's name—that you worked with earlier in this chapter. The order schedule file also contains an item number. Add to the query the description of the item and quantity on hand as listed in the item master file. As with the prior example, the files are defined in Table 5.26.

First, you will need to add the item description and on-hand quantity to the dummy physical file used to format the data as shown in Table 5.27.

Next, add the ITEMMAS file to the list of files to be queried and a join specification to tie ITEMMAS to ORDSKED. Because field ITMNBR is found in both ORDSKED and ITEMMAS, add a MAPFLD entry to tell OPNQRYF to use the value of ITMNBR in the order schedule file. See Figure 5.49.

Table 5.26: Files for Joining More Than Two Files.		
ORDSKED		
	ORDNBR	Order number
	CUSNBR	Customer number
	ITMNBR	Item number
	ORDQTY	Quantity ordered
CUSMAS		
	CUSNBR	Customer number
	CUSNAM	Customer name
ITEMMAS		
	ITMNBR	Item number
	ITMDSC	Description
	QOH	Quantity on hand
	ORDPT	Order point
	STKLOC	Stock location

You may join up to 32 physical file members in a single OPNQRYF command. However, you cannot always code 32 files in the FILE parameter. Suppose you are joining two physical files to a join logical (which is itself over four physical files). You would list three files in the FILE parameter, but they would account for six physical files.

The maximum number of join field pairs you can code is 50. You don't need a join field pair to cover all the files. If there is no join field pair for a file, it will be joined as a Cartesian product.

In the example shown in Figure 5.50, SALESSUM and CUSTOT are joined on a common customer number. Each product of that join will be joined to each record of the SALESTOT file because SALESTOT is not referenced in the JFLD parameter.

Table 5.27: Dummy Physical File for Joining Three Files.	
ORDSKED	
ORDNBR	Order number
CUSNBR	Customer number
ITMNBR	Item number
ORDQTY	Quantity ordered
ITMDSC	Item description
QOH	Quantity on hand

```
OPNQRYF    FILE((ORDSKED) (CUSMAS) (ITEMMAS)) +
           FORMAT(SKEDWRK) +
           JFLD((1/CUSNBR 2/CUSNBR) +
               (1/ITMNBR 3/ITMNBR)) +
           MAPFLD((CUSNBR '1/CUSNBR')
               (ITMNBR '1/ITMNBR'))
```

Figure 5.49: Example of joining more than two files.

```
OPNQRYF    FILE((SALESSUM) (CUSTTOT) (SALESTOT)) +
           FORMAT(WORK2) +
           JFLD((1/CUSNBR 2/CUSNBR)) +
           KEYFLD((CUSNBR) (YEAR))
```

Figure 5.50: A three-file join that includes a Cartesian product.

PERFORMANCE CONSIDERATIONS

OPNQRYF prefers to join files with fewer selected records to those with more selected records. For example, if you are joining a customer master file of 26,000 records to a sales representative file of 50 records, and you are selecting all records from each, OPNQRYF prefers to use the salesrep file as the primary file.

INNER JOINS VERSUS LEFT OUTER JOINS

If the file with more records is specified as primary, and you are using an inner join, and the JORDER parameter has a value of *ANY, the system could decide to rearrange the order of the files. To return to the example in the previous paragraph, OPNQRYF may treat the salesrep file as primary (regardless of the order of the two files in the file parameter).

Because OPNQRYF cannot rearrange the order of the files if you specify JORDER(*FILE), use a left outer join, or use a default join, or you should use inner joins when possible. And, unless you have some compelling reason, don't use the JORDER parameter.

Sometimes you can change left outer joins to inner joins by adding "bogus" values to a file. For example, if a customer who is not assigned a salesrep is routinely assigned a salesrep number of zero, add a salesrep 0 to the salesrep master file. Although there is no salesrep with the number 0, you may be able to use an inner join instead of an outer join if salesrep 0 exists in the salesrep file.

This technique won't work in cases where truly bogus salesrep numbers have been entered into the customer file. However, if you can ensure that each customer has a valid salesrep number or a zero, it will work.

ACCESS PATHS

The query processor requires that secondary join files have an appropriate index over the join fields. If no such index already exists, the system will build a temporary one. You can often speed up a join by creating a logical file with an index the system can use.

For example, suppose you are joining the salesrep master file (primary) to the customer master (secondary) on salesrep number. You can create a logical file over the customer master keyed on salesrep number. Therefore, the system won't have to create that access path every time your query runs.

The system could decide to change the join order. If it decides to use a secondary file as primary, you will need an access path over the file you specified as primary.

Keep in mind that the system sometimes will change the join order and, at other times, will retain the join order you specify. In such cases, it is advantageous to create indexes on the join fields of both the primary and secondary files. However, you shouldn't automatically create such logical files. You should first decide whether or not the expense of maintaining the logical is worth the cost. If this query runs frequently, you will probably need to create the extra logical. If it only runs once a month, it is probably not worth the cost.

DUPLICATE TEST CONDITIONS

If a field tested in the QRYSLT parameter is found in more than one file, you can speed up data retrieval by testing the field in each file. (Note: The field doesn't have to have the same name in each file, but it may have the same name.) In the example shown in Figure 5.51, customer number is found in both files. Therefore, both files are tested in the QRYSLT parameter.

```
OVRDBF      FILE(SKEDWORK) TOFILE(ORDSKED)SHARE(*YES)
OPNQRYF     FILE((ORDSKED) (CUSMAS)) FORMAT (SKEDWORK) +
            QRYSLT('1/CUSNBR=4051 & 2/CUSNBR=4051') +
            JFLD((1/CUSNBR 2/CUSNBR)) JDFTVAL(*YES)* +
            MAPFLD((CUSNBR '1/CUSNBR'))
```

Figure 5.51: An example of coding for duplicate test conditions.

KEY FIELDS FROM MORE THAN ONE FILE

OPNQRYF permits you to specify key fields from more than one file, but that privilege carries a penalty. Before the system can order your data, it must create a temporary physical file with all the fields in the joined format. Copying all that data can take quite a while. Use this feature if you need it, but don't use it unnecessarily. When you do sort on fields from more than one file, you can get better performance by specifying ALWCPYDTA(*OPTIMIZE) , which lets the system use a sort routine.

SUMMARY

OPNQRYF can dynamically join files, which is often a viable replacement for rarely used join logical files. This capability also is necessary for carrying out exception joins, which aren't supported by join logicals.

OPNQRYF supports three join types. Inner joins return records only when the primary join file finds matching records in the secondary join files. Left outer joins return records for all primary file records (whether or not they are matched in the secondary join files). The exception join only returns primary records that have no secondary file matches.

Two record types may be joined on more than one field. A file may be joined to itself. Records may be joined on any relational condition.

When joining over fields of incompatible data types, it is necessary to map one or more fields to change the data type. If a field cannot be mapped to a satisfactory data value, an intermediary file is required.

The Cartesian product of two files is formed when all records of one file are joined to all records of another file. Cartesian products are rarely useful unless restricted by the QRYSLT parameter. One great disadvantage of joining through Cartesian product is that the inner join is the only type of join permitted.

6

❖ Date and Time Data Types

Dealing with the date, time, and time stamp data types is not really any different than working with character data but, for some reason, people think it is dissimilar. Date, time, and time stamp literals are like character literals—in that they are surrounded by quotation marks—but they differ from character literals in that they can only have certain values. This chapter explains how to use these three data types with OPNQRYF.

LITERALS

Time stamp literals are coded in the format shown in Figure 6.1.

```
     YYYY-MM-DD-hh.mm.ss.mmmmmm
       ^   ^   ^  ^  ^  ^   ^
Year ---+   |   |  |  |  |   +------- Microsecond
Month -----+   |  |  |  +---------- Second
Day ----------+  |  +------------- Minute
                 +--------------- Hour
```

Figure 6.1: Format of a time stamp literal.

Here is an example of a time stamp literal:
'1991-12-31-04.12.28.000342'

It represents 28 and 342 millionths seconds after 4:12 o'clock on the morning of December 31, 1991.

Date literals have several representations because people throughout the world write dates in different ways. All date types except Julian have year, month, and day portions. Julian has year and day portions only. (These examples presume that the job's date separator character, DATSEP, has a value of "/".) Table 6.1 shows the different date formats with examples of each.

Table 6.1: Examples of Date Formats.				
Format	**Length**	**Order**	**Delimiter**	**Example**
*ISO, JIS	10	yyyymmdd	.	1992.04.15
*USA	10	mmddyyyy	/	04/15/1992
*EUR	10	ddmmyyyy	.	15.04.1992
*YMD	8	yymmdd	DATSEP	92/04/15
*MDY	8	mmddyy	DATSEP	04/15/92
*DMY	8	ddmmyy	DATSEP	15/04/92
*JUL	7	yyddd	DATSEP	92/106

Time literals also have several forms (see Table 6.2) and all have hour and minute portions. All of them include seconds, except for *USA, which ends with "AM" or "PM". (These examples presume that the job's time separator character, TIMSEP, has a value of ":".)

Duration literals represent an interval of time. The three types of duration literals are:

❖ Date.

❖ Time.

❖ Time stamp.

Table 6.2: Examples of Time Formats.				
Format	**Length**	**Order**	**Delimiter**	**Example**
*ISO, *EUR	8	hhmmss	.	20.02.35
*JIS	8	hhmmss	:	20:02:35
*USA	8	hhmm xM	:	08:02 PM
*HMS	8	hhmmss	TIMSEP	20:02:35

All duration literals are decimal numbers. They are used for date/time arithmetic.

Date duration literals are eight-digit decimal numbers with no decimal places. The first four positions represent years, the next two are months, and the last two are days. The date duration literal 00021114 means an interval of two years, 11 months, and 14 days.

Time duration literals have six digits (none of which are decimal places). The first two digits are hours, the next two are minutes, and the final two are seconds. For example, 130258 stands for 13 hours, two minutes, and 58 seconds.

Time-stamp duration literals are 20 digits long. The last six are decimal places that represent microseconds. The 14 digits to the left of the decimal point are divided into increments as follows:

- ❖ Years, four digits.
- ❖ Months, two digits.
- ❖ Days, two digits.
- ❖ Hours, two digits.
- ❖ Minutes, two digits.
- ❖ Seconds, two digits.

Therefore, 00040302111009.757643 means an interval of four years, three months, two days, 11 hours, 10 minutes, nine and 757,643 millionths seconds.

Don't confuse dates, times, and time stamps with durations. Dates, times, and time stamps stand for points of time (such as 3:30 in the afternoon of April 9, 1990 or the day of April 3, 1992). Durations are intervals of time, such as two hours and 18 minutes.

Let's look of some examples of OPNQRYF using date and time data types. The first example, shown in Figure 6.2, uses a field called REQDT, which is a date field in *ISO format. This expression selects orders that customers have requested for shipment on June 30, 1992.

```
OPNQRYF     FILE((CUSORDH)) +
              QRYSLT('REQDT *EQ ''1992-06-30''')
```

Figure 6.2: Selecting records based on a date field in *ISO format.

If REQDT were in *USA format, the correct expression would look like the code shown in Figure 6.3.

```
OPNQRYF     FILE((CUSORDH)) +
              QRYSLT('REQDT *EQ ''06/30/1992''')
```

Figure 6.3: Selecting records based on a date field in *USA format.

CMPTIM (completion time) is a time-stamp field. The expression shown in Figure 6.4 selects operations completed before June 1, 1992.

```
OPNQRYF     FILE((MACHIS)) +
              QRYSLT('CMPTIM *LT ''1992-06-01-00.00.00.000000''')
```

Figure 6.4: Selecting records based on a time-stamp field.

As shown in Figure 6.5, TTIME is a field of type time. This query retrieves records where TTIME is 11 A.M. or later.

```
OPNQRYF     FILE((CHRON)) +
              QRYSLT(''TTIME *GE "11:00:00"')
```

Figure 6.5: Selecting records based on a time field.

The expression also could have been written as shown in Figure 6.6 regardless of the format of TTIME.

```
        QRYSLT('TTIME *GE "11:00 AM"')
or
        QRYSLT('TTIME *GE "11.00.00"')
```

Figure 6.6: Alternative notations for time.

While OPNQRYF requires that date literals have the same format as the date fields they are compared to, it is lenient with time fields.

DATE, TIME, AND TIME-STAMP FUNCTIONS

The functions that operate with fields of type DATE, TIME, and TIME STAMP can be divided into categories of constant, extraction, conversion, and duration functions. A complete list of these functions is provided in appendix C. The functions are examined briefly in the following sections.

CONSTANT FUNCTIONS

Three constant functions, %CURDATE, %CURTIME, and %CURTIMESTP, return the current date or time. Figure 6.7 shows an example where all orders with a due date on or before the current date will be read by the high-level language program.

```
OPNQRYF      FILE((ORDERS)) QRYSLT('DUEDAT *LE %CURDATE')
```

Figure 6.7: An example of using %CURDATE to select records.

The %CURTIMEZONE function returns the value stored in system value QUTCOFFSET (Offset from Coordinated Universal Time, or Greenwich Mean Time) as a time duration. Local time minus %CURTMEZONE equals UTC.

EXTRACTION FUNCTIONS

Another group of functions extracts portions of a date, time, or time stamp. They are:

❖ %DATE.

❖ %YEAR.

❖ %MONTH.

- ❖ %DAY.
- ❖ %TIME.
- ❖ %HOUR.
- ❖ %MINUTE.
- ❖ %SECOND.
- ❖ %MICSEC.

Presuming time-stamp field STAMP has the value 1990-05-23-14.16.19.000025, the functions in Table 6.3 yield the following values.

Table 6.3: Examples of Date, Time, and Time-Stamp Functions.	
%DATE(STAMP)	1990-05-23
%TIME(STAMP)	14.16.19
%YEAR(STAMP)	1990
%MONTH(STAMP)	05
%DAY(STAMPS)	23
%HOUR(STAMP)	14
%MINUTE(STAMP)	16
%SECOND(STAMP)	19
%MICSEC(STAMP)	25

CMPTIM (completion time) is a time-stamp field that contains the date and time of completion of a machining operation. To select the operations completed in June 1992, you can use the code shown in Figure 6.8.

CONVERSION FUNCTIONS

Some functions convert date, time, time-stamp data to or from other data types. They are:

- ❖ %TIMESTP.
- ❖ %DATE.

❖ %TIME.

❖ %CHAR.

❖ %DAYS.

```
OPNQRYF   ... +
            QRYSLT('%DATE(CMPTIM) *EQ +
                    %RANGE("1992-06-01" "1992-06-30")')

        or QRYSLT('%YEAR(CMPTIM) = 1992 & %MONTH(CMPTIM) = 6')
```

Figure 6.8: Selecting records based on a time-stamp field.

The %TIMESTP function takes two arguments—a date and a time—and combines them into a time stamp.

For example, if field GDATE contains the date August 2, 1955, and GTIME is 6:30 P.M., then %TIMESTP(GDATE GTIME) is 1955-08-02-18.30.00.000000.

The %DATE function can convert either character or numeric data to a date field. If you give it a character argument, the argument must be the external representation of the date (e.g., %DATE ('11/17/1988')).

If the argument is numeric, it must be a whole number in the range of 1 to 3,652,059, which stands for the number of the day on a continuous calendar dating from January 1, 1 A.D. In this sense, the %DATE function is the opposite of the %DAYS function.

The %TIME function can convert character data that contains the character representation of a time to a time field.

The %CHAR function returns the character representation of a date/time argument according to the format specified in the second argument.

Suppose the date July 30, 1957 is stored in date field HDATE. The value of %CHAR(HDATE "ISO") returns the value 1957-07-30.

The %DAYS function returns an integer value for a date. Each day's value is one more than the previous day's value. The values listed in Table 6.4 are supplied as points of reference.

Table 6.4: Sample %DAYS Function Values.	
January 1, 1 AD	1
January 1, 1000	364,878
January 1, 1990	726,468
January 1, 1995	728,294
January 1, 2000	730,120

DURATION FUNCTIONS

The duration functions return intervals of time. For example, %DURYEAR(2) means a duration, or interval, of two years. Duration functions are used for date, time, and time-stamp arithmetic. The duration functions are:

- ❖ %DURYEAR.
- ❖ %DURMONTH.
- ❖ %DURDAY.
- ❖ %DURHOUR.
- ❖ %DURMINUTE.
- ❖ %DURSEC.
- ❖ %DURMICSEC.

You might find it easier to understand durations if you read them as they are written in SQL: as a number followed by a unit of time. For example, read %DURYEAR(2) as "two years" and %DURSEC(50) as "50 seconds."

DATE, TIME, AND TIME-STAMP ARITHMETIC

If date, time and time-stamp arithmetic were not supported, storing data in date, time, and time-stamp fields would offer little, if any, advantage over storing them in character and numeric fields—as has been done for many years.

If you have been doing date or time arithmetic with data stored in numeric or character fields, you might consider using the DATE, TIME, and TIME STAMP fields instead. While some high-level languages don't have the capability to carry out the arithmetic, OPNQRYF has functions that should let you do just about any type of date or time arithmetic you want.

Date/time arithmetic involves three quantities. Two of the quantities must be date/time/ time stamps, and the other quantity is a duration. For example, you can subtract one date from another and get a duration. Or you can add a duration to (or subtract a duration from) one date to get another date.

Obviously, you cannot add December 12, 1979 to February 17, 1977, and get anything meaningful. You can, however, subtract February 17, 1977, from December 12, 1979, and get the interval of time between the two dates. Or you can add four days to December 30, 1990, to get January 3, 1991.

You can perform three operations with dates, times, and time stamps:

1. You can add a duration to a date/time/time stamp to get another date/time/time stamp.
2. You can subtract a duration from a date/time/time stamp to get another date/time/time stamp.
3. You can subtract one date/time/time stamp from another to get a duration.

The duration can be expressed with one function (such as, %DURDAY(3)) or with a combination of functions (%DURDAY(1) + %DURHOUR(4)). In either case, it is still one duration of time.

If you do use two functions to express a single duration, don't group the two within parentheses. Doing so would cause the system to try to add two durations (which is not permitted). A duration may only be added to date, time, or time-stamp data. Examples of the right and wrong way to express multiple functions are shown in Figure 6.9.

```
Wrong: QRYSLT('DUED *LE ODATE + (%DURMONTH(2) + %DURDAY(15))')
Right: QRYSLT('DUED *LE ODATE + %DURMONTH(2) + %DURDAY(15)')
```

Figure 6.9: Right and wrong ways to express multiple-duration functions.

Example 1

The query shown in Figure 6.10 selects records where the due date is on or before the date one month from the current date.

```
OPNQRYF     FILE((ORDERS)) +
            QRYSLT('DUEDAT *LE %CURDATE + %DURMONTH(1))')
```

Figure 6.10: Selection using multiple functions.

You can read this expression as "1 month past the current date" or, if you prefer, "1 month from today." In any case, adding the %DURMONTH function to a date returns the same day of the next month. August 2, 1955 plus one month yields September 2, 1955. In the case of a nonexistent date, OPNQRYF returns the last date of the month. For example, August 31 plus one month returns September 30 because there is no September 31.

Example 2

Although they do return the same result in many cases, %DURMONTH(1) and %DURDAY(30) aren't equivalent. The query shown in Figure 6.11 selects orders due within the coming 30 days. Past due orders are not selected.

```
OPNQRYF     FILE((ORDERS)) +
            QRYSLT('DUEDAT *EQ
                   %RANGE(%CURDATE %CURDATE + %DURDAY(30)')
```

Figure 6.11: Selecting records within a 30-day window regardless of the month.

Example 3

The query shown in Figure 6.12 selects orders due on or before the date one month from the current date. Past due orders are included.

```
OPNQRYF     FILE((ORDERS)) +
            QRYSLT('DUEDAT *LE %CURDATE + %DURMONTH(1)')
```

Figure 6.12: Selecting records within one month of the current date.

Example 4

File MACHHIS (machining history) has two time fields: start and stop times for a machining operation. The query shown in Figure 6.13 finds all operations that lasted more than 15 minutes.

DATE AND TIME DATA TYPES

```
OPNQRYF     FILE((MACHHIS)) +
            QRYSLT('STPTIM - STRTIM > %DURMINUTE(15)')
```

Figure 6.13: Selecting records based on %DURMINUTE.

Example 5

The query shown in Figure 6.14 finds all operations that lasted less than 30 seconds.

```
OPNQRYF     FILE((MACHHIS)) +
            QRYSLT('STPTIM - STRTIM < %DURSEC(30)')
```

Figure 6.14: Selecting records based on %DURSEC.

Example 6

File MOPHIS (machining operation history) has two time-stamp fields: STRTIM (start time) and CMPTIM (completion time). The code shown in Figure 6.15 selects the operations that lasted four minutes or less.

```
    OPNQRYF     FILE((MOPHIS)) +
                QRYSLT('CMPTIM - STRTIM *LE 00000000000400.000000')
                    or 'CMPTIM - STRTIM *LE 400.000000'
                    or 'CMPTIM - STRTIM *LE 400'
                    or 'STRTIM + %DURMINUTE(4) *GE CMPTIM'
                    or 'CMPTIM - %DURMINUTE(4) *LE STRTIM'
                    or 'CMPTIM - 00000000000400.000 *LE STRTIM'
or OPNQRYF      FILE((MOPHIS)) +
                QRYSLT('CMPTIM - FOURMINS *LE STRTIM') +
                MAPFLD((FOURMINS '400' *DEC 20 6))
```

Figure 6.15: Selecting records based on calculation of duration in minutes.

Example 7

REQDAT (request date) is the date a customer requests for shipment of an order. ACKDAT (acknowledged date) is the date the order can be shipped. The code shown in Figure

6.16 selects the orders that you plan to ship more than one day after the requested ship date.

```
OPNQRYF     FILE((CUSORDH)) +
            QRYSLT('%DAYS(ACKDAT) - %DAYS(REQDAT) *GT 1')
              or 'ACKDAT - %DURDAY(1) *GT REQDT'
              or 'ACKDAT - REQDT *GT 00000001'
              or 'ACKDAT - REQDT *GT 1'
```

Figure 6.16: Selecting records based on multiple criteria.

These examples should be sufficient to give you an idea of some different forms of time-stamp arithmetic.

7

❖ Summary Processing

The preceding chapters discuss OPNQRYF's detail-processing capabilities. Each record sent to the high-level language program represents data from only one record of each of the input files. This chapter examines cases in which one query file record represents a group of records in the input files. OPNQRYF does representative processing in two ways: processing by unique key fields and processing by group.

UNIQUE KEY PROCESSING

The UNIQUEKEY parameter instructs OPNQRYF to select only one record to represent a group of records that have a common key. For example, if you sort an order schedule file on customer number, you can tell OPNQRYF to send only one record per customer number to the high-level language program that reads the queried data. Each record read by the high-level language program will contain data from one order schedule record only, but that one record acts as the sole representative for that customer.

Because the default value for UNIQUEKEY is *NONE, all eligible records will be read by the high-level language program. To use unique key processing, you must place in the UNIQUEKEY parameter the special value *ALL or a whole number with a value that ranges from one to the number of key fields in your query. This value tells OPNQRYF how many key fields to check for uniqueness. Suppose that file SKEDWORK has the data listed in Table 7.1. Each line represents one sales order. Figure 7.1 shows an example of processing by unique key.

Table 7.1: Data for the File SKEDWORK.			
ORDNO	**CUSNO**	**Date**	**Amount**
01	C11	91/10/20	200.00
02	C22	91/10/20	50.00
03	C33	91/10/20	25.00
04	C11	91/10/21	450.00
05	C33	91/10/21	20.00
06	C11	91/10/21	125.00

```
OPNQRYF     FILE((SKEDWORK)) +
            KEYFLD ((CUSNO) (AMOUNT *DESC)) +
            UNIQUEKEY(1)
```

Figure 7.1: Processing a file by unique key.

The command retrieves the record with the highest amount for each customer. See Table 7.2. UNIQUEKEY (1) means that only one key field, CUSNO, is to be checked for uniqueness.

Table 7.2: Results of the Query Shown in Figure 7.1.			
ORDNO	**CUSNO**	**Date**	**Amount**
04	C11	91/10/21	450.00
02	C22	91/10/20	50.00
03	C33	91/10/20	25.00

In contrast, the command shown in Figure 7.2 uses the special value *ALL (or UNIQUEKEY(2)) to retrieve one record for each customer on each date. Here all (both) key fields are checked for uniqueness. The retrieved records are shown in Table 7.3.

```
OPNQRYF   FILE((SKEDWORK)) +
          KEYFLD((CUSNO) (DATE)) +
          UNIQUEKEY(*ALL)
```

Figure 7.2: Retrieving one record for each customer on each date.

TABLE 7.3: RESULTS OF QUERY IN FIGURE 7.2.			
ORDNO	**CUSNO**	**Date**	**Amount**
01	C11	91/10/20	200.00
04	C11	91/10/21	450.00
02	C22	91/10/20	50.00
03	C33	91/10/20	25.00
05	C33	91/10/21	20.00

Order 06 was dropped because it was not the first order processed by OPNQRYF for customer C11 on October 21, 1991. In some situations, because OPNQRYF may not always process the data in the same sequence, OPNQRYF might drop order O4. If you want to ensure that the first order is the one OPNQRYF processes, you must add ORDNO to the list of key fields and change the UNIQUEKEY parameter value from *ALL to 2.

GROUP PROCESSING

Group processing, like unique key processing, causes OPNQRYF to build one query file record to represent a group of records. While each unique key record represents the group with its own data, group records use data from all records in the group.

To give you an idea of what group processing is all about, several scenarios are presented in the following sections. For example, you might like to know total sales for each customer. You could summarize sales by customer number as in Example 1 listed in Table 7.4. Each summary record represents a group of detail records with a common customer number; note that there won't be a date field. Or you could summarize sales by customer number and date as shown in Example 2. Additionally, as shown in Example 3, you

Table 7.4: File with Sales Summarized in Various Ways.

Example 1: Data summarized by Customer Number

CUSNO	Amount
C11	775.00
C22	50.00
C33	45.00

Example 2: Data summarized by Customer Number and Date

CUSNO	Date	Amount
C11	91/10/20	200.00
C11	91/10/21	575.00
C22	91/10/20	50.00
C33	91/10/20	25.00
C33	91/10/21	20.00

Example 3: Data summarized as one group with total on Amount

870.00

Example 4: Number of sales per customer, and the average amount of sale

CUSNO	Count	Average
C11	3	258.33
C22	1	50.00
C33	2	22.50

could summarize sales as one large group. If you wanted to, as shown in Example 4, you also could get the number of sales per customer and the average amount of sale.

For group processing, you must specify at least one grouping function in the MAPFLD parameter. Refer to appendix C for a complete list of the grouping functions. You can group data in two ways. You can group records that share common field values or you can group an entire file into one record.

GROUPING BY COMMON FIELD VALUES

OPNQRYF'S grouping feature summarizes common values from one or more fields into one record. For example, consider the following data stored in file HISTJL4 as shown in Table 7.5. File HISTJL4, a join logical file, has four fields:

❖ CUSNO (customer number).

❖ INVDAt (invoice date).

❖ UNTPR (unit price).

❖ QTYSLD (quantity sold) among others.

Table 7.5: Data in HISTJL4 File.				
INVDAT	**CUSNO**	**UNTPR**	**QTYSLD**	**Sale**
19910405	11111	1.00	1	1.00
19910405	22222	33.00	2	66.00
19910405	11111	36.75	1	36.75
19910406	33333	50.00	4	200.00
19910406	11111	7.49	1	7.49
19910406	11111	15.00	3	45.00

Each record represents one item sold to one customer. SALE is a virtual field, not stored in the database, but calculated by OPNQRYF. The other fields are stored in the database.

If you group this data by customer number, you will get three records. You will get one record for customers 11111, 22222, and 33333.

If you group the data by invoice date, you will get two records: one each for the fifth and sixth of April, 1991.

If you group it by customer number and invoice date, you will get four records: one for each of the combinations listed in Table 7.6.

Table 7.6: Data Grouped by Customer Number and Invoice Date.	
CUSNO	INVDAT
11111	19910405
11111	19910406
22222	19910405
33333	19910406

Grouping, therefore, gives one record for each distinct combination of group field values. You can tell OPNQRYF to group data with the GRPFLD (group field) parameter. To group by customer number, use the code shown in Figure 7.3.

```
OPNQRYF     FILE((HISTJL4)) ... GRPFLD(CUSNO)
```

Figure 7.3: Grouping records by CUSNO.

To group by customer number and invoice date, use the code shown in Figure 7.4.

```
OPNQRYF     FILE((HISTJL4)) ... GRPFLD(CUSNO INVDAT)
```

Figure 7.4: Grouping records by CUSNO and INVDAT.

Group field names can be qualified with a file name, a file number, or the special value *MAPFLD. You shouldn't need to qualify them because you will have to use the MAPFLD parameter to resolve any ambiguous field names.

Now that you have the data grouped, what do you want to know about it? OPNQRYF provides a variety of summary functions for groups. It can tell you how many records are in each group (%COUNT); the total of all values of a numeric field or expression (%SUM); and the minimum (%MIN), maximum (%MAX), or average (%AVG) value of a field or expression in the group. If you are interested in statistics, you can ask OPNQRYF for the variance (%VAR) or standard deviation (%STDDEV).

If you group the data listed above by customer number, you might count the records in each group, average number of units sold, average sale amount, largest sale, smallest sale, and total sales. OPNQRYF would present the data shown in Figure 7.5.

Cust	Ct	Avg units	Avg sale	Largest sale	Smallest sale	Total sales
11111	4	1.5	22.56	45.00	1.00	90.24
22222	1	2	66.00	66.00	66.00	66.00
33333	1	4	200.00	200.00	200.00	200.00

Figure 7.5: Example of output of grouped data.

Now, look at what it takes to process this data in summary form. First, you must have a file with a record layout that corresponds to the data as just presented. Because it is unlikely that there is such a file in the database, you will have to create a dummy physical file with the desired record layout. Figure 7.6 contains the DDS for the work file, SUMWRK.

```
A          R SUMWRKR                    TEXT('SUMMARY WORK FILE')
A            CUSNO      R               REFFLD(CUSNO HISTJL4)
A            COUNT         5  0
A            AVGUNT        5  0
A            AVGSAL        9  2
A            LRGSAL        9  2
A            SMLSAL        9  2
A            SUMSAL       11  2
A          K CUSNO
```

Figure 7.6: The DDS for work file to hold summarized data.

Create the file with no members [MBR(*NONE)] and write an RPG program, GRPPROG, to read it. Figure 7.7 shows the RPG IV file description to read the created file.

Although you know that the SUMWRK file doesn't have any data in it, the RPG program doesn't know that. Now you need a CL program to run it. See Figure 7.8.

```
F*** Program GRPPROG-sales summary report
F***
FSUMWRK    IF   E                 DISK
FSUMRPT    0    E                 PRINTER OFLIND(*IN88)
```

Figure 7.7: File description specifications of the RPG IV program to read summarized file.

```
PGM
OVRDBF     FILE(SUMWRK) TOFILE(HISTJL4) SHARE(*YES)
OPNQRYF    FILE((HISTJL4)) +
             FORMAT(SUMWRK) +
             KEYFLD(CUSNO) +
             GRPFLD(CUSNO) +
             MAPFLD((SALE    'UNTPR * QTYSLD') +
                    (COUNT   '%COUNT') +
                    (AVGUNT  '%AVG(UNTPR)') +
                    (AVGSAL  '%AVG(SALE)') +
                    (LRGSAL  '%MAX(SALE)') +
                    (SMLSAL  '%MIN(SALE)') +
                    (SUMSAL  '%SUM(SALE)'))
CALL       PGM(GRPPROG)
CLOF       OPNID(HISTJL4)
DLTOVR     FILE(SUMWRK)
ENDPGM
```

Figure 7.8: CL program to run summarizing program.

The %COUNT function returns a count of the selected records. The %SUM and %AVG functions return the sum and average of field SALE in the selected records. The %MAX and %MIN functions return the highest and lowest value of SALE found in the selected records.

SELECTING GROUPS

You don't have to process all the group records. You can have OPNQRYF omit the groups you don't want by coding an expression in the Group Select (GRPSLT) parameter. With the exception that it tests fields calculated with summary functions, GRPSLT works just like QRYSLT.

Suppose you only want to read summary records with more than one sale. You could add the clause GRPSLT('COUNT *GT 1') to the OPNQRYF in the previous example. See Figure 7.9.

```
OPNQRYF      FILE((HISTJL4)) +
             FORMAT(SUMWRK) +
             KEYFLD(CUSNO) +
             GRPFLD(CUSNO) +
             GRPSLT('COUNT *GT 1') +
             MAPFLD((SALE     'UNTPR * QTYSLD') +
                    (COUNT    '%COUNT') +
                    (AVGUNT   '%AVG(UNTPR)') +
                    (AVGSAL   '%AVG(SALE)') +
                    (LRGSAL   '%MAX(SALE)') +

                    (SMLSAL   '%MIN(SALE)') +
                    (SUMSAL   '%SUM(SALE)'))
```

Figure 7.9: Selecting specific groups of summarized data.

If you wanted only those customers whose average sale was not over $100.00, you could use the GRPSLT parameter shown in Figure 7.10.

```
GRPSLT('AVGSAL *LE 100')
```

Figure 7.10: Use the GRPSLT parameter to select average sales of $100.00 and less.

GRPSLT VERSUS QRYSLT

If you wanted only a certain range of customer numbers, you would put the test in the QRYSLT parameter (see Figure 7.11) rather than in the GRPSLT parameter because the value of CUSNO is not calculated with a summary function.

```
QRYSLT('CUSNO = %RANGE(1111 19999)')
```

Figure 7.11: Selecting within the QRYSLT parameter.

OPNQRYF would not return an error if you used GRPSLT, but the job would run less efficiently because OPNQRYF would calculate group figures that it would eventually discard.

Use the QRYSLT parameter to exclude records from the grouping function. For example, adding this QRYSLT expression causes OPNQRYF to build the summary figures from January 1991 records. Figure 7.12 shows an example.

```
QRYSLT('INVDAT=%RANGE(19910101 19910131)')
```

Figure 7.12: An example of using QRYSLT to exclude records from the grouping function.

A good rule to remember is not to put a test in the GRPSLT parameter if you can put it in the QRYSLT parameter instead.

GROUPING INTO ONE RECORD

You also can have OPNQRYF treat an entire file as one large group that produces grand summary totals only. To do so, omit the GRPFLD and GRPSLT parameters.

You can write a program to display the number of sales records, the average amount sold, the smallest and largest sales records, and the total amount sold.

Because the record format for HISTJL4 doesn't match the summarized data, you'll have to create a dummy physical file that does describe the summary fields. See Figure 7.13. (Remember, when you create dummy physical files to serve as record formats for OPNQRYF, specify MBR(*NONE).)

```
A* FILE SUMWRK (SUMMARY WORK)
A           R SUMWRKR
A             COUNT      5  0
A             SUM       12  2
A             AVG       10  2
A             HISALE    10  2
A             LOSALE    10  2
```

Figure 7.13: The DDS for dummy file to describe summary fields.

Use the MAPFLD parameter to calculate each sale as unit price times quantity sold and to calculate each summary figure as shown in Figure 7.14.

OPNQRYF returns only one record. You could write an RPG program to display the data, but another option is to have a CL program read the query file and show the results to the user in a message.

```
MAPFLD((SALE    'UNTPR * QTYSLD') +
        (COUNT  '%COUNT') +
        (SUM    '%SUM(SALE)') +
        (AVG    '%AVG(SALE)') +
        (HISALE '%MAX(SALE)') +
        (LOSALE '%MIN(SALE)'))
```

Figure 7.14: Using MAPFLD to calculate sales and summarize.

The program shown in Figure 7.15 accepts one parameter (a date) and sends the results to the user in a message.

```
PGM     PARM(&DATE)
DCL     VAR(&DATE)      TYPE(*DEC)  LEN(8) /* YYYYMMDD */
DCL     VAR(&CHARDATE)  TYPE(*CHAR) LEN(8)
DCL     VAR(&QRYSLT)    TYPE(*CHAR) LEN(256)
DCL     VAR(&MSG)       TYPE(*CHAR) LEN(160)
DCL     VAR(&NUMIN )    TYPE(*DEC)  LEN(15)
DCL     VAR(&NUMOUT)    TYPE(*CHAR) LEN(22)
DCLF    FILE(SUMWRK)
IF (&DATE *NE 0) THEN(DO)
     CHGVAR  VAR(&CHARDATE) VALUE(&DATE)
     CHGVAR  VAR(&QRYSLT) +
             VALUE('INVDAT *EQ' *BCAT &CHARDATE)
ENDDO
ELSE DO
     CHGVAR  VAR(&QRYSLT) VALUE(*ALL)
ENDDO
OVRDBF      FILE(SUMWRK) TOFILE(HISTJL4) SHARE(*YES)
OPNQRYF     FILE((HISTJL4)) +
            FORMAT(SUMWRK) +
            QRYSLT(&QRYSLT) +
            MAPFLD((SALE 'UNTPR * QTYSLD') +
                   (COUNT '%COUNT') +
                   (SUM '%SUM(SALE)') +
                   (AVG '%AVG(SALE)') +
                   (HISALE '%MAX(SALE)') +
                   (LOSALE '%MIN(SALE)'))
RCVF
MONMSG      MSGID(CPF5104) /* no data found */
CLOF        OPNID(HISTJL4)
DLTOVR      FILE(SUMWRK)
```

Figure 7.15: A CL program to read the query file and show results to the user in a message.

```
IF (&COUNT *GT 0) THEN(DO)
    EDTVAR  CHROUT(&NUMOUT) NUMINP(&COUNT)
    CHGVAR  VAR(&MSG) VALUE('Count=' *CAT &NUMOUT)
    CHGVAR  VAR(&NUMIN) VALUE(&SUM * 100)
    EDTVAR  CHROUT(&NUMOUT) NUMINP(&NUMIN) NBRDEC(2)
    CHGVAR  VAR(&MSG) +
              VALUE(&MSG *BCAT 'Sum=' *CAT &NUMOUT)
    CHGVAR  VAR(&NUMIN) VALUE(&AVG * 100)
    EDTVAR  CHROUT(&NUMOUT) NUMINP(&NUMIN) NBRDEC(2)
    CHGVAR  VAR(&MSG) +
              VALUE(&MSG *BCAT 'Average=' *CAT  &NUMOUT)
    CHGVAR  VAR(&NUMIN) VALUE(&HISALE * 100)
    EDTVAR  CHROUT(&NUMOUT) NUMINP(&NUMIN) NBRDEC(2)
    CHGVAR  VAR(&MSG) +
              VALUE(&MSG *BCAT 'Hi sale=' *CAT &NUMOUT)
    CHGVAR  VAR(&NUMIN) VALUE(&LOSALE * 100)
    EDTVAR  CHROUT(&NUMOUT) NUMINP(&NUMIN) NBRDEC(2)
    CHGVAR  VAR(&MSG) +
              VALUE(&MSG *BCAT 'Lo sale=' *CAT &NUMOUT)
ENDDO
ELSE DO
    CHGVAR  VAR(&MSG) +
              VALUE('No sales data found for' *BCAT &CHARDATE)
ENDDO
SNDPGMMSG  MSG(&MSG)
ENDPGM
```

Figure 7.15: A CL program to read the query file and show results to the user in a message. (Continued)

(Note: The Edit Variable (EDTVAR) command, incidentally, is not an OS/400 command, but is from the TAATOOL library).

If HISTJL4 has the data listed in Table 7.7, you could call the CL program and pass it the value 19910405, which would result in the output shown in Figure 7.16. (The system displays the message under the function key legend.)

If you use a date of all zeros, the message instead becomes the output shown in Figure 7.17.

If you use a date of 19910409, for which there are no sales, the message is as shown in Figure 7.18.

One more point deserves attention here. This example uses group processing in an interactive program. With small files, or when only a small number of records will be re-

Table 7.7: Data in HISTJL4 File.			
INVDAT	**CUSNO**	**UNTPR**	**QTYSLD**
19910404	11111	1.00	1
19910405	22222	33.00	2
19910405	11111	36.75	1
19910406	33333	50.00	4
19910406	11111	7.49	1
19910407	11111	15.00	3

```
MYMENU                                    MY MENU
Select one of the following:
    1. Display sales statistics for one day
    2. another option
    3. yet another option


Selection or command_
===>>_____

F3=Exit    F4=Prompt    F9=Retrieve    F12=Cancel
Count=2 Sum=102.75 Average=51.37 Hi sale=66.00 Lo sale=36.75
```

Figure 7.16: Sample output from a CL program.

```
Count=6 Sum=356.24 Average=59.37 Hi sale=200.00 Lo sale=7.49
```

Figure 7.17: Sample output from a CL program using a date of all zeros.

```
No sales data found for 19910409
```

Figure 7.18: Sample output using a date for which there are no sales.

trieved, this technique is acceptable. However, you should generally avoid group processing with interactive programs because the system will have to read hundreds or even thousands of records before the program can write to the screen.

RANDOM ACCESS

OPNQRYF doesn't permit random access to query files that use unique key or group processing. However, you can use another method to achieve the same results.

You should create a file to hold the data from the query file. This file should be keyed on the fields needed for the random access. You then must load the file with the queried data. You can write a program to do this or use the CPYFRMQRYF command. Your high-level language program should read this temporary file randomly.

SUMMARY

OPNQRYF supports two distinct types of summary processing. Unique key processing uses data from one record to represent a group of records.

Group processing uses data from a group of records to prepare summary figures for the entire group. Examples of summary functions are sum, average, variance, and standard deviation.

Only grouping fields and summary fields are permitted in the FORMAT file of a grouping query. When all selected records are being summarized into one total record, there are no grouping fields.

Summary figures may be used for record selection in the GRPSLT parameter. Grouping fields may also be tested in the GRPSLT parameter, but it is more efficient to test them in the QRYSLT parameter instead.

Random processing is not supported for unique key or group processing. Instead, the data must be copied to a temporary database file which can be accessed randomly.

8

❖ Reusing an Open Data Path

At one time or another, you probably will want to call two or more high-level language programs to run against a single execution of OPNQRYF. You can either use the Position Database File (POSDBF) command or high-level language commands that position the file pointer. You don't have to re-execute an identical OPNQRYF command before you call the second or subsequent high-level language program.

The techniques presented here apply to more than just OPNQRYF processing. They will work in any application in which a shared open data path is used. You can use these techniques without understanding how programs can share an open data path, but you cannot master something you don't understand.

SHARED OPEN DATA PATHS

When a program opens a file to read it sequentially, it sets an imaginary pointer at the first record in the file as shown in Figure 8.1.

As the program reads the file, it advances that pointer to the next record. The program continues to advance the pointer with each read, until it tries to read the end of file marker.

Suppose you have two programs, PGMA and PGMB, that read FILEX sequentially. PGMA reads two records and quits. PGMB reads the entire file.

```
                        beginning of file marker
---------------->>Record 1
   |------------->>Record 2
      |---------->>Record 3
         |------->>Record 4
            |--->>Record 5
               |->>end of file marker
```

Figure 8.1: Pointer set to first record in file.

If you call both programs back to back, as shown in Figure 8.2, PGMA will read records 1 and 2. PGMB will read all five records.

```
CALL    PGM(PGMA)
CALL    PGM(PGMB)
```

Figure 8.2: Example of calling two programs, back to back.

However, if you tell the two programs to share an open data path, as in Figure 8.3, PGMA will read records 1 and 2. PGMB will begin reading FILEX at record 3 and continue through record 5. PGMB won't use its own pointer, but will share the pointer of the existing open data path (which was left pointing to record 3 by PGMA).

```
OVRDBF    FILE(FILEX) SHARE(*YES)
OPNDBF    FILE(FILEX)
CALL      PGM(PGMA)
CALL      PGM(PGMB)
```

Figure 8.3: An example of the same two programs sharing an open data path.

Now think about the previous OPNQRYF examples. The OPNQRYF command in Figure 8.4 creates an open data path that the high-level language program shares.

When HLLPGM starts running, the file pointer for FILEX points to the first record to be retrieved. When HLLPGM ends, it is pointing at the end of file marker. Because FILEX is shared, another program reading FILEX will read the end of file marker on the first read.

Before another program can read from FILEX, the record pointer must be relocated from the end of file marker—unless the second program wants to read FILEX backwards.

```
OVRDBF     FILE(FILEX) SHARE(*YES)
OPNQRYF    FILE((FILEX)) QRYSLT('FLDX=4') KEYFLD (FLDY)
CALL       PGM(HLLPGM)
```

Figure 8.4: Using OPNQRYF *to create an open data path for a HLL program to use.*

THE POSDBF COMMAND

The POSDBF command positions the file pointer of an open data path to the beginning or end of a file. This command provides one way to run more than one high-level language program against the open data path created by an OPNQRYF command. See the example shown in Figure 8.5.

```
DCLF       FILE(FILEX)
OVRDBF     FILE(FILEX) SHARE(*YES)
OPNQRYF    FILE((FILEX)) QRYSLT('FLDX=35') +
             OPTIMIZE(*MINWAIT)
CALL       PGM(ONE)
POSDBF     OPNID(FILEX) POSITION(*START)
CALL       PGM(TWO)
CLOF       OPNID(FILEX)
DLTOVR     FILE(FILEX)
```

Figure 8.5: Repositioning an open data path pointer with POSDBF.

Programs ONE and TWO both read the query file sequentially, from top to bottom. When ONE finishes execution, the file pointer for FILEX is pointing to the end of file marker. The POSDBF command makes the pointer point to the first record instead. When TWO begins to run, it will start with the first record.

RESETTING THE FILE POINTER
FROM A HIGH-LEVEL LANGUAGE PROGRAM

You also can use high-level language commands that change the position of the file pointer, such as the RPG operation SETLL (set lower limit) and the COBOL verb START. The program fragment shown in Figure 8.6 is part of program THREE.

The SETLL operation eliminates the need to reposition the file pointer before calling this program. Therefore, you could run this program immediately after ONE, as shown in Figure 8.7.

```
FFileX     IF  E     K Disk
FXReport   O   E         Printer OflInd(*IN88)

C*... XREPORT has record formats named HDR, DTL, and TAIL
C                     Write     HDR

C       *LOVAL        SetLL     FileXR
C                     Read      FileXR
C                     DoW       not %eof
C*            ... more calculations ...
C                     Write     DTL
C                     Read      FileXR
C                     EndDo
C                     Write     TAIL
C                     Eval      *inLR = *on
```

Figure 8.6: Using SETLL to reposition the file pointer.

```
OVRDBF     FILE(FILEX) SHARE(*YES)
OPNQRYF    FILE((FILEX)) QRYSLT('FLDX=35') +
             OPTIMIZE(*MINWAIT)
CALL       PGM(ONE)
CALL       PGM(THREE)
CLOF       OPNID(FILEX)
DLTOVR     FILE(FILEX)
```

Figure 8.7: CL program where program ONE repositions file pointer with SETLL.

THE OPTIMIZE PARAMETER

The default value of the OPTIMIZE parameter is *ALLIO. This value tells the query optimizer to consider the time to:

1. Access the data.
2. Process the data with a high-level language program.

When you reuse an open data path and your query doesn't select all the records in the file, you can improve performance by specifying OPTIMIZE(*MINWAIT). This parameter will cause the query optimizer to use an access path, which can be used by all the high-level language programs, for record selection.

The first high-level language program will still go through both steps, access and process, but subsequent high-level language programs will only go through the process stage.

SUMMARY

You don't need to re-execute an identical OPNQRYF command within a job because the open data path exists until the job ends. Two methods can be used to reprocess an OPNQRYF file. One method is to use the POSDBF command in a CL program. The other method is to have the high-level language program reposition the file pointer.

Generally, it is a good idea to use the OPTIMIZE(*MINWAIT) parameter when you create an OPNQRYF file that is to be re-used. This parameter forces the operating system to create an access path over the queried data.

9

❖ The CPYFRMQRYF Command

The Copy From Query File (CPYFRMQRYF) command can read the open data path created by OPNQRYF and write to a physical file, a program-described printer file, a distributed data management (DDM) file, a tape file, or a diskette file. The FROMOPNID parameter must match the OPNID parameter of the OPNQRYF command, which defaults to the first file name in the file parameter. Copying to *PRINT sends the results to QSYSPRT. The other parameters work as they do for CPYF. Refer to the *CL Reference* manual for the complete syntax of CPYFRMQRYF. Because CPYFRMQRYF doesn't open the shared file, the SHARE(*YES) attribute isn't needed. Other system commands—such as CPYF and DSPPFM—won't share an open data path and, as a result, they may not be used with OPNQRYF.

DEBUGGING

You can use CPYFRMQRYF instead of (or in addition to) a high-level language program during program development. Once the OPNQRYF command is working correctly, you can begin work on the high-level language program and know that during testing your program is reading the data correctly.

Instead of copying to a printer file, dump the data to a disk file in QTEMP. Then display or print it with the RUNQRY command. (You can use RUNQRY even if Query/400 isn't installed on your system.) The advantage to this approach is that your data will appear in a format you can read.

If you use CPYFRMQRYF after calling a high-level language program, be sure to run a POSDBF command before running CPYFRMQRYF. If the open data path is at the end of file when CPYFRMQRYF is executed, you will get error CPF2971.

COPYING TO A FILE

If you write a read-a-record, write-a-record program to get the results of the query into a disk file, you can see one use for CPYFRMQRYF. Not only will CPYFRMQRYF write to disk, it also can build diskette, tape, and DDM files.

OPNQRYF will send the data to a high-level language program in a format different from that of the files containing the data. In most cases, this capability eliminates the need to build work files.

USING CPYFRMQRYF IN RECAP PROGRAMS

Writing programs that print recaps is a chore. Two basic approaches can be used to build recap programs:

- ❖ Accumulating recap figures in arrays.
- ❖ Accumulating recap figures in work files.

The CPYFRMQRYF command can take much of the drudgery out of writing recap programs. Actually, with CPYFRMQRYF, recap programs are not difficult to write.

The following sample application, with three recaps at the end of the report, prints a sales-history report. The sales data is in a join logical file named HISTJL1. The fields are listed in Table 9.1. You need a work file in which to store the summarized data. Let's call it SLS122PF (see Figure 9.1).

Figure 9.2 shows CL program SLS2122CL, which runs the recap job. SLS122CL runs grouping queries that build temporary files in QTEMP. Let's examine it in more detail.

Step 1: Copy the desired billing data into a temporary work file in QTEMP. This has two benefits. First, it ensures that the detail data and recaps are in sync. If someone were to add data to the underlying physical files while this program is running, it's possible that the recaps would not match the detail records printed on the report. Second, it speeds up processing by creating a smaller file over which the OPNQRYF commands can run.

Table 9.1: Fields in Join Logical File HISTJL1.

Field Name	Type	Length	Decimals	Comment
REPNO	Packed	3	0	Sales rep number
REPNAM	Character	15		Sales rep name
CUSNO	Packed	5	0	Customer numberl
CUSNAM	Character	20		Customer name
INVNO	Zoned	6	0	Invoice number
INVDAT	Packed	8	0	Invoice date (YYYYMMDD)
INVLN	Packed	2	0	Invoice line number
ITMNO	Character	7		Item number
ITMDSC	Character	22		Item description
UNTPR	Packed	5	2	Unit price
QTYSLD	Packed	5	0	Quantity sold

```
     ** WORK FILE FOR RECAPS PRINTED BY PROGRAM SLS122RG
     **
A         R RECAPREC
A           RTITLE       40
A           RVALUE       40
A           RQTY    R    +2           REFFLD(QTYSLD HISTJL1)
A           RAMT    R    +3           REFFLD(UNTPR  HISTJL1)
```

Figure 9.1: DDS for work file SLS122PF.

```
/*===============================================================*/
/* Billing history report with recaps                           */
/*                                                               */
/* CPP for SLS122 command                                        */
/*                                                               */
/*===============================================================*/
PGM         PARM(&FROMDATE &THRUDATE)
    DCL     &LIB        *CHAR   10
    DCL     &FROMDATE   *CHAR   7            /* CYYMMDD */
```

Figure 9.2: CL program SLS122CL.

```
DCL      &THRUDATE   *CHAR    7            /* CYYMMDD */
DCL      &FROM_C     *CHAR    8            /* YYYYMMDD */
DCL      &THRU_C     *CHAR    8            /* YYYYMMDD */
DCL      &FROM_N     *DEC     8            /* YYYYMMDD */
DCL      &THRU_N     *DEC     8            /* YYYYMMDD */
DCL      &ERRBYTES   *CHAR    4       VALUE(X'00000000')
DCL      &ERROR      *LGL             VALUE('0')
DCL      &MSGKEY     *CHAR    4
DCL      &MSGTYPCTR  *CHAR    4       VALUE(X'00000001')
DCL      &MSGTYP     *CHAR   10       VALUE('*DIAG')
DCL      &PGMMSGQ    *CHAR   10       VALUE('*')
DCL      &STKCTR     *CHAR    4       VALUE(X'00000001')
MONMSG   MSGID(CPF0000) EXEC(GOTO ERROR_RTN)

CHGVAR     VAR(&FROM_N) VALUE(&FROMDATE)
CHGVAR     VAR(&FROM_N) VALUE(&FROM_N + 19000000)
CHGVAR     VAR(&FROM_C) VALUE(&FROM_N)
CHGVAR     VAR(&THRU_N) VALUE(&THRUDATE)
CHGVAR     VAR(&THRU_N) VALUE(&THRU_N + 19000000)
CHGVAR     VAR(&THRU_C) VALUE(&THRU_N)

/* Copy the selected data */
CPYF       FROMFILE(HISTJL1) TOFILE(QTEMP/TEMPWORK) +
             MBROPT(*REPLACE) CRTFILE(*YES) +
             INCREL((*IF INVDAT *GE &FROM_C) +
                (*AND INVDAT *LE &THRU_C))

/* Create the recap file in QTEMP */
CLRPFM     FILE(QTEMP/SLS122PF)
MONMSG CPF3142 EXEC(DO)
 RTVOBJD    OBJ(SLS122PF) OBJTYPE(*FILE) RTNLIB(&LIB)
 CRTDUPOBJ  OBJ(SLS122PF) FROMLIB(&LIB) OBJTYPE(*FILE) +
             TOLIB(QTEMP)
ENDDO

/* Summarize by customer */
OPNQRYF    FILE((QTEMP/TEMPWORK)) FORMAT(SLS122PF) +
             KEYFLD((RTITLE) (RVALUE)) +
             GRPFLD(RVALUE) +
             MAPFLD((RTITLE '"Customer"') +
                (RVALUE '%DIGITS(CUSNO)') +
                (RQTY   '0') +
                (RAMT   '%SUM((QTYSLD * UNTPR))'))
CPYFRMQRYF FROMOPNID(TEMPWORK) TOFILE(QTEMP/SLS122PF) +
             MBROPT(*ADD) FMTOPT(*MAP)
CLOF       OPNID(TEMPWORK)

/* Summarize by item */
OPNQRYF    FILE((QTEMP/TEMPWORK)) FORMAT(SLS122PF) +
             KEYFLD((RTITLE) (RVALUE)) +
             GRPFLD(RVALUE) +
             MAPFLD((RTITLE '"Item"') +
```

Figure 9.2: CL program SLS122CL. (Continued)

```
                             (RVALUE  'ITMNO') +
                             (RQTY   '%SUM(QTYSLD)') +
                             (RAMT   '%SUM((QTYSLD * UNTPR))')'))
         CPYFRMQRYF  FROMOPNID(TEMPWORK) TOFILE(QTEMP/SLS122PF) +
                       MBROPT(*ADD) FMTOPT(*MAP)
         CLOF        OPNID(TEMPWORK)
         /* Summarize by sales rep */
         OPNQRYF     FILE((QTEMP/TEMPWORK)) FORMAT(SLS122PF) +
                       KEYFLD((RTITLE) (RVALUE)) +
                       GRPFLD(RVALUE) +
                       MAPFLD((RTITLE '"Sales Rep"') +
                             (RVALUE '%DIGITS(REPNO) *CAT " " *CAT REPNAM') +
                             (RQTY   '0') +
                             (RAMT   '%SUM((QTYSLD * UNTPR))'))
         CPYFRMQRYF  FROMOPNID(TEMPWORK) TOFILE(QTEMP/SLS122PF) +
                       MBROPT(*ADD) FMTOPT(*MAP)
         CLOF        OPNID(TEMPWORK)

         /* Summarize by sales rep & item */
         OPNQRYF     FILE((QTEMP/TEMPWORK)) FORMAT(SLS122PF) +
                       KEYFLD((RTITLE) (RVALUE)) +
                       GRPFLD(RVALUE) +
                       MAPFLD((RTITLE '"Sales Rep & Item"') +
                             (RVALUE '%DIGITS(REPNO) *CAT " " *CAT ITMNO') +
                             (RQTY   '%SUM(QTYSLD)') +
                             (RAMT   '%SUM((QTYSLD * UNTPR))'))
         CPYFRMQRYF FROMOPNID(TEMPWORK) TOFILE(QTEMP/SLS122PF) +
                       MBROPT(*ADD) FMTOPT(*MAP)
         CLOF        OPNID(TEMPWORK)

         /* Print the report */
         OVRDBF      FILE(HISTJL1) TOFILE(QTEMP/TEMPWORK)
         OVRDBF      FILE(SLS122PF) TOFILE(QTEMP/SLS122PF)
         CALL        PGM(SLS122RG) PARM(&FROM_N &THRU_N)
         DLTOVR      FILE(HISTJL1 SLS122PF)
         RETURN

ERROR_RTN:
         IF          COND(&ERROR) THEN(GOTO ERRDONE)
         CHGVAR      VAR(&ERROR) VALUE('1')
/* Move *DIAG messages to previous program queue */
         CALL        PGM(QMHMOVPM) PARM(&MSGKEY &MSGTYP +
                       &MSGTYPCTR &PGMMSGQ &STKCTR &ERRBYTES)

/* Resend last escape message */
ERRDONE:
         CALL        PGM(QMHRSNEM) PARM(&MSGKEY &ERRBYTES)
         MONMSG      MSGID(CPF0000) EXEC(DO)
           SNDPGMMSG  MSGID(CPF3CF2) MSGF(QCPFMSG) +
                       MSGDTA(QMHRSNEM) MSGTYPE(*ESCAPE)
           MONMSG     MSGID(CPF0000)

         ENDDO
ENDPGM
```

Figure 9.2: CL program SLS122CL. *(Continued)*

Step 2: Create or clear the recap work file in QTEMP. If the work file already exists in QTEMP, it is cleared. Otherwise, it is created from an empty template sitting in the production library.

Step 3: Build the recaps. To build a recap, the program must use the MAPFLD parameter to assign values to the four recap fields. RTITLE describes the recap, providing a way for the RPG print program to distinguish one recap from another. RVALUE is the character version of the values by which the file is being summarized. That is, if you are summarizing by item number, RVALUE will have an item number. If you summarize by a numeric field, like CUSNO, OPNQRYF uses the %DIGITS function to place character representations of CUSNO into RVALUE.

Step 4: Print the report. For this step, the CL program calls upon RPG IV program SLS122RG shown in Figure 9.3). The program reads two files: the join logical HISTJL1 and the recap work file in QTEMP.

```
  * Billing history report with recaps

FHistJL1    if    e           k disk     rename(HISTJL1R:HistRec)
FSls122PF   if    e           k disk     rename(RECAPREC:RecapRec)
FSls122P1   o     e             printer OflInd(*IN88)

D FromDt            s            8 0
D ThruDt            s            8 0
D STitle            s                    like(RTitle)
D                   sds
D   S#PGM                     1  10
D   S#LIB                    81  90

C       *ENTRY      plist
C                   parm                  FromDt          8 0
C                   parm                  ThruDt          8 0
  *
C                   exsr      INIT
C                   exsr      REPORT
C                   exsr      RECAP
C                   eval      *inLR = *on
  ***********
C       REPORT      BegSR
  *
C                   write     PageHd
```

Figure 9.3: The RPG IV program SLS122RG prints the report.

```
C                        write     RptHd
C                        eval      *in88 = *off
   *
C                        read      HistRec                             91
C                        dow       not *in91
C                        if        *in88
C                        write     PageHd
C                        write     RptHd
C                        eval      *in88 = *off
C                        endif
C                        eval      XPrice = QtySld * UntPr
C                        write     DtlLn
C                        read      HistRec                             91
C                        enddo
   *
C                        EndSr
   ***********
C        RECAP           BegSR
   *
C                        eval      STitle = *loval
   *
C                        read      RecapRec                            91
C                        dow       not *in91
C                        if        (RTitle <> STitle) or *in88
C                        write     PageHd
C                        write     RecapHd
C                        eval      Stitle = RTitle
C                        eval      *in88 = *off
C                        endif
C                        write     RecapLn
C                        read      RecapRec                            91
C                        enddo
   *
C                        EndSr
   ***********
C        INIT            BegSR
   *
C                        eval      PGMNAM = %trim(S#LIB) + '/' + S#PGM
   *
C                        EndSr
```

Figure 9.3: The RPG IV program SLS122RG prints the report. (Continued)

The REPORT subroutine reads through the selected billing data and prints it out. Then subroutine RECAP reads the recapped work file and checks for a control break on RTITLE. When the subroutine finds another value in RTITLE, it knows it is to begin another recap.

There are no calculations in the RPG program to accumulate the quantity and extended amount fields because those accumulations have already been done by OPNQRYF and placed into the recap work file. The RPG program only prints them out. Figure 9.4 shows the printer file that describes the report.

```
A                                              REF(HISTJL1)
 ** REPORT BODY LINES
A           R PAGEHD                           SKIPB(03)
A                                              1'Billing History ('
A             FROMDT        8  0               +0EDTWRD('      -  - ')
A                                              +1'thru'
A             THRUDT        8  0               +1EDTWRD('      -  - ')
A                                              +0')'
A                                              85'Page'
A                                              +1PAGNBR EDTCDE(4)
A                                              97'ID:'
A             PGMNAM       21                  +1
A                                                SPACEA(2)
 ** REPORT BODY LINES
A           R RPTHD
A                                              1'Invoice'
A                                              14'Date'
A                                              24'Cust'
A                                              31'Rep'
A                                              37'Item'
A                                              50'Qty'
A                                              58'Price'
A                                              70'Extended'
A                                                SPACEA(2)
A           R DTLLN                              SPACEA(1)
A             INVNO         R                  1EDTCDE(3)
A             INVDAT        R                  +3EDTWRD('      -  - ')
A             CUSNO         R                  +4EDTCDE(3)
A             REPNO         R                  +3EDTCDE(4)
A             ITMNO         R                  +3
A             QTYSLD        R                  +3EDTCDE(K)
A             UNTPR         R                  +3EDTCDE(J)
A             XPRICE        R                  +3REFFLD(RAMT    SLS122PF)
A                                              EDTCDE(J)
 ** RECAP LINES
A           R RECAPHD
A                                              1'Recap by'
A             RTITLE        R                  +1REFFLD(RTITLE  SLS122PF)
A                                                SPACEA(2)
A                                              50'Qty'
```

Figure 9.4: The DDS for the report.

```
A                                              70'Extended'
A                                              SPACEA(2)
A           R RECAPLN                          SPACEA(1)
A             RVALUE    R                      1REFFLD(RVALUE   SLS122PF)
A             RQTY      R                      44REFFLD(RQTY    SLS122PF)
A                                              EDTCDE(K)
A             RAMT      R                      67REFFLD(RAMT    SLS122PF)
A                                              EDTCDE(J)
```

Figure 9.4: The DDS for the report. (Continued)

Figure 9.5 shows a command to put it all in motion.

```
/*===================================================================*/
/* To compile:                                                       */
/*                                                                   */
/*          CRTCMD    CMD(XXX/SLS122) PGM(XXX/SLS122CL) +            */
/*                    SRCFILE(XXX/QCMDSRC) MSGF(OURMSGF)             */
/*                                                                   */
/*===================================================================*/
           CMD       PROMPT('Billing history with recap')
           PARM      KWD(FROM) TYPE(*DATE) MIN(1) PROMPT('From +
                     date')
           PARM      KWD(THRU) TYPE(*DATE) MIN(1) PROMPT('Through +
                     date')
           DEP       CTL(*ALWAYS) PARM((&FROM *LE &THRU)) +
                     MSGID(OUR0101)
```

Figure 9.5: The command to run the program for a billing history recap.

The text of message OUR0101 reads "From date must not be after thru date." The report results looks like Figure 9.6.

To add another recap to the report, just add another OPNQRYF-CPYFRMQRYF-CLOF command to the CL program. You won't have to change the other objects. Adding another recap to an application that has been designed this way should take only a few minutes.

```
Billing History (1998-04-01 thru 1998-04-07)      Page   1      ID: XYZ/SLS122RG

Invoice     Date        Cust     Rep     Item        Qty    Price          Extended
100002    1998-04-05    2345     111    EF-1212        3    12.25            36.75
100002    1998-04-05    2345     111    CD-4667       12     5.50            66.00
100003    1998-04-06    3456     222    EF-1212        2    12.00            24.00
100003    1998-04-06    3456     222    AB-4567       50    .4.00           200.00
100004    1998-04-06    1234     111    DE-5678        1     7.49             7.49
100005    1998-04-06    5678     444    DE-5678        1     7.49             7.49
100005    1998-04-06    5678     444    EF-1212        4    12.00            48.00
100005    1998-04-06    5678     444    AB-4567        2     3.75             7.50
100006    1998-04-07    2345     111    AB-4567        1     4.10             4.10

Billing History (1998-04-01 thru 1998-04-07)      Page   2      ID: XYZ/SLS122RG

Recap by Customer

                                                    Qty                    Extended

01234                                                                          7.49
02345                                                                        106.85
03456                                                                        224.00
05678                                                                       · 62.99

Billing History (1998-04-01 thru 1998-04-07)      Page   3      ID: XYZ/SLS122RG

Recap by Item

                                                    Qty                    Extended

AB-4567                                              53                      211.60
CD-4667                                              12                       66.00
DE-5678                                               2                       14.98
EF-1212                                               9                      108.75

Billing History (1998-04-01 thru 1998-04-07)      Page   4      ID: XYZ/SLS122RG

Recap by Sales Rep

                                                    Qty                    Extended

111 JONES                                                                   114.34
222 SMITH                                                                   224.00
444 GREEN                                                                    62.99

Billing History (1998-04-01 thru 1998-04-07)      Page   5      ID: XYZ/SLS122RG

Recap by Sales Rep & Item

                                                    Qty                    Extended

111 AB-4567                                           1                        4.10
111 CD-4667                                          12                       66.00
111 DE-5678                                           1                        7.49
111 EF-1212                                           3                       36.75
222 AB-4567                                          50                      200.00
222 EF-1212                                           2                       24.00
444 AB-4567                                           2                        7.50
444 DE-5678                                           1                        7.49
444 EF-1212                                           4                       48.00
```

Figure 9.6: A sample billing history recap report.

USING CPYFRMQRYF
FOR RANDOM ACCESS OVER GROUP QUERIES

As mentioned in chapter 7, a query file cannot be accessed randomly if group processing or unique-key processing is involved. A handy way to get around this limitation is to use the CPYFRMQRYF command to build a temporary keyed file that can be used for random access. You can summarize file HISTJL1 (an order history file) by customer number, and then read the summary file randomly. Figure 9.7 shows the DDS for the summary file, CUSSUM. Because the RPG program will be reading it randomly by customer number, you must make CUSNO the key field.

```
A* Physical file CUSSUM
A                                   REF(DICTIONARY)
A          R CUSSUMR                TEXT('CUSTOMER SUMMARY WORK FILE')
A            CUSNO     R
A            XAMT      R  +4        TEXT('AMOUNT SOLD')
A                                   REFFLD(UNTPR)
A          K CUSNO
```

Figure 9.7: The DDS for summary file CUSSUM.

The part of the RPG program that will read the summarized data is shown in Figure 9.8.

```
FOrdSked    if  e           k disk
FCusSum     if  e           k disk
FRaxSumP    o   e             printer    oflind(*in77)
C    CusNo          chain     CusSumR                              91
... etc.
```

Figure 9.8: An RPG IV program fragment for reading the summary file.

The CL program creates a duplicate of CUSSUM in library QTEMP. Doing this avoids conflicts between users running this job concurrently. Because the temporary file is a duplicate object of the permanent file, it also is keyed on CUSNO.

Once the CL program has built the temporary file, it issues an override to cause the RPG program to use the temporary file instead of the pattern. The CL program is shown in Figure 9.9.

```
        PGM
        DCL       VAR(&RTNLIB) TYPE(*CHAR) LEN(10)
        RTVOBJD   OBJ(CUSSUM) OBJTYPE(*FILE) RTNLIB(&RTNLIB)
        CRTDUPOBJ OBJ(CUSSUM) FROMLIB(&RTNLIB) OBJTYPE(*FILE) +
                    TOLIB(QTEMP)
        MONMSG    MSGID(CPF2104) /* ALREADY EXISTS */
/* Build summary file by customer */
        OPNQRYF   FILE((HISTJL1)) FORMAT(CUSSUM) GRPFLD(CUSNO) +
                    MAPFLD((XPR 'QTYSLD * UNTPR') (XAMT +
                      '%SUM(XPR)'))
        CPYFRMQRYF FROMOPNID(HISTJL1) TOFILE(QTEMP/CUSSUM) +
                    MBROPT(*REPLACE)
        CLOF      OPNID(HISTJL1)
/* Print report */
        OVRDBF    FILE(CUSSUM) TOFILE(QTEMP/CUSSUM)
        CALL      PGM(RAXSUMR)
        DLTOVR    FILE(CUSSUM)
        ENDPGM
```

Figure 9.9: A CL program.

SUMMARY

The CPYFRMQRYF command writes queried data to physical, DDM, tape, diskette, and program-described printer files. The command often eliminates the need to write high-level language programs that read and write records without other processing. It also simplifies certain difficult programming tasks such as writing recap programs, and overcomes the limitation that OPNQRYF cannot support random access for grouping and unique-key queries. The FROMOPNID parameter must match the OPNID parameter of the OPNQRYF command. Because CPYFRMQRYF doesn't open the shared file, the primary query file doesn't have to have the shared attribute.

10

❖ Using OPNQRYF in Interactive Programs

Although OPNQRYF is primarily used in batch programming, it also can be effectively used with interactive programs as well. You may find yourself changing some of your programming habits, however. For example, you'll probably have to open more files, rather than let the RPG cycle open them for you. This chapter focuses on how you should code certain parameters when you run OPNQRYF in an interactive job.

THE OPTIMIZE PARAMETER

The OPTIMIZE parameter gives the programmer a way to help OPNQRYF speed up record selection processing (and, to a lesser degree, join processing). In interactive jobs, you probably will want to set this value to *FIRSTIO, as shown in Figure 10.1.

```
OPNQRYF    FILE((ORDERS)) QRYSLT(&SELECT) KEYFLD((TDATE)) +
             OPTIMIZE(*FIRSTIO) ...
```

Figure 10.1: Using OPTIMIZE(*FIRSTIO) to improve performance.

This parameter tells the query processor that you want it, as quickly as possible, to retrieve the first buffer of records, even if it has to do something that will cause performance to suffer as more records are retrieved from the file.

THE SEQONLY PARAMETER

In interactive programs that use OPNQRYF you should also try to avoid random access. You shouldn't use any random reads, such as the RPG CHAIN operation, or set the file pointer to start at a certain limit (as the RPG SETLL and SETGT op codes do). Instead, you should read the file sequentially, from the beginning, and stop when you reach the end of the file or when the screen fills up—whichever comes first.

You can tell OPNQRYF that you are going to process the query file sequentially by coding SEQONLY(*YES N), where N is the number of records needed to fill the screen. (See Figure 10.2.)

```
OPNQRYF     FILE((ORDERS)) QRYSLT(&SELECT) KEYFLD((TDATE)) +
            OPTIMIZE(*FIRSTIO) SEQONLY(*YES 12)
```

Figure 10.2: Using SEQONLY(*YES) to process the query file sequentially.

For example, suppose you are writing an inquiry program that will display 15 records from a history file at a time and, 95 percent of the time this program is run, the record the user is looking for is in the first group of 15. You need a way to tell OPNQRYF to do whatever it can to get that first group of 15 records as quickly as possible. Therefore, your OPNQRYF command needs to look something like the one in Figure 10.3.

```
OPNQRYF     FILE((HISTFILE)) QRYSLT(&QRYSLT) +
            KEYFLD((&KEY)) OPTIMIZE(*FIRSTIO) +
            SEQONLY(*YES 15)
```

Figure 10.3: Using SEQONLY to read 15 records to fill the screen quickly.

MECHANICS

OPNQRYF is used in interactive jobs in two ways. One way is to prompt for sort and record selection criteria outside of the high-level language program, execute the OPNQRYF command and then call the high-level language program. This process is the same as the one used for the report jobs described in chapter 9. The only difference is that the high-level language program writes to a display station rather than to a printer. The other method is to include the prompt for query criteria within the high-level language program. To illustrate these methods, consider a simple job that queries a history file. The user is presented with a prompt screen, as shown in Figure 10.4.

```
8/12/98              Order history inquiry              20:39:02

To select records, fill in one or more blanks and press Enter.

     Customer number:    3579
     Item number:        _____
     Invoice number:     _____
     Invoice date:       _____    (yyyymmdd format)
     Sales rep number:

     Sort sequence:      2           0=any
                                     1=Customer number
                                     2=Item number
                                     3=Invoice number


     F3=Exit    F12=Cancel
```

Figure 10.4: Prompt screen for order-history inquiry.

When the user presses the Enter key, the CL program generates a query selection string based on any blanks he filled in, executes the OPNQRYF command and calls the high-level language program. The user then sees the results of the query (Figure 10.5).

```
8/12/98              Order history inquiry              20:39:03

Customer                    Invoice Item              Price   Qty   Rep
3579 JIM'S CAR WASH         100005 AB-4567 MOP         3.75     2   444
3579 JIM'S CAR WASH         100005 DE-5678 DUSTER      7.49     2   444
3579 JIM'S CAR WASH         100005 EF-1212 WASTE CAN  12.00     4   444
```

Figure 10.5: An example that shows the results of a query.

The following code gives an example of the first approach. CL program ORDIQY1C prompts for record-selection criteria and a sort sequence using display file ORDIQY1P. It then runs the OPNQRYF command and calls program ORDIQY1R, which fills a subfile and displays it. (To reduce size and complexity, roll key processing has been omitted.) Figure 10.6 shows the DDS for prompt screen ORDIQY1P. Figure 10.7 shows CL program ORDIQY1C.

```
*=============================================================
* Order history inquiry - Version 1
*=============================================================
* To compile:
*
*      CRTDSPF FILE(XXX/ORDIQY1P) SRCFILE(XXX/QDDSSRC)
*
*=============================================================
A                                    DSPSIZ(24 80 *DS3)
A                                    REF(HISTJL1)
A          R PROMPT
A                                    TEXT('Prompt user for criteria -
A                                    for query')
A                                    CA03(03
A                                    PRINT
A                                  1  3DATE
A                                    EDTCDE(Y)
A                                  1 27'Order history inquiry'
A                                  1 72TIME
A                                  3  2'To select records, fill in one -
A                                    or -
A                                    more blanks and press Enter.'
A                                  5  5'Customer number:'
A            CUSNO    R         B  5 24
A                                  6  5'Item number:'
A            ITMNO    R         B  6 24
A                                  7  5'Invoice number:'
A            INVNO    R         B  7 24
A                                  8  5'Invoice date:'
A            INVDAT   R         B  8 24
A                                  9  5'Sales rep number:'
A            REPNO    R         B  9 24
A                                  8 36'(yyymmdd format)'
A                                 23  5'F3=Exit'
A                                 23 16'F12=Cancel'
A                                 11  5'Sort sequence:'
A            SRTSEQ   1        OB 11 24
A                                 12 36'1=Customer number'
A                                 13 36'2=Item number'
A                                 14 36'3=Invoice number'
A                                 11 36'0=any'
```

Figure 10.6: The DDS for prompt screen ORDIQY1P.

The RPG program ORDIQY1R reads HISTJL1 through OPNQRYF and displays up to 16 records. Figure 10.8 shows the RPG III code and Figure 10.9 has the RPG IV equivalent. Figure 10.10 shows the DDS for display file ORDIQY1D, used by program ORDIQY1R.

```
/*================================================================*/
/* Order history inquiry - Version 1                             */
/*================================================================*/
/* To compile:                                                   */
/*                                                               */
/* (OPM)    CRTCLPGM    PGM(XXX/ORDIQY1C) SRCFILE(XXX/QCLSRC)     */
/* (ILE)    CRTBNDCL    PGM(XXX/ORDIQY1C) SRCFILE(XXX/QCLSRC) +   */
/*                      DFTACTGRP(*NO)                            */
/*                                                               */
/*================================================================*/

        PGM

        DCLF        FILE(ORDIQY1P) RCDFMT(PROMPT)
        DCL         VAR(&QRYSLT) TYPE(*CHAR) LEN(256)
        DCL         VAR(&KEYFLD) TYPE(*CHAR) LEN( 10)
        DCL         VAR(&INVNOA) TYPE(*CHAR) LEN(  6)
        DCL         VAR(&CUSNOA) TYPE(*CHAR) LEN(  4)
        DCL         VAR(&INVD)   TYPE(*CHAR) LEN(  8)
        DCL         VAR(&REPNOA) TYPE(*CHAR) LEN(  3)
        DCL         VAR(&CONJ)   TYPE(*CHAR) LEN(  4)

PROMPT:
        SNDRCVF     RCDFMT(PROMPT)
        IF (&IN03) +
            THEN(RETURN)

/* Build QRYSLT parameter */
        CHGVAR      VAR(&QRYSLT) VALUE(' ')
        CHGVAR      VAR(&CONJ)        VALUE(' ')
/* Invoice number                                                */
/*     If an invoice number was entered, do not look at other fields */
        IF (&INVNO *NE 0) THEN(DO)
            CHGVAR  VAR(&INVNOA) VALUE(&INVNO)
            CHGVAR  VAR(&QRYSLT) VALUE('INVNO=' *CAT &INVNOA)
            GOTO    SELECTSORT
        ENDDO

/* Customer number                                               */
        IF (&CUSNO *NE 0) THEN(DO)
            CHGVAR  VAR(&CUSNOA) VALUE(&CUSNO)
            CHGVAR  VAR(&QRYSLT) VALUE('CUSNO=' *CAT &CUSNOA)
            CHGVAR  VAR(&CONJ)     VALUE(*AND)
        ENDDO

/* Item number                                                   */
        IF (&ITMNO *NE ' ') THEN(DO)
            CHGVAR  VAR(&QRYSLT) +
```

Figure 10.7: A CL program to run the query.

177

```
                          VALUE(&QRYSLT *BCAT &CONJ *BCAT +                    */
                               'ITMNO="' *CAT &ITMNO *CAT '"')
              CHGVAR  VAR(&CONJ)   VALUE(*AND)
       ENDDO
/* Invoice date                                                              */
       IF (&INVDAT *NE 0) THEN(DO)
              CHGVAR  VAR(&INVD  ) VALUE(&INVDAT)
              CHGVAR  VAR(&QRYSLT) +
                          VALUE(&QRYSLT *BCAT &CONJ *BCAT +
                               'INVDAT=' *CAT &INVD)
              CHGVAR  VAR(&CONJ)   VALUE(*AND)
       ENDDO

/* Sales rep number                                                          */
       IF (&REPNO *NE 0) THEN(DO)
              CHGVAR  VAR(&REPNOA) VALUE(&REPNO)
              CHGVAR  VAR(&QRYSLT) +
                          VALUE(&QRYSLT *BCAT &CONJ *BCAT +
                               'REPNO=' *CAT &REPNOA)
       ENDDO

SELECTSORT:
       IF (&SRTSEQ *EQ 1) +
              THEN(CHGVAR  VAR(&KEYFLD) VALUE(CUSNO))
       ELSE IF (&SRTSEQ *EQ 2) +
                 THEN(CHGVAR  VAR(&KEYFLD) VALUE(ITMNO))
            ELSE IF (&SRTSEQ *EQ 3) +
                       THEN(CHGVAR  VAR(&KEYFLD) VALUE(INVNO))
                    ELSE CHGVAR VAR(&KEYFLD) VALUE(*NONE)

RUN:
       IF (&QRYSLT *EQ ' ') +
              THEN(CHGVAR  VAR(&QRYSLT) VALUE(*ALL))

       OVRDBF       FILE(HISTJL1) SHARE(*YES)
       OPNQRYF      FILE((HISTJL1)) QRYSLT(&QRYSLT) +
                       KEYFLD((&KEYFLD)) OPTIMIZE(*FIRSTIO) +
                       SEQONLY(*YES 16)
       CALL         PGM(ORDIQY1R)
       CLOF         OPNID(HISTJL1)
       DLTOVR       FILE(HISTJL1)
       GOTO         PROMPT

       ENDPGM
```

Figure 10.7: A CL program to run the query. (Continued)

```
*================================================================
* Order history inquiry - Version 1
*================================================================
* To compile:
*
*       CRTRPGPGM  PGM(XXX/ORDIQY1R) SRCFILE(XXX/QRPGSRC)
*
*================================================================
FHISTJL1 IF E                      DISK
FORDIQY1DCF E                      WORKSTN
F                                       RRN   KSFILE SFL
C                   READ HISTJL1R                    91
C         *IN91     DOWEQ*OFF
C         RRN       ANDLE16
C                   MOVELCUSNAM   CUSNM2
C                   MOVELITMDSC   ITMDS2
C                   ADD  1        RRN       30
C                   WRITESFL
C                   READ HISTJL1R                    91
C                   ENDDO
C*
C         RRN       IFGT *ZERO
C                   MOVE *ON      *IN22     DSPLY SUBFILE
C                   ENDIF
C                   MOVE *ON      *IN21     DSPLY CTL REC
C*
C                   EXFMTCTL
C*
C                   MOVE *ON      *INLR
```

Figure 10.8: RPG III code to read the history file and display results to the user.

```
*================================================================
* Order history inquiry - Version 1
*================================================================
* To compile:
*
*       CRTBNDRPG  PGM(XXX/ORDIQY1R) SRCFILE(XXX/QRPGLESRC) +
*                  DFTACTGRP(*NO)
*
*================================================================

FHistJL1  if    e         disk    rename(HistJL1r: HistRec)
FOrdIqy1d cf    e         workstn sfile(sfl: rrn)

D rrn           s         4 0
```

Figure 10.9: RPG IV code to read HISTJL1 and display records to the user.

```
C            read        HistRec                              91
C            dow         (not *in91) and (rrn <= 16)
C            eval        CusNm2 = Cusnam
C            eval        ItmDs2 = ItmDsc
C            eval        rrn = rrn + 1
C            write       sfl
C            read        HistRec                              91
C            enddo
C
C            eval        *in22 = (rrn > *zero)
C            eval        *in21 = *on
C
C            exfmt       ctl
C
C            eval        *inLR = *on
```

Figure 10.9: RPG IV code to read HISTJL1 and display records to the user. (Continued)

```
*=============================================================
* Order history inquiry - Version 1
*=============================================================
* To compile:
*
*      CRTDSPF    FILE(XXX/ORDIQY1D) SRCFILE(XXX/QDDSSRC)
*
*=============================================================
A                                      DSPSIZ(24 80 *DS3)
A                                      REF(*LIBL/HISTJL1)
A          R SFL                       SFL
A            CUSNO     R      0  4  2
A            CUSNM2    R  -2  0  4   7REFFLD(CUSNAM)
A            INVNO     R      0  4  26
A            ITMNO     R      0  4  33
A            ITMDS2    R  -2  0  4  41REFFLD(ITMDSC)
A            UNTPR     R      0  4  62EDTCDE(L)
A            QTYSLD    R      0  4  70EDTCDE(L)
A            REPNO     R      0  4  78
A          R CTL                       SFLCTL(SFL)
A                                      SFLSIZ(0018)
A                                      SFLPAG(0017)
A                                      TEXT('Subfile record')
A                                      CA03
A                                      CA12
A                                      PRINT
A     22                               SFLDSP
A     21                               SFLDSPCTL
```

Figure 10.10: DDS for display file to display records to the user.

```
A                              1   3DATE
A                                  EDTCDE(Y)
A                              1  27'Order history inquiry'
A                              1 72TIME
A                              3   2'Customer'
A                              3  25'Invoice'
A                              3  33'Item'
A                              3  63'Price'
A                              3  72'Qty    Rep'
```

Figure 10.10: DDS for display file to display records to the user. (Continued)

While this program works, it could be more efficient. Terminating the program and calling it again creates overhead. This limitation suggests a second method, which is to include the prompt for the record selection and sequence criteria within the high-level language program.

The five-step logic used so far (OVRDBF, OPNQRYF, CALL, CLOF DLTOVR) must be modified. In interactive programs, you can still override the file before you call the program, and you can still delete the override after the program ends, but you will have to move the OPNQRYF and CLOF commands inside the program you call.

The following example is the same program, but the prompt screen has been added to the program's display file. Now the RPG program must execute the OPNQRYF and CLOF commands. Because the database file must be closed when the OPNQRYF command is executed, the RPG cycle can no longer open and close it. Instead, the programmer must open and close the database file at the appropriate time.

Figures 10.11 and 10.12 show the RPG III and RPG IV versions of the RPG program ORDIQY2R. The DDS for display file ORDIQY2D is shown in Figure 10.13.

```
*==================================================================
* Order history inquiry - Version 2
*==================================================================
* To compile:
*
*      CRTRPGPGM  PGM(XXX/ORDIQY2R) SRCFILE(XXX/QRPGSRC)
*
*==================================================================
```

Figure 10.11: An efficient version of RPG III code to read the file HISTJL1 and display records to the user.

```
FHISTJL1 IF  E                           DISK                              UC
FORDIQY2DCF  E                           WORKSTN
F                                                RRN  KSFILE SFL
E                          C      1    2  80            CL COMMANDS
E                          KFN    4    4  10            KEY FIELD NAMES
I* These literals are used to build the OPNQRYF command
I              'QRYSLT('''               C         LIT01
I              'INVNO='                  C         LIT02
I              'CUSNO='                  C         LIT03
I              'ITMNO='''''              C         LIT04
I              'INVDAT='                 C         LIT05
I              'REPNO='                  C         LIT06
I              '''''                     C         LIT07
I              ''')'                     C         LIT08
I              'KEYFLD('                 C         LIT99
C                          EXFMTPROMPT                   PROMPT
C              *IN03       DOWEQ'0'
C                          EXSR BLDCMD                   BUILD COMMAND
C                          EXSR SHWDTA                   SHOW DATA
C                          EXFMTPROMPT                   PROMPT
C                          ENDDO
C*
C                          MOVE '1'       *INLR
C***********
C              BLDCMD      BEGSR                          BLD/EXEC CMD
C*
C* MOVE THE OPNQRYF COMMAND, WITH PARAMETERS THAT DO NOT CHANGE,
C*   INTO VARIABLE CMD
C                          MOVE *BLANKS   CMD   256
C                          MOVELC,1       CMD
C*
C* BUILD THE QRYSLT PARAMETER
C                          MOVE *BLANKS   QRYSLT 96
C                          MOVE *BLANK    CONJ   1
C*
C* TEST FOR INVOICE NUMBER
C              INVNO1      IFNE *ZERO
C                          MOVE *BLANKS   ALPHA  8       ALPHA WRK FLD
C                          MOVELINVNO1    ALPHA
C              QRYSLT      CAT  LIT02:0   QRYSLT
C              QRYSLT      CAT  ALPHA:0   QRYSLT
C                          GOTO BLDM50
C                          ENDIF
C*
C* TEST FOR CUSTOMER NUMBER
C              CUSNO1      IFNE *ZERO
C                          MOVE *BLANKS   ALPHA  8       ALPHA WRK FLD
C                          MOVELCUSNO1    ALPHA
C              QRYSLT      CAT  LIT03:0   QRYSLT
C              QRYSLT      CAT  ALPHA:0   QRYSLT
C                          MOVE '&'       CONJ
C                          ENDIF
C*
```

Figure 10.11: An efficient version of RPG III code to read the file HISTJL1 *and display records to the user. (Continued)*

```
C* TEST FOR ITEM NUMBER
C           ITMNO1    IFNE *BLANKS
C           QRYSLT    CAT  CONJ:1    QRYSLT
C           QRYSLT    CAT  LITO4:1   QRYSLT
C           QRYSLT    CAT  ITMNO1:0  QRYSLT
C           QRYSLT    CAT  LITO7:0   QRYSLT
C                     MOVE '&'       CONJ
C                     ENDIF
C*
C* TEST FOR INVOICE DATE
C           INVDT1    IFNE *ZERO
C                     MOVE *BLANKS   ALPHA     8    ALPHA WRK FLD
C                     MOVELINVDT1    ALPHA
C           QRYSLT    CAT  CONJ:1    QRYSLT
C           QRYSLT    CAT  LITO5:1   QRYSLT
C           QRYSLT    CAT  ALPHA:0   QRYSLT
C                     MOVE '&' CONJ
C                     ENDIF
C*
C* TEST FOR SALES REP NUMBER
C           REPNO1    IFNE *ZERO
C                     MOVE *BLANKS   ALPHA     8    ALPHA WRK FLD
C                     MOVELREPNO1    ALPHA
C           QRYSLT    CAT  CONJ:1    QRYSLT
C           QRYSLT    CAT  LITO6:1   QRYSLT
C           QRYSLT    CAT  ALPHA:0   QRYSLT
C                     MOVE '&'       CONJ
C                     ENDIF
C*
C           BLDM50    TAG
C*
C* ADD THE QRYSLT PARAMETER TO CMD
C*
C           QRYSLT    IFNE *BLANKS
C           CMD       CAT  LITO1:1   CMD
C           CMD            CAT  QRYSLT:0 CMD
C           CMD       CAT  LITO8:0   CMD
C                     ENDIF
C*
C* BUILD THE KEYFLD PARAMETER
C                     MOVE *BLANKS      KEYFLD 10
C           SRTSEQ    IFGE 1
C           SRTSEQ    ANDLE3
C                     MOVE KFN,SRTSEQKEYFLD
C                     ELSE
C                     MOVEL'*FILE'      KEYFLD
C                     ENDIF
C*
C* ADD THE KEYFLD PARAMETER TO CMD
C           CMD            CAT  LIT99:1   CMD
C           CMD            CAT  KEYFLD:0  CMD
C           CMD            CAT  ')':0 CMD
C*
C                     ENDSR
```

Figure 10.11: An efficient version of RPG III code to read the file HISTJL1 and display records to the user. (Continued)

```
C***********
C            SHWDTA    BEGSR                              SHOW DATA
C*
C* EXECUTE THE OPNQRYF COMMAND
C                      CALL 'QCMDEXC'
C                      PARM CMD          ###CMD256
C                      PARM 256          ###LEN 155
C*
C* OPEN THE DATA FILE
C                      OPEN HISTJL1
C*
C* CLEAR SUBFILE
C                      MOVE *OFF         *IN21
C                      MOVE *OFF         *IN22
C                      MOVE *ON          *IN26
C                      WRITECTL
C                      MOVE *OFF         *IN26
C*
C* FILL SUBFILE
C                      MOVE *ZERO        RRN       30
C                      READ HISTJL1R                         91
C            *IN91     DOWEQ*OFF
C            RRN       ANDLE16
C                      MOVELCUSNAM       CUSNM2
C                      MOVELITMDSC       ITMDS2
C                      ADD  1            RRN
C                      WRITESFL
C                      READ HISTJL1R                         91
C                      ENDDO
C*
C* DISPLAY THE RETRIEVED DATA
C            RRN       IFGT *ZERO
C                      MOVE *ON          *IN22
C                      ENDIF
C                      MOVE *ON          *IN21
C                      EXFMTCTL
C*
C* CLOSE THE DATA FILE
C                      CLOSEHISTJL1
C*
C* EXECUTE THE CLOF COMMAND TO CLOSE THE QUERY FILE
C                      CALL 'QCMDEXC'
C                      PARM C,2          ###CMD
C                      PARM 256          ###LEN
C*
C                      ENDSR
** C - COMMAND STRINGS
OPNQRYF FILE((HISTJL1)) OPTIMIZE(*FIRSTIO) SEQONLY(*YES 16)
CLOF OPNID(HISTJL1)
** KFN - KEY FIELD NAMES
CUSNO    ITMNO    INVNO     *NONE
```

Figure 10.11: An efficient version of RPG III code to read the file HISTJL1 and display records to the user. (Continued)

```
*=================================================================
* Order history inquiry - Version 2
*=================================================================
* To compile:
*
*       CRTBNDRPG PGM(XXX/ORDIQY2R) SRCFILE(XXX/QRPGLESRC) +
*                 DFTACTGRP(*NO)
*
*=================================================================

FHistJL1   if   e               disk      rename(HistJL1R: HistRec)
F                                          UsrOpn
FOrdIqy2d  cf   e               workstn sfile(sfl: rrn)

D QCmdExc        pr                        ExtPgm('QCMDEXC')
D  Command                      2000
D  Length                         15 5
D
D AppendExpr     pr
D  Expr                         2000
D  NewExpr                        80     value
D
D KeyFieldNames  S               10     DIM(3) CTDATA PERRCD(4)
D rrn            s                4 0
D Cmd            s             2000
D CmdSize        s               15p 5 inz(%Size(Cmd))
D QrySlt         s             2000
D alpha          s                8

C                    exfmt     prompt
C                    dow       not *in03
C                    exsr      BuildCommand
C                    exsr      ShowData
C                    exfmt     prompt
C                    enddo
C*
C                    eval      *inLR = *on
C***********
C     BuildCommand   BegSR
C*
C* Build the QRYSLT parameter value
C                    eval      QrySlt = *blanks
C*
C* Test for invoice number
C                    if        InvNo1 <> *zero
C                    movel (p) InvNo1          alpha
C                    callp     AppendExpr (QrySlt : 'INVNO=' + Alpha)
C
C                    else
C*
```

Figure 10.12: An efficient version of RPG IV code to read file HISTJL1 and display records to the user.

```
C* Test for customer number
C                    if        CusNo1 <> *zero
C                    movel (p) CusNo1        alpha
C                    callp     AppendExpr (QrySlt : 'CUSNO=' + Alpha)
C                    endif
C*
C* Test for item number
C                    if        ItmNo1 <> *blanks
C                    callp     AppendExpr (QrySlt :
C                                          'ITMNO="' + ItmNo1 + '"')
C                    endif
C*
C* Test for invoice date
C                    if        InvDt1 <> *zero
C                    movel (p) InvDt1        alpha
C                    callp     AppendExpr (QrySlt : 'INVDAT=' + Alpha)
C                    endif
C*
C* Test for sales rep number
C                    if        RepNo1 <> *zero
C                    movel (p) RepNo1        alpha
C                    callp     AppendExpr (QrySlt : 'REPNO=' + Alpha)
C                    endif
C*
C                    endif
C*
C* Move the OPNQRYF command, with parameters that do not change,
C*   into variable CMD
C                    eval      Cmd = 'OPNQRYF FILE((HISTJL1)) +
C                                    OPTIMIZE(*FIRSTIO) +
C                                    SEQONLY(*YES 16)'
C*
C*
C* Add the QRYSLT parameter to CMD
C*
C                    if        QrySlt <> *blanks
C                    eval      Cmd = %trim(Cmd) + ' ' +
C                                    'QRYSLT(''' + %trim(QrySlt) + ''')'
C                    endif
C*
C* Build the KEYFLD parameter
C                    if        SrtSeq >= 1 and SrtSeq <= 3
C                    eval      Cmd = %trim(Cmd) + ' ' + 'KEYFLD(' +
C                                    KeyFieldNames (SrtSeq) + ')'
C                    endif
C*
C                    EndSR
C***********
C    ShowData        BegSR
```

Figure 10.12: An efficient version of RPG IV code to read file HISTJL1 and display records to the user. (Continued)

```
C*
C* Execute the OPNQRYF command
C                    callp    QCmdExc (Cmd : CmdSize)
C
C* Open the data file
C                    open     HistJL1
C
C* Clear the subfile
C                    eval     *in21 = *off
C                    eval     *in22 = *off
C                    eval     *in26 = *on
C                    write    ctl
C                    eval     *in26 = *off
C
C* Fill the subfile
C                    eval     rrn = *zero
C                    read     HistRec                              91
C                    dow      (not *in91) and (rrn <= 16)
C                    eval     CusNm2 = Cusnam
C                    eval     ItmDs2 = ItmDsc
C                    eval     rrn = rrn + 1
C                    write    sfl
C                    read     HistRec                              91
C                    enddo
C
C                    eval     *in22 = (rrn > *zero)
C                    eval     *in21 = *on
C
C                    exfmt    ctl
C
C* Close the data file
C                    close    HistJL1
C*
C* Close the query file
C                    eval     Cmd = 'CLOF OPNID(HISTJL1)'
C                    callp    QCmdExc (Cmd : CmdSize)
C*
C                    EndSR
 *
P AppendExpr       b
D                  pi
D Expr                        2000
D NewExpr                       80     value
D WorkExpr        s           128
D
C                    eval     WorkExpr = '(' + %trim(NewExpr) + ')'
C                    if       Expr = *blanks
C                    eval     Expr = Workexpr
C                    else
```

Figure 10.12: An efficient version of RPG IV code to read file HISTJL1 and display records to the user. (Continued)

```
        C                      eval      Expr = %trim(Expr) + '&' + WorkExpr
        C                      endif
        C
        P              e

   **ctdata KeyFieldNames
   CUSNO     ITMNO     INVNO
```

Figure 10.12: An efficient version of RPG IV code to read file HISTJL1 and display records to the user. (Continued)

```
*===============================================================
* Order history inquiry - Version 2
*===============================================================
* To compile:
*
*     CRTDSPF    FILE(XXX/ORDIQY2D) SRCFILE(XXX/QDDSSRC)
*
*===============================================================
A                                      REF(HISTJL1)
A                                      DSPSIZ(24 80 *DS3)
A          R PROMPT
A                                      TEXT('Prompt user for criteria -
A                                      for query')
A                                      CA03(03)
A                                      CA12(03)
A                                      PRINT
A                                    1  3DATE
A                                      EDTCDE(Y)
A                                    1 27'Order history inquiry'
A                                    1 72TIME
A                                    3  2'To select records, fill in one -
A                                      or more blanks and press Enter.'
A                                    5  5'Customer number:'
A          CUSNO1     R          B   5 24REFFLD(CUSNO)
A                                    6  5'Item number:'
A          ITMNO1     R          B   6 24REFFLD(ITMNO)
A                                    7  5'Invoice number:'
A          INVNO1     R          B   7 24REFFLD(INVNO)
A                                    8  5'Invoice date:'
A          INVDT1     R          B   8 24REFFLD(INVDAT)
A                                    9  5'Sales rep number:'
```

Figure 10.13: The DDS for version two of the RPG program shown in Figure 10.11 and 10.12.

```
A         .   REPNO1    R           B  9 24REFFLD(REPNO)
A                                      8 36'(yyyymmdd format)'
A                                     23  5'F3=Exit'
A                                     23 16'F12=Cancel'
A                                     11  5'Sort sequence:'
A             SRTSEQ    1         OB 11 24
A                                     12 36'1=Customer number'
A                                     13 36'2=Item number'
A                                     14 36'3=Invoice number'
A                                     11 36'0=any'
A       R SFL                                SFL
A             CUSNO     R           O  4  2
A             CUSNM2    R -2        O  4  7REFFLD(CUSNAM)
A             INVNO     R           O  4 26
A             ITMNO     R           O  4 33
A             ITMDS2    R -2        O  4 41REFFLD(ITMDSC)
A             UNTPR     R           O  4 62EDTCDE(L)
A             QTYSLD    R           O  4 70EDTCDE(L)
A             REPNO     R           O  4 78
A       R CTL                            SFLCTL(SFL)
A                                        TEXT('Subfile record')
A                                        CA03 CA12 PRINT
A  22                                    SFLDSP
A  21                                    SFLDSPCTL
A  26                                    SFLCLR
A                                        SFLSIZ(0018)
A                                        SFLPAG(0017)
A                                      1  3DATE
A                                        EDTCDE(Y)
A                                      1 27'Order history inquiry'
A                                      1 72TIME
A                                      3  2'Customer'
A                                      3 25'Invoice'
A                                      3 33'Item'
A                                      3 63'Price'
A                                      3 72'Qty   Rep'
```

Figure 10.13: The DDS for version two of the RPG program shown in Figure 10.11 and 10.12. (Continued)

If you prefer, you can have the high-level language program carry out the OVRDBF and DLTOVR commands. If you do that, you will no longer need the CL program. Figure 10.14 shows the RPG III program modified to carry out the override commands. The modified lines are highlighted. Figure 10.15 has the same program coded in RPG IV.

Remember, because the RPG program is taking care of the override, there is no need for a CL program.

```
*===================================================================
* Order history inquiry - Version 3
*===================================================================
* To compile:
*
*     CRTRPGPGM  PGM(XXX/ORDIQY2R)  SRCFILE(XXX/QRPGSRC)
*
*===================================================================
FHISTJL1 IF  E                      DISK                         UC
FORDIQY2DCF  E                      WORKSTN
F                                         RRN  KSFILE SFL
```

```
E                   C         1    4 80              CL COMMANDS
E                   KFN       4    4 10              KEY FIELD NAMES
I          'QRYSLT('''            C       LIT01
I          'INVNO='               C       LIT02
I          'CUSNO='               C       LIT03
I          'ITMNO='''''           C       LIT04
I          'INVDAT='              C       LIT05
I          'REPNO='               C       LIT06
I          ''''''                 C       LIT07
I          ''')'                  C       LIT08
I          'KEYFLD('              C       LIT99
```

```
C* OVERRIDE THE FILE TO BE QUERIED
C                    CALL 'QCMDEXC'
C                    PARM C,3      ###CMD
C                    PARM 256      ###LEN
```

```
C*
C                    EXFMTPROMPT               PROMPT
C          *IN03     DOWEQ'0'
C                    EXSR BLDCMD               BUILD COMMAND
C                    EXSR SHWDTA               SHOW DATA
C                    EXFMTPROMPT               PROMPT
C                    ENDDO
C*
C                    MOVE '1'     *INLR
```

```
C* DELETE THE OVERRIDE
C                    CALL 'QCMDEXC'
C                    PARM C,4      ###CMD
C                    PARM 256      ###LEN
```

```
C***********
C          BLDCMD    BEGSR                     BULD/EXEC CMD
C*
C* MOVE THE OPNQRYF COMMAND, WITH PARAMETERS THAT DO NOT CHANGE,
C*   INTO VARIABLE CMD
C                    MOVE *BLANKS CMD      256
C                    MOVELC,1     CMD
C*
C* BUILD THE QRYSLT PARAMETER
C                    MOVE *BLANKS  QRYSLT  96
```

Figure 10.14: RPG III program modified to handle the override.

```
     C                      MOVE *BLANK   CONJ      1
C*
C* TEST FOR INVOICE NUMBER
     C          INVNO1      IFNE *ZERO
     C                      MOVE *BLANKS  ALPHA     8     ALPHA WRK FLD
     C                      MOVELINVNO1   ALPHA
     C          QRYSLT      CAT  LIT02:0  QRYSLT
     C          QRYSLT      CAT  ALPHA:0  QRYSLT
     C                      GOTO BLDM50
     C                      ENDIF
C*
C* TEST FOR CUSTOMER NUMBER
     C          CUSNO1      IFNE *ZERO
     C                      MOVE *BLANKS  ALPHA     8     ALPHA WRK FLD
     C                      MOVELCUSNO1   ALPHA
     C          QRYSLT      CAT  LIT03:0  QRYSLT
     C          QRYSLT      CAT  ALPHA:0  QRYSLT
     C                      MOVE '&'      CONJ
     C                      ENDIF
C*
C* TEST FOR ITEM NUMBER
     C          ITMNO1      IFNE *BLANKS
     C          QRYSLT      CAT  CONJ:1   QRYSLT
     C          QRYSLT      CAT  LIT04:1  QRYSLT
     C          QRYSLT      CAT  ITMNO1:0 QRYSLT
     C          QRYSLT      CAT  LIT07:0  QRYSLT
     C                      MOVE '&'      CONJ
     C                      ENDIF
C*
C* TEST FOR INVOICE DATE
     C          INVDT1      IFNE *ZERO
     C                      MOVE *BLANKS  ALPHA     8     ALPHA WRK FLD
     C                      MOVELINVDT1   ALPHA
     C          QRYSLT      CAT  CONJ:1   QRYSLT
     C          QRYSLT      CAT  LIT05:1  QRYSLT
     C          QRYSLT      CAT  ALPHA:0  QRYSLT
     C                      MOVE '&'      CONJ
     C                      ENDIF
C*
C* TEST FOR SALES REP NUMBER
     C          REPNO1      IFNE *ZERO
     C                      MOVE *BLANKS  ALPHA     8     ALPHA WRK FLD
     C                      MOVELREPNO1   ALPHA
     C          QRYSLT      CAT  CONJ:1   QRYSLT
     C          QRYSLT      CAT  LIT06:1  QRYSLT
     C          QRYSLT      CAT  ALPHA:0  QRYSLT
     C                      MOVE '&'      CONJ
     C                      ENDIF
C*
     C          BLDM50      TAG
C*
C* ADD THE QRYSLT PARAMETER TO CMD
C*
     C          QRYSLT      IFNE *BLANKS
```

Figure 10.14: RPG III program modified to handle the override. (Continued)

```
C                 CMD         CAT  LIT01:1   CMD
C                 CMD         CAT  QRYSLT:0  CMD
C                 CMD         CAT  LIT08:0   CMD
C                             ENDIF
C*
C* BUILD THE KEYFLD PARAMETER
C                             MOVE *BLANKS   KEYFLD 10
C                 SRTSEQ      IFGE 1
C                 SRTSEQ      ANDLE3
C                             MOVE KFN,SRTSEQKEYFLD
C                             ELSE
C                             MOVEL'*FILE'   KEYFLD
C                             ENDIF
C*
C* ADD THE KEYFLD PARAMETER TO CMD
C                 CMD         CAT  LIT99:1   CMD
C                 CMD         CAT  KEYFLD:0  CMD
C                 CMD         CAT  ')':0     CMD
C*
C                             ENDSR
C***********
C                 SHWDTA      BEGSR                       SHOW DATA
C*
C* EXECUTE THE OPNQRYF COMMAND
C                             CALL 'QCMDEXC'
C                             PARM CMD       ###CMD256
C                             PARM 256       ###LEN 155
C*
C* OPEN THE DATA FILE
C                             OPEN HISTJL1
C*
C* CLEAR SUBFILE
C                             MOVE '0'       *IN21
C                             MOVE '0'       *IN22
C                             MOVE '1'       *IN26
C                             WRITECTL
C                             MOVE '0'       *IN26
C*
C* FILL SUBFILE
C                             MOVE *ZERO     RRN     30
C                             READ HISTJL1R                   91
C                 *IN91       DOWEQ*OFF
C                 RRN         ANDLE16
C                             MOVELCUSNAM    CUSNM2
C                             MOVELITMDSC    ITMDS2
C                             ADD  1         RRN
C                             WRITESFL
C                             READ HISTJL1R                   91
C                             ENDDO
C*
C* DISPLAY THE RETRIEVED DATA
C                 RRN         IFGT *ZERO
C                             MOVE *ON       *IN22
C                             ENDIF
```

Figure 10.14: RPG III program modified to handle the override. (Continued)

```
C                         MOVE *ON      *IN21
C                         EXFMTCTL
C*
C* CLOSE THE DATA FILE
C                         CLOSEHISTJL1
C*
C* EXECUTE THE CLOF COMMAND TO CLOSE THE QUERY FILE
C                         CALL 'QCMDEXC'
C                         PARM C,2      ###CMD
C                         PARM 256      ###LEN
C*
C                         ENDSR
** C - COMMAND STRINGS
OPNQRYF FILE((HISTJL1)) OPTIMIZE(*FIRSTIO) SEQONLY(*YES 16)
CLOF OPNID(HISTJL1)
OVRDBF FILE(HISTJL1) SHARE(*YES)
DLTOVR FILE(HISTJL1)
** KFN - KEY FIELD NAMES
CUSNO    ITMNO    INVNO    *NONE
```

Figure 10.14: RPG III program modified to handle the override. (Continued)

```
*===============================================================
* Order history inquiry - Version 3
*===============================================================
* To compile:
*
*       CRTBNDRPG PGM(XXX/ORDIQY2R) SRCFILE(XXX/QRPGLESRC) +
*                 DFTACTGRP(*NO)
*
*===============================================================

FHistJL1 if   e            disk      rename(HistJL1R: HistRec)
F                                    UsrOpn
FOrdIqy2d cf  e            workstn   sfile(sfl: rrn)

D QCmdExc       pr                   ExtPgm('QCMDEXC')
D   Command            2000
D   Length               15  5
D
D AppendExpr    pr
D   Expr               2000
D   NewExpr              80   value
D
D KeyFieldNames S         10         DIM(3) CTDATA PERRCD(4)
D rrn           s          4  0
D Cmd           s       2000
D CmdSize       s         15p  5inz(%Size(Cmd))
D QrySlt        s       2000
D alpha         s          8
```

Figure 10.15: RPG IV program modified to handle the override.

```
C* Override the file to be queried
C                    eval      Cmd = 'OVRDBF FILE(HISTJL1) SHARE(*YES)'
C                    callp     QCmdExc (Cmd : CmdSize)
C
C                    exfmt     prompt
C                    dow       not *in03
C                    exsr      BuildCommand
C                    exsr      ShowData
C                    exfmt     prompt
C                    enddo
C
C                    eval      *inLR = *on
C* Delete the override
C                    eval      Cmd = 'DLTOVR FILE(HISTJL1)'
C                    callp     QCmdExc (Cmd : CmdSize)
C***********
C       BuildCommand  BegSR
C*
C* Build the QRYSLT parameter value
C                    eval      QrySlt = *blanks
C*
C* Test for invoice number
C                    if        InvNo1 <> *zero
C                    movel (p)InvNo1       alpha
C                    callp     AppendExpr (QrySlt : 'INVNO=' + Alpha)
C
C                    else
C*
C* Test for customer number
C                    if        CusNo1 <> *zero
C                    movel (p)CusNo1       alpha
C                    callp     AppendExpr (QrySlt : 'CUSNO=' + Alpha)
C                    endif
C*
C* Test for item number
C                    if        ItmNo1 <> *blanks
C                    callp     AppendExpr (QrySlt :
C                                          'ITMNO="' + ItmNo1 + '"')
C   endif
C*
C* Test for invoice date
C                    if        InvDt1 <> *zero
C                    movel (p)InvDt1       alpha
C                    callp     AppendExpr (QrySlt : 'INVDAT=' + Alpha)
C                    endif
C*
C* Test for sales rep number
C                    if        RepNo1 <> *zero
C                    movel (p)RepNo1       alpha
C                    callp     AppendExpr (QrySlt : 'REPNO=' + Alpha)
C                    endif
C*
C                    endif
```

Figure 10.15: RPG IV program modified to handle the override. (Continued)

```
C*
C* Move the OPNQRYF command, with parameters that do not change,
C*   into variable CMD
C                     eval      Cmd = 'OPNQRYF FILE((HISTJL1)) +
C                                     OPTIMIZE(*FIRSTIO) +
C                                     SEQONLY(*YES 16)'
C*
C*
C* Add the QRYSLT parameter to CMD
C*
C                     if        QrySlt <> *blanks
C                     eval      Cmd = %trim(Cmd) + ' ' +
C                                     'QRYSLT(''' + %trim(QrySlt) + ''')'
C                     endif
C*
C* Build the KEYFLD parameter
C                     if        SrtSeq >= 1 and SrtSeq <= 3
C                     eval      Cmd = %trim(Cmd) + ' ' + 'KEYFLD(' +
C                                     KeyFieldNames (SrtSeq) + ')'
C                     endif
C*
C                     EndSR
C***********
C       ShowData      BegSR
C*
C* Execute the OPNQRYF command
C                     callp     QCmdExc (Cmd : CmdSize)
C
C* Open the data file
C                     open      HistJL1
C
C* Clear the subfile
C                     eval      *in21 = *off
C                     eval      *in22 = *off
C                     eval      *in26 = *on
C                     write     ctl
C                     eval      *in26 = *off
C
C* Fill the subfile
C                     eval      rrn = *zero
C                     read      HistRec                            91
C                     dow       (not *in91) and (rrn <= 16)
C                     eval      CusNm2 = Cusnam
C                     eval      ItmDs2 = ItmDsc
C                     eval      rrn = rrn + 1
C                     write     sfl
C                     read      HistRec                            91
C                     enddo
C
C                     eval      *in22 = (rrn > *zero)
C                     eval      *in21 = *on
C
C                     exfmt     ctl
C
```

Figure 10.15: RPG IV program modified to handle the override. (Continued)

```
C* Close the data file
C                          close     HistJL1
C*
C* Close the query file
C                          eval      Cmd = 'CLOF OPNID(HISTJL1)'
C                          callp     QCmdExc (Cmd : CmdSize)
C*
C                          EndSR
*
P AppendExpr              b
D                         pi
D  Expr                             2000
D  NewExpr                            80    value
D  WorkExpr               s          128
D
C                          eval WorkExpr = '(' + %trim(NewExpr) + ')'
C                          if   Expr = *blanks
C                          eval Expr = Workexpr
C                          else
C                          eval Expr = %trim(Expr) + '&' + WorkExpr
C                          endif
C
P                         e

**ctdata KeyFieldNames
CUSNO    ITMNO    INVNO
```

Figure 10.15: RPG IV program modified to handle the override. (Continued)

ACCESS PATHS

OPNQRYF uses existing access paths when possible. When you are running OPNQRYF interactively, you can tell whether or not OPNQRYF is using an existing access path by watching the status messages. Sometimes a status message will tell you it is building an access path. Other times, the number of records processed will slowly increment by a large number, such as 2000, while fewer records are selected. In this case, the system is scanning the entire file, ignoring access paths.

If the file has only a few thousand records, using this method probably is not a problem. If the file is large or response time to the query is unacceptable, you should consider building one or more logical files over the fields used in the select and sequence criteria. Unfortunately, there are no hard-and-fast rules to follow, and sometimes you will just have to experiment until you find a logical that works. Improving performance is discussed further in chapter 16.

Summary

OPNQRYF is best suited for batch processing, but with careful planning, it can be used effectively in interactive programs. Interactive programs must not open the file before the OPNQRYF is executed. Performance of interactive programs may often be improved by proper coding of the OPTIMIZE(*FIRSTIO) and SEQONLY parameters. Another way to improve performance is to create permanent access paths that OPNQRYF can use.

11

❖OPNQRYF in the Integrated Language Environment

Running OPNQRYF in ILE programs is different than running OPNQRYF in OPM programs. This chapter describes how OPNQRYF works under ILE. You'll see the difference is great, but not difficult to handle. Because activation groups didn't exist under OPM, many AS/400 programmers still don't understand them. Yet, activation groups are one of the key concepts behind ILE, and you must understand them if you intend to make ILE work as it should.

ACTIVATION GROUPS

An activation group is a division of a job. While every job has at least one activation group, a job may have more than one activation group. Just as jobs aren't objects, activation groups are not objects. Just as two jobs can run without conflicting for resources, two activation groups within a job can run without conflicting for resources.

For example, let's suppose two users—Bill and Mary—both run a certain accounts payable inquiry program at the same time. Bill enters vendor number 13579 into a prompt screen of some sort; OPNQRYF runs and selects open purchase orders for that vendor. Mary, sitting at the next desk, enters vendor number 24680 into the prompt screen; OPNQRYF runs, and she sees open purchase orders for that vendor.

The two jobs didn't conflict with one another because they are separate jobs. Bill's job never sees the ODP (open data path) created by Mary's job, and Mary's job never sees the ODP created by Bill's job. However, if Bill runs two programs that access the purchase order file within the same job, it is possible that one will see the ODP of the other. ILE allows a single job to be divided into "subjobs," called *activation groups*, that behave to an extent as two distinct jobs would.

SCOPE

The term *scope* refers to the amount of influence something has within a job. When IBM introduced ILE, they added an OPNSCOPE (open scope) parameter to OPNQRYF so you could specify the way an OPNQRYF is to affect the job within which it runs.

The default value of OPNSCOPE is *ACTGRPDFN (defined by the activation group). If the OPNQRYF runs in a program running in the default activation group, the scope is to the call level. If the program is running in a named activation group, the OPNQRYF only has influence within the activation group.

All OPM programs run in the default activation group. ILE programs may run in the default activation group as well. In general, ILE applications should be designed in such a way that ILE programs run in named activation groups—not in the default activation group. However, in a mixed OPM-ILE environment, it is common and fitting that many ILE programs would run in the default activation group.

If you want to limit the scope of an OPNQRYF command to the activation group, you can specify OPNSCOPE(*ACTGRP). Shared opens within the activation group will use the ODP created by the OPNQRYF. The ODP will exist until it is closed with CLOF or until the activation group is destroyed.

If you use named activation groups, you probably won't have to specify OPNSCOPE (*ACTGRP) because that is the way OPNQRYF works within named activation groups anyway.

You may also scope an ODP to the job. Any shared open within the job, no matter what activation group it is in, will share the ODP created by ONPQRYF. Because this defeats the purpose of ILE and activation groups, scoping to a job should be avoided as a rule.

CONVERSION FROM OPM TO ILE

Figure 11.1 shows part of a CL program that runs OPNQRYF and calls an RPG program.

```
OVRDBF      FILE(CUSFILE) SHARE(*YES)
OPNQRYF     FILE((CUSFILE)) +
              QRYSLT('CUSNO = %RANGE(2 9)') +
              KEYFLD((STATE) (TERRCD) (ZIPCD))
CALL        PGM(CILEX1RG)
CLOF        OPNID(CUSFILE)
DLTOVR      FILE(CUSFILE)
```

Figure 11.1: An example of OPNQRYF that runs under OPM.

If you want to convert this set of programs to run under ILE instead of OPM, what do you need to do differently? The easy method is to recompile the programs as ILE programs that run in the same activation group. The code in Figure 11.2 shows how to do that.

```
CRTBNDCL   PGM(OQFMAGIC/CILEX1CL) SRCFILE(XXX/QCLSRC) SRCMBR(CILEX1CL) +
             DFTACTGRP(*NO) ACTGRP(CILEX1)
CRTBNDRPG  PGM(OQFMAGIC/CILEX1RG) SRCFILE(XXX/QRPGLESRC) +
             SRCMBR(CILEX1RG) DFTACTGRP(*NO) ACTGRP(CILEX1)
```

Figure 11.2: Commands to recompile programs as ILE programs running in activation group CILEX1.

If this RPG IV program runs under different CL programs, you could choose to let it run in the caller's activation group, whatever that happens to be, as shown in Figure 11.3.

```
CRTBNDRPG PGM(OQFMAGIC/CILEX1RG) SRCFILE(XXX/QRPGLESRC) +
            SRCMBR(CILEX1RG) DFTACTGRP(*NO) ACTGRP(*CALLER)
```

Figure 11-3: The command to recompile the RPG program to run in the caller's activation group.

Either method makes the CL and RPG programs run in the same activation group. However, if this CL program is the only one that calls this RPG program, then you might prefer to compile them into modules and bind the two together into one program. You must change the CL program slightly. The CALL command becomes a CALLPRC (Call Procedure) command as shown in Figure 11.4.

```
CALLPRC     PRC(CILEX2RG)
```

Figure 11-4: An example of a CALLPRC command.

Now to create the program, build modules and bind them together as shown in Figure 11.5.

```
CRTCLMOD  MODULE(XXX/CILEX2CL) SRCFILE(XXX/QCLSRC) SRCMBR(CILEX2CL)
CRTRPGMOD MODULE(XXX/CILEX2RG) SRCFILE(XXX/QRPGLESRC) SRCMBR(CILEX2RG)
CRTPGM    PGM(XXX/CILEX2) MODULE(XXX/CILEX2CL XXX/CILEX2RG)
```

Figure 11-5: An example of creating modules and then binding them together.

ANOTHER EXAMPLE

Just to help ensure that you understand how activation groups work, let's consider one more example. Suppose you have an ILE CL program named CILEX3CL that runs OPNQRYF over file CUSFILE and calls ILE RPG program CILEX3RG1 to process the queried data. Let's further suppose that this RPG program calls another RPG program, CILEX3RG2, that also uses CUSFILE, but shouldn't share the ODP. How could you set this up? Here is one method.

- ❖ Compile the CL program CILEX3CL to run in named activation group QILE.
- ❖ Compile the RPG program CILEX3RG1 to run in activation group *CALLER. This means it also will run in QILE.
- ❖ Compile the RPG program CILEX3RG2 to run in a *NEW activation group. Because it won't run in QILE, it won't share the ODP.

Converting from OPM to ILE is more than using RPG IV and changing CL CALL commands to CALLPRC commands. Before you begin to convert programs that use OPNQRYF, master activation groups.

12

❖Using OPNQRYF in CL Programs

A CL program can read an OPNQRYF file just as a high-level language program can. The Receive File (RCVF) command, unlike most system commands, can share an open data path. Probably the main reason that programmers don't often use OPNQRYF with CL programs is that CL programs can work with only one file at a time. Report programs generally require at least two files: one for input, and one for output.

One approach you could use to overcome this limitation is to have the CL program call a subprogram to print the report. This philosophy is behind the PRINT command in QUSRTOOL and is the approach used in the following examples.

Another approach is to have the data sent to an object—such as a message queue, data queue, or data area—that is not a file. This method is feasible when the OPNQRYF returns only one or a few records, but not for large volumes of data.

You can use two methods to process the query file. One method uses two CL programs; the other uses only one CL program. The two methods are examined in greater detail in the following sections.

USING TWO CL PROGRAMS

When you use two CL programs to process an OPNQRYF file, one program runs the OPNQRYF command and calls the second one, which reads the data and builds the output. This approach is like the high-level language examples throughout this book. The difference is that you call a CL program that could just as easily be an RPG or COBOL program.

Figure 12.1 shows a CL program that runs an OPNQRYF command and then calls another program (CUSLIST) to print the report.

```
/* This program prints a customer master list for a state */
        PGM       PARM(&STATE)
        DCL       VAR(&QRYSLT) TYPE(*CHAR) LEN(80) +
                    VALUE('CUSSTT="XX"')
        DCL       VAR(&STATE) TYPE(*CHAR) LEN(2)
        CHGVAR    VAR(%SST(&QRYSLT 9 2)) VALUE(&STATE)
        OPNQRYF   FILE((CUSMAS)) QRYSLT(&QRYSLT) +
                    KEYFLD((CUSCIT) (CUSNAM))
        OVRDBF    FILE(CUSMAS) SHARE(*YES)
        CALL      PGM(CUSLIST)
        DLTOVR    FILE(CUSMAS)
        CLOF      OPNID(CUSMAS)
        ENDPGM
```

Figure 12-1: An example of using two CL programs to process an OPNQRYF file.

CUSLIST could be an RPG or COBOL program. In this case, CUSLIST is the CL program shown in Figure 12.2.

```
/* This program may run stand-alone or under OPNQRYF */
/* If it runs stand-alone and no overrides are in effect, it lists  */
/* the customer master file in customer number order                */
        PGM
        DCLF      FILE(CUSMAS)
        DCL       VAR(&PLINE)  TYPE(*CHAR) LEN(132)
        DCL       VAR(&TITLE)  TYPE(*CHAR) LEN( 80) +
                    VALUE('CUSTOMER MASTER LISTING')
        CHGVAR    VAR(&PLINE) VALUE('NAME')
        CHGVAR    VAR(%SST(&PLINE 22  4)) VALUE('NBR')
        CHGVAR    VAR(%SST(&PLINE 27 14)) VALUE('CITY')
        CHGVAR    VAR(%SST(&PLINE 42  2)) VALUE('ST')
        CHGVAR    VAR(%SST(&PLINE 45  3)) VALUE('ZIP')
        PRINT     ACTION(*OPN) TITLE(&TITLE) COLHD1(&PLINE)
READDATA:
        RCVF
```

Figure 12-2: A program that is called from the initial program.

```
        MONMSG      MSGID(CPF0864) EXEC(GOTO ENDPRINT)
                            /* CPF0864 means end of file */
        CHGVAR      VAR(&PLINE) VALUE(' ')
        CHGVAR      VAR(%SST(&PLINE  1 20)) VALUE(&CUSNAM)
        CHGVAR      VAR(%SST(&PLINE 22  4)) VALUE(&CUSNO)
        CHGVAR      VAR(%SST(&PLINE 27 12)) VALUE(&CUSCIT)
        CHGVAR      VAR(%SST(&PLINE 42  2)) VALUE(&CUSSTT)
        CHGVAR      VAR(%SST(&PLINE 45 10)) VALUE(&CUSZIP)
        PRINT       LINE(&PLINE)
        GOTO        READDATA
ENDPRINT:
        PRINT       ACTION(*CLO)
        ENDPGM
```

Figure 12-2: A program that is called from the initial program. (Continued)

USING ONE CL PROGRAM

The first program doesn't need to call a separate CL program. They can be combined into one like the example shown in Figure 12.3.

```
        PGM         PARM(&STATE)
        DCLF        FILE(CUSMAS)
        DCL         VAR(&PLINE)  TYPE(*CHAR) LEN(132)
        DCL         VAR(&TITLE)  TYPE(*CHAR) LEN( 80) +
                        VALUE('CUSTOMER MASTER LISTING')
        DCL         VAR(&QRYSLT) TYPE(*CHAR) LEN(80) +
                        VALUE('CUSSTT="XX"')
        DCL         VAR(&STATE) TYPE(*CHAR) LEN(2)
/* Open the query file */
        CHGVAR      VAR(%SST(&QRYSLT 9 2)) VALUE(&STATE)
        OPNQRYF     FILE((CUSMAS)) QRYSLT(&QRYSLT) +
                        KEYFLD((CUSCIT) (CUSNAM))
        OVRDBF `     FILE(CUSMAS) SHARE(*YES)
/* Print the report */
        CHGVAR      VAR(&PLINE) VALUE('NAME')
        CHGVAR      VAR(%SST(&PLINE 22  4)) VALUE('NBR')
        CHGVAR      VAR(%SST(&PLINE 27 14)) VALUE('CITY')
        CHGVAR      VAR(%SST(&PLINE 42  2)) VALUE('ST')
        CHGVAR      VAR(%SST(&PLINE 45  3)) VALUE('ZIP')
        PRINT       ACTION(*OPN) TITLE(&TITLE) COLHD1(&PLINE)
READDATA:
        RCVF
```

Figure 12-3: An example of combining the two programs into one.

```
      MONMSG    MSGID(CPF0864) EXEC(GOTO ENDPRINT)
                /* CPF0864 means end of file */
      CHGVAR    VAR(&PLINE) VALUE(' ')
      CHGVAR    VAR(%SST(&PLINE  1 20)) VALUE(&CUSNAM)
      CHGVAR    VAR(%SST(&PLINE 22  4)) VALUE(&CUSNO)
      CHGVAR    VAR(%SST(&PLINE 27 12)) VALUE(&CUSCIT)
      CHGVAR    VAR(%SST(&PLINE 42  2)) VALUE(&CUSSTT)
      CHGVAR    VAR(%SST(&PLINE 45 10)) VALUE(&CUSZIP)
      PRINT     LINE(&PLINE)
      GOTO      READDATA
ENDPRINT:
      PRINT     ACTION(*CLO)
/* The report has been printed. Clean up and end the job */
      DLTOVR    FILE(CUSMAS)
      CLOF      OPNID(CUSMAS)
      ENDPGM
```

Figure 12-3: An example of combining the two programs into one. (Continued)

The first execution of RCVF opens the file to the CL program. The OPNQRYF command must be executed and the file must have the share open data path attribute before the RCVF command is executed.

Just as a high-level language file declaration must match the FORMAT parameter, the DCLF must match OPNQRYF'S FORMAT parameter.

SUMMARY

CL programs, like high-level language programs, also can benefit from the OPNQRYF command. The important thing to remember is that the OPNQRYF command must be executed, and the file made to share the open data path, before the first RCVF command is executed. OPNQRYF can be processed in a CL program in two ways. One way is to use two programs (one of which functions as a high-level language program). The other method is to combine all OPNQRYF and high-level language functions in one program.

13

❖ OPNQRYF and the Year 2000 Issue

I this chapter, you'll find some ways to sequence and select six-digit dates that span centuries. OPNQRYF cannot solve the Year 2000 challenge for you, but it might be able to help in two ways:

❖ You might be able to avoid converting some of your date fields to an unambiguous format.

❖ You might be able to buy some time until you can properly convert a date field in the database.

Suppose a file contains manufacturing order information, including the date a manufacturing order is due to be finished. A person looking at orders from this file in December of 1999 will see orders due on dates such as 991221 and 000111. There is no doubt that the first order is due in 1999 and the second is due in 2000.

If production is scheduled three months in advance, and orders are always produced on time, then the file will contain dates for both years 1999 and 2000 for only the last three months of 1999. If shipments are running late, then this problem could last into the beginning of 2000. However, at some point, there will be no more orders for 1999 in the file. All orders in the file will be for years 2000 or after, and six-digit dates in that file won't present a problem for another 99 years.

The following sections offer some techniques that might help in such situations. First, consider ways of sequencing (sorting) records based on six-digit dates. Then look at the challenge of record selection.

SORTING RECORDS

Is it necessary to change a file and all the programs that use it because one date won't sort correctly for only three months? Maybe not.

Suppose you have a report program that sorts by a date field. People have already started putting dates for the Year 2000 into the file, but you won't be able to convert the date to eight-digit dates for a few months. What do you do in the meantime?

SEQUENCING TECHNIQUE 1: ADJUST THE YEAR

One possibility is to convert years to another range of numbers. For example, you might presume that years of 40 or greater are in the twentieth century, and years of 39 or less are in the twenty-first century. If so, you would convert dates in the year 1940 to year 00 and dates in the year 2039 to year 99.

To do this conversion, make OPNQRYF modify the date by adding 60 to the year and dropping any overflow into the hundreds column. Years 40-99 become 00-59 and 00-39 become 60-99.

Figure 13.1 shows the code to convert field DUEDAT (in YYMMDD format) in file MANUFORD.

```
OPNQRYF  FILE((MANUFORD)) KEYFLD((DUEDAT) (SEQ)) +
           MAPFLD((DUEDAT '(1/DUEDAT + 600000) // 1000000'))
```

Figure 13.1: Using OPNQRYF to convert dates with MAPFLD.

The MAPFLD (Mapped Field) parameter redefines DUEDAT. Adding 600,000 to the DUEDAT value from the MANUFORD file modifies the year but could cause the date to overflow into the millions. The // operator returns the remainder of dividing by 1,000,000. In this case, // removes the millions and leaves a six-digit date with the modified year.

It is important to understand that this doesn't change the way data is stored in the database file. It only changes the way OPNQRYF, and any programs that run under OPNQRYF, view the data.

Because programs that read the MANUFORD file under the control of OPNQRYF will see the modified date, not the real one, each HLL program should convert the modified date back to something usable. For example, you can make an RPG III program convert the modified date to the correct date in YYYYMMDD format as shown in Figure 13.2.

```
C           DUEDAT    ADD   19400000  DATE2    80
```

Figure 13.2: RPG III code to convert a modified date to YYYYMMDD format.

Or you can make the program convert the modified date to the correct date in YYMMDD format as shown in Figure 13.3.

```
C                     ADD   400000    DUEDAT
```

Figure 13.3: RPG III code to convert a modified date to YYMMDD format.

If DUEDAT were in MMDDYY format, you'd have to change the OPNQRYF command a little (Figure 13.4).

```
OPNQRYF  FILE((MANUFORD)) KEYFLD((DUEDAT) (SEQ)) +
           MAPFLD((YEAR1 '1/XDATE // 100' *DEC 2 0) +
                  (MONTHDAY1 '(1/DUEDAT - YEAR1) * 0.01' *DEC 4 0) +
                  (YEAR2 '(YEAR1 + 60) // 100' *DEC 2 0) +
                  (DUEDAT '(YEAR2 * 10000) + MONTHDAY1'))
```

Figure 13.4: The OPNQRYF command when DUEDAT is in MMDDYY format.

SEQUENCING TECHNIQUE 2: GENERATE A CENTURY DIGIT

Another way to sort six-digit dates properly is to generate a century digit and sort on it ahead of the date field. Like the previous technique, it's ugly but it works. Presume the same file of manufacturing orders, MANUFORD, with field DUEDAT in MMDDYY format. The data would look something like Table 13.1.

Create a physical file that includes all the fields from MANUFORD, plus a century digit field as in Figure 13.5. This field won't contain data and doesn't have to have a member.

Write your RPG program to use this file instead of MANUFORD, and then make the CL program generate the century digit as shown in Figure 13.6.

Table 13.1: Sample Data for File MANUFORD.		
Order Number	Customer Number	Due Date
101	2	12-15-99
102	4	10-31-99
103	5	01-15-00
104	8	12-31-99
105	8	11-30-99
106	4	01-31-00
107	3	01-15-00

```
A* File MOWORK01
A* Dummy format file for OPNQRYF
A                                              REF(MANUFORD)
A          R WORKREC
A            MONBR      R
A            MOCUST     R
A            DUEDAT     R
A            CDIGIT       1S 0
```

Figure 13.5: The DDS for a dummy physical file to hold the century digit.

The MAPFLD accomplishes two things. So that the field sorts properly, MAPFLD reformats the due-date field from MMDDYY format to YYMMDD. MAPFLD also generates the century digit. If you have to use this technique to keep an existing program working, the existing program should already include some method to make a MMDDYY date sort properly. Therefore, you will probably have to add only the calculations to generate the century digit. The RPG program sees the data as if it were stored as shown in Table 13.2.

One last point needs to be made. If your file includes dates with special values, such as all zeros or all 9s, the output won't be sequenced in the way people are used to seeing it. People are accustomed to viewing dates of zero first, valid dates second, and dates of all

```
OVRDBF      FILE(MOWORK01) TOFILE(MANUFORD) SHARE(*YES)
OPNQRYF     FILE((MANUFORD)) FORMAT(MOWORK01) +
              KEYFLD((CDIGIT) (DUEDAT)) +
              MAPFLD(+
                (DUE_MDY_C '%DIGITS(1/DUEDAT)' *CHAR 6) +
                (DUEYR_C   '%SST(DUE_MDY_C 5 2)' *CHAR 2) +
                (DUE_YMD_C 'DUEYR_C *CAT +
                            %SST(DUE_MDY_C 1 4)' *CHAR 6) +
                (DUEDAT    'DUE_YMD_C') +
                (DUEYR_Z   'DUEYR_C' *ZONED 2 0) +
                (CDIGIT    '((139 - DUEYR_Z) / 100)') +
              )
CALL        PGM(CY2KX1RG)
CLOF        OPNID(MANUFORD)
DLTOVR      FILE(MOWORK01)
```

Figure 13.6: CL program to generate century digit.

Table 13.2: Data Sent to RPG Program.			
Order Number	Customer Number	Due Date	Century
102	4	99-10-31	0
105	8	99-11-30	0
101	2	99-12-15	0
104	8	99-12-31	0
103	5	00-01-15	1
107	3	00-01-15	1
106	4	00-01-31	1

9s last. Now the records with special date values will be embedded somewhere within the report, and users might overlook them.

SEQUENCING TECHNIQUE 3: JOINING

The preceding techniques transform the date from one format to another. An alternative is to join to a file of dates and sequence on fields from that file. For instance, consider the file DATEFL that is introduced in the chapter 5 and further developed in appendix D. If you put both six-digit and eight-digit dates in that file, you can transform a six-digit date to an eight-digit one simply by joining files.

Returning to the manufacturing orders file example, sort on the six-digit due date. As long as there's a field of the same format in DATEFL, the format doesn't matter.

Because all sort fields have to be in the record format, create a work file containing all the fields from MANUFORD, plus the sort fields. See Figure 13.7. In this case, there's only one sort field (an eight-digit date field in YYYYMMDD format). Let's call the work file MOWORK02.

```
A* Dummy format file for OPNQRYF
A                                                    REF(MANUFORD)
A          R WORKREC
A            MONBR        R
A            MOCUST       R
A            DUEDAT       R
A            DUEDT8              8
```

Figure 13.7: The DDS for the dummy work file to contain all sort fields.

Of course, the RPG program will be coded as if it will read this file (not MANUFORD). OPNQRYF joins the files to sort. See Figure 13.8.

```
OVRDBF     FILE(MOWORK02) TOFILE(MANUFORD) SHARE(*YES)
OPNQRYF    FILE((MANUFORD)) (DATEFL)) FORMAT(MOWORK02) +
             KEYFLD((DUEDT8)) JFLD((DUEDAT YMDN)) +
             MAPFLD((DUEDT8 'YMDC8'))
CALL       PGM(CY2KX2RG)
CLOF       OPNID(MANUFORD)
DLTOVR     FILE(MOWORK02)
```

Figure 13.8: A CL program with OPNQRYF joining files and sequencing before the RPG program.

Because the eight-digit character date field in YYYYMMDD format is called YMDC8 in DATEFL, that's the field you assign to DUEDT8. The resulting data looks like Table 13.3.

Table 13.3: Result of CL Program Shown in Figure 13.8.			
Order Number	Customer Number	Due Date	Eight-Digit Date Field
102	4	99-10-31	19991031
105	8	99-11-30	19991130
101	2	99-12-15	19991215
104	8	99-12-31	19991231
103	5	00-01-15	20000115
107	3	00-01-15	20000115
106	4	00-01-31	20000131

RECORD SELECTION

Now let's consider the problem of record selection.

SELECTION TECHNIQUE 1: CONVERT DATES

Suppose you use the first sequencing technique listed in this chapter to adjust the year by adding 60 (or whatever adjustment you prefer) and drop overflow into the hundreds column. The result is that the year portion of the dates is off by 40 years. To select records, you'll have to adjust the year portion of each date value used in the QRYSLT parameter.

For example, to select manufacturing orders for December 1, 1999 through January 31, 2000, you'd have to select records where due dates ranged from 591201 through 600131. Here are a couple of ways to handle this.

❖ Remove the record selection from the QRYSLT parameter and add it to the RPG program. Let the RPG program reformat the dates back to their original values and then carry out record selection.

❖ Write a utility program that adjusts dates from their actual values to their adjusted values. Have CL programs that run OPNQRYF call this utility program to adjust the dates, and use the adjusted dates in the QRYSLT parameter.

You might think of other ways to adjust dates, but you are creating a lot of work for yourself by avoiding fixing the database. If you have only a very few programs that do such record selection, using this technique could be worthwhile.

SELECTION TECHNIQUE 2: ALTER THE BOOLEAN LOGIC

Suppose you have a program that selects manufacturing orders for a range of dates (Figure 13.9).

```
DCL        &FROMDATE   *CHAR     6   /* YYMMDD FORMAT */
DCL        &THRUDATE   *CHAR     6   /* YYMMDD FORMAT */

OVRDBF     FILE(MANUFORD) SHARE(*YES)
OPNQRYF    FILE((MANUFORD)) +
             QRYSLT('DUEDAT = %RANGE(' *CAT +
                 &FROMDATE *BCAT &THRUDATE *CAT ')') +
             KEYFLD((MOCUST))
CALL       PGM(CY2KX3RG)
CLOF       OPNID(MANUFORD)
DLTOVR     FILE(MANUFORD)
```

Figure 13.9: A program to select within a range of dates using QRYSLT.

This works fine if &FROMDATE is 980101 and &THRUDATE is 991231, but not when &FROMDATE is 990101 and &THRUDATE is 001231. An easy way to solve this problem is to take advantage of the relational and logical operators available with OPNQRYF. The revised code is shown in Figure 13.10.

```
DCL        &FROMDATE   *CHAR     6   /* YYMMDD FORMAT */
DCL        &THRUDATE   *CHAR     6   /* YYMMDD FORMAT */
DCL        &QRYSLT     *CHAR   256   /* YYMMDD FORMAT */

IF (&FROMDATE *LE &THRUDATE) DO
   CHGVAR  &QRYSLT ('DUEDAT = %RANGE(' *CAT +
                      &FROMDATE *BCAT &THRUDATE *CAT ')')
ENDDO
ELSE DO
   CHGVAR  &QRYSLT ('(DUEDAT *GE' *BCAT &FROMDATE *BCAT '*OR +
                      DUEDAT *LE' *BCAT &THRUDATE *CAT ')')
```

Figure 13.10: Using relational and logical operators with CHGVAR to format a date for OPNQRYF QRYSLT.

```
ENDDO

OVRDBF   FILE(MANUFORD) SHARE(*YES)
OPNQRYF  FILE((MANUFORD)) QRYSLT(&QRYSLT) KEYFLD((MOCUST))
CALL     PGM(CY2KX3RG)
CLOF     OPNID(MANUFORD)
DLTOVR   FILE(MANUFORD)
```

Figure 13.10: Using relational and logical operators with CHGVAR to format a date for OPNQRYF QRYSLT. (Continued)

Moving the record selection logic to variable &QRYSLT gives us the flexibility needed to make this work. If &FROMDATE is less than or equal to &THRUDATE, the record selection logic is unchanged. But if &FROMDATE is greater than &THRUDATE, the program assumes the dates span centuries, and gets all records with due dates greater than or equal to &FROMDATE or due dates less than or equal to &THRUDATE.

Selecting orders from December 15, 1999 through January 15, 2000 gives results like the data shown in Table 13.4. Of course, this isn't an idiot-proof technique. A user wanting orders for all of December, 1999 might enter a &FROMDATE value of 991231 and a &THRUDATE of 991201. The penalty for the lack of common sense results in the opposite of what the user wanted.

Table 13.4: Results of Query in Figure 13.13.		
Order Number	Customer Number	Due Date
101	2	99-12-15
107	3	00-01-15
103	5	00-01-15
104	8	99-12-31
105	8	99-11-30

14

❖ Other Parameters
of the OPNQRYF Command

In the preceding chapters, the parameters most often used by OPNQRYF are examined. In contrast, this chapter discusses the parameters that you will use less frequently. While it's possible you might not even use some of these parameters, you at least should be aware of them.

OPTION (OPEN OPTION)

In most cases, you will use OPNQRYF to read data from a file. However, if there is no join, union, unique key, or grouping involved, you also can issue output operations to the queried database file.

When the shared open data path is first opened, it must be opened for all types of processing for which it will be used. The OPTION parameter gives you a way to tell OPNQRYF how you intend to use the file. The default value, *INP, tells the processor that the file is an input file only. You can use three more modes along with *INP. *UPD means you want to update existing records. To add new records, use the special value *OUT. If you want to delete records in the database file, you must use the *DLT value.

Figure 14.1 shows the standard option with the *INP default. The file may be opened only for input by programs that use the opened query file.

```
OPNQRYF     FILE((MYFILE)) OPTION(*INP) KEYFLD(&KEY)
```

*Figure 14.1: Specifying *INP on the OPTION keyword.*

If you want to perform other operations on the queried database file, you may code either OPTION(*INP *OUT *UPD *DLT) or OPTION(*ALL). Figure 14.2 shows examples.

```
OPNQRYF   ... OPTION(*OUT)        output only

OPNQRYF   ... OPTION(*OUT *INP)     input and output

OPNQRYF   ... OPTION(*INP *UPD *DLT)   read, update, delete
```

Figure 14.2: Examples of specifying different OPTION parameters.

The high-level language program must not try to open the file in a way that is inconsistent with the OPTION parameter. If the OPNQRYF option is *INP, for example, the RPG F specification must specify a file type of "I" (column 17 in RPG IV; column 15 in RPG III).

If you want to update records in a file, consider the I/O capabilities of the language you are using. RPG, for example, requires that you read a record before you update it. For RPG update programs, you will have to use both *INP and *UPD options. The same is true of deletions. If the language you are using requires you to read a record before deleting it, you will have to have the *INP option in addition to *DLT.

A high-level language program doesn't have to use all the specified options. The OPNQRYF command could specify OPTION(*ALL), for example, but an RPG program might process it as input only.

Opening a query file for more than input is quite useful for selective updates. For example, you might want to zero out a field based on the value of another field. Figure 14.3 shows the CL for a short job that lets you assign a sales representative to all customers in a state. Figure 14.4 shows the RPG program that processes and updates the file.

To assign sales rep 404 to all customers in Louisiana, you would use the parameters shown in Figure 14.5. A nice aspect of this technique is that the RPG program doesn't lock records that it isn't going to update.

```
/*==============================================================*/
/* Assign a sales rep to all customers in a certain state       */
/*==============================================================*/
/* To compile:                                                  */
/*                                                              */
/*            CRTCLMOD  MODULE(XXX/UPDREPCL) SRCFILE(XXX/QCLSRC) */
/*            CRTPGM    PGM(XXX/UPDREP) MODULE(UPDREPCL UPDREPRG)*/
/*                                                              */
/*==============================================================*/

       PGM          PARM(&STATE &REP)

       DCL          VAR(&STATE) TYPE(*CHAR) LEN(2)
       DCL          VAR(&REP)   TYPE(*CHAR) LEN(3)
       OPNQRYF      FILE((CUSTOMERS)) OPTION(*INP *UPD) +
                      QRYSLT('CUSSTATE = "' *CAT &STATE *CAT '"')
       OVRDBF       FILE(CUSTOMERS) SHARE(*YES)
       CALLPRC      PRC(UPDREPRG) PARM(&REP)
       DLTOVR       FILE(CUSTOMERS)
       CLOF         OPNID(CUSTOMERS)

       ENDPGM
```

Figure 14.3: A CL module to select customer records for an update.

```
*================================================================
* To compile:
*
*      CRTRPGMOD  MODULE(XXX/XXX001RG) SRCFILE(XXX/QRPGLESRC)
*      CRTPGM     PGM(XXX/UPDREP) MODULE(UPDREPCL UPDREPRG)
*
*================================================================
* This module sets the REPNO field to the value of
*    parameter NEWREP.
*
* It should be run under OPNQRYF with a QRYSLT parameter,
*    unless all records are to be updated.
*================================================================

FCustomers uf    e             disk

D NewRep             s              3
D thereAreCustomers...
D                    s              n   inz(*on)
```

Figure 14.4: An RPG module to update the assignment of sales representatives.

```
C        *Entry        plist
C                      parm                        NewRep
C
C                      dow           thereAreCustomers
C                      read          Customer
C                      if            %eof
C                      leave
C                      endif
C                      eval          RepNo = NewRep
C                      update        Customer
C                      enddo
C
C                      eval          *inLR = *on
```

Figure 14.4: An RPG module to update the assignment of sales representatives. (Continued)

```
CALL     PGM(UPDREP) PARM('LA' '404')
```

Figure 14.5: Calling a program with parameters.

ALWCPYDTA (ALLOW COPY DATA)

Sometimes the query processor cannot carry out a task without copying records from a file into a work file. This occurs when the system is building key fields from two or more files, and in certain grouping functions. The only problem is that changes made to a queried database file after the copy is made won't be reflected in the results of the query.

If the ALWCPYDTA parameter has a value of *YES (its default value), it will copy data to work files when necessary. The *NO option prohibits the system from copying the data.

*OPTIMIZE: The system can use a sort routine to sequence the data but this option has certain restrictions. Included among the restrictions is that the query file must be processed as a sequential input file and the KEYFLD parameter must have a value other than *FILE and *NONE. For more details, refer to the discussion of OPNQRYF in the *CL Reference* manual.

IGNDECERR (IGNORE DECIMAL ERRORS)

If your database is in good shape, you probably will never have to use the IGNDECERR parameter. If you do have some files from another system that have non-numeric data in numeric fields, you can have OPNQRYF change the data to valid numeric values (which might not be the values you expected).

OPNID (OPEN ID)

The identifier of the OPNQRYF file defaults to the name of the first file in the FILE parameter. You may use another name by coding the OPNID parameter. The file ID in the CPYFRMQRYF (copy from query file), POSDBF (position database file), and CLOF (close file) commands must match OPNQRYF's file ID. The example in Figure 14.6 shows how the file IDs correspond.

```
PGM
OVRDBF          FILE(JOIN11) TOFILE(CUSMAS) SHARE(*YES)
OPNQRYF         FILE((CUSMAS) (CUSORD)) +
                  FORMAT(JOIN11) +
                  KEYFLD((CUSNO)) +
                  JFLD((1/CUSNO) (2/CUSNO)) +
                  JDFTVAL(*YES) +
                  MAPFLD((CUSNO '1/CUSNO')) +
                  OPTIMIZE(*MINWAIT) +
                  OPNID(JOINFILE)                    <<---
CPYFRMQRYF      OPNID(JOINFILE) TOFILE(*PRINT)       <<---
CALL            PGM(MYPROG)
POSDBF          OPNID(JOINFILE) POSITION(*START)     <<---
CALL            PGM(HISPROG)
CLOF            OPNID(JOINFILE)                      <<---
DLTOVR          FILE(JOIN11)
ENDPGM
```

Figure 14.6: Specifying file IDs.

Without the OPNID parameter, the query file's ID would be CUSMAS. If you decided to change the order of the two files so that CUSORD would be the primary join file, you also would have to change the CPYFRMQRYF, POSDBF, and CLOF commands. Using the OPNID parameter, you wouldn't have to change those commands.

COMMIT (COMMITMENT CONTROL)

If the high-level language program uses commitment control with the queried file, OPNQRYF must know about it. You must use COMMIT(*YES) when working with commitment control. The default value, COMMIT(*NO), means that no commitment control is to be used.

TYPE (OPEN TYPE)

The Open Type (TYPE) parameter affects the way the Reclaim Resource (RCLRSC) command works. The code shown in Figure 14-7 illustrates use of the RCLRSC command.

```
OVRDBF      FILE(MYFILE) SHARE(*YES)
OPNQRYF     FILE((MYFILE)) ...etc.
CALL        PGM(MYPROG)
RCLRSC
```

Figure 14.7: An example of the default value of TYPE.

If the OPNQRYF command specifies TYPE(*NORMAL), the default value, the RCLRSC command will close the OPNQRYF file. If the TYPE parameter has the value *PERM, the RCLRSC command won't close the OPNQRYF file. Instead, the OPNQRYF file will be closed by a CLOF command or at the end of the routing step.

The TYPE parameter is only applicable to programs running in the default-activation group, using the default value of the OPNSCOPE parameter.

DUPKEYCHK (CHECK FOR DUPLICATE KEYS)

The Check for Duplicate Keys (DUPKEYCHK) parameter is for COBOL programmers only. The special value *YES tells OPNQRYF to return duplicate key feedback information on I/O operations.

SRTSEQ (SORT SEQUENCE)

The Sort Sequence (SRTSEQ) parameter indicates the sorting sequence used in record selection, joining operations, group selection, key fields, unique key processing, and the minimum and maximum functions. Having the default value *JOB means that this parameter uses the sort sequence of the job in which the OPNQRYF is running.

You also may use the values *HEX (sort by hexadecimal values), *LANGIDUNQ (use a unique-weight sort table), and *LANGIDSHR (use a shared-weight sort table).

If you use one of the *LANGIDXXX values along with KEYFLD(*FILE), the system will sort the records in some order other than the file's actual sequence.

LANGID (LANGUAGE IDENTIFIER)

The Language Identifier (LANGID) parameter is only used with SRTSEQ(*LANGIDUNQ) or SRTSEQ(*LANGIDSHR). It allows you to specify the identifier of the language to use when sorting.

OPTALLAP (OPTIMIZE ALL ACCESS PATHS)

When looking for an efficient way to access data, the query processor will consider as many access paths as it can until an internal timeout internal is exceeded. Specifying OPTALLAP(*YES) forces the query optimizer to consider all access paths and ignore time-out values.

15

❖ Comparing OPNQRYF to FMTDTA Data

M any midrange professionals believe the Format Data (FMTDTA) command
should be used only to replace the sort routines in software ported from other
IBM midrange systems such as the System/36. In native applications, they reason, OPNQRYF should be used instead. OPNQRYF and FMTDTA are similar in what they do.
Both prepare data to be read by a high-level language program by selecting records and
sorting. Both also can produce detail or summary records. Although they are similar, they
are not equivalent. Because they are not equivalent, one cannot completely replace the
other. The purpose of this chapter is to discuss the differences between the two tools and
to provide some guidelines to help you decide when to use each one.

CONTRASTING OPNQRYF AND FMTDTA

Table 15.1 lists the major differences between OPNQRYF and FMTDTA, as used in the
AS/400 native environment. These distinctions can be summed up in one statement:
FMTDTA is a sort/merge package; OPNQRYF is a query tool.

ADVANTAGES OF OPNQRYF

One advantage OPNQRYF has over FMTDTA is that OPNQRYF works with database data by
field name, not by column position. This capability minimizes the effort required to modify the database. For example, suppose file REQUEST has a packed decimal field called
LIMIT, which is defined as seven digits (two of which are decimal positions). LIMIT is
found in columns 73 through 76 of each data record. An OPNQRYF command to sort the
file by LIMIT would look like the example shown in Figure 15.1.

Table 15.1: Differences between OPNQRYF and FMTDTA.	
OPNQRYF	**FMTDTA**
Recognizes external file definitions	Ignores external file definitions
Fields are referenced by field name	Fields are referenced by column position in file
Joins files	Merges files
Record selection and sort criteria coded in parameters	Record selection and sort criteria are coded in sequence specifications and stored in a separate source member
Sort and selection may be changed at run time	Sort and sequence criteria are hard coded in the sequence specs

```
OPNQRYF     FILE((REQUEST)) KEYFLD(LIMIT)
```

Figure 15.1: An example of using KEYFLD(LIMIT) in OPNQRYF.

FMTDTA would need the sequence specifications shown in Figure 15.2.

```
HSORTR      7A          X
I
FNP  73  76
FDC   1 135
```

Figure 15.2: Sequence specifications for FMTDTA.

Some time later, when the LIMIT field needs to be increased by two digits, the record length increases to 136 bytes, and LIMIT now occupies positions 73 through 77.

The OPNQRYF command requires no modification, but the sequence specifications must be completely modified (as shown in Figure 15.3). In the control specification, the key field length has to be changed to 9. The control field specification must be modified to reflect the new ending position (77) of the LIMIT field. The data field specification must

```
HSORTR      9A           X
I
FNP   73   77
FDC    1  136
```

Figure 15.3: Changes to FMTDTA's sequence specifications.

be changed to reflect the new record length: 136. If any include/omit specifications tested the field LIMIT, they also would have to be changed.

Another advantage of OPNQRYF is that key fields and record selection can be specified at runtime. Hard coding the sequence specifications prevents them from being changed. To use different sort sequences or record selection criteria, you must code multiple sequence specification members and use a CL variable in the SRCMBR parameter of the FMTDTA command.

OPNQRYF also has an advantage when it comes to calculating virtual fields. While OPNQRYF has a rich variety of built-in functions, FMTDTA is limited to testing a substring of a field, concatenating adjacent fields, and forcing control and data fields to a constant value.

OPNQRYF is a more powerful tool when two or more files must be joined. OPNQRYF can join two or more files, select records based on fields from more than one file, and sort on fields from different files. To do that type of task with FMTDTA, you often have to code a high-level language program to build a work file that serves as input to the sort.

HOW NOT TO CONVERT FMTDTA TO OPNQRYF

You might have discovered that OPNQRYF can be used with program-described files. Any file created with the BLDFILE procedure or CRTPF command has an external definition, automatically provided by the system. You can use the %SST function to select and sort records. For example, the sequence specs in Figure 15.4 can be translated to the OPNQRYF specifications in Figure 15.5.

FLATFILE was created with the System/36 BLDFILE procedure as an indexed file of 80-byte records with a four-byte key starting in position 1. The file's external definition consists of two fields: K00001 in positions 1 through 4, and F00001 in positions 5 through 80. WORKFILE is a file of 105-byte records created with the DDS shown in Figure 15.6.

```
HSORTR      4A          X
I C    5    5EQC1
FNP   16   19
FDC    1   80
```

Figure 15.4: FMTDTA sequence specifications that correspond to OPNQRYF in Figure 15.5.

```
OVRDBF    FILE(FLATFILE) SHARE(*YES)
OPNQRYF   FILE((FLATFILE)) FORMAT(WORKFILE) +
            QRYSLT('%SST(DATFLD 5 1) *EQ "1"') +
            KEYFLD((KEYFLD)) +
            MAPFLD((DTAFLD 'K00001 *CAT F00001') +
                (KEYFLD '%SST(DATFLD 16 4)'))
CALL      PGM(QRYFLATR)
      ...etc.
```

Figure 15.5: The OPNQRYF command that corresponds to the FMTDTA sequence specifications shown in Figure 15.4.

```
A         R WORKFILE
A           DTAFLD      80
A           KEYFLD      25
A         K KEYFLD
```

Figure 15.6: The DDS for a 105-byte WORKFILE record.

Native RPG III program QRYFLATR (S/36-compatible programs will not work) defines the file as shown in Figure 15.7.

```
FFLATFILEIP  F      80  1AI        1 DISK
```

Figure 15.7: The definition for a flat file in RPG III.

The preceding technique works, but you shouldn't use it to convert your sort jobs to OPNQRYF. You would be much better off spending your time and energy creating external definitions for your files.

You might use the technique with files uploaded from a microcomputer, for example, or with source files or with spool files copied to disk files. However, don't use this technique with database files. Save it for some situation in which it is impossible or impractical to build an external definition.

SUMMARY

OPNQRYF and FMTDTA are often compared because they perform some of the same functions. The two are quite different; one cannot completely replace the other. FMTDTA is a sort/merge package and OPNQRYF is a query tool.

OPNQRYF's strength lies in its flexibility. OPNQRYF queries usually need no modification when the database description changes. Another strength is its power. OPNQRYF provides a host of built-in functions and it can join files.

16

❖ Performance Considerations

Performance is discussed in the preceding chapters. Those ideas won't be repeated here. Instead, this chapter describes how you can try to speed up an OPNQRYF job and will attempt to put performance in perspective. Unfortunately, "acceptable" performance is a relative term. What is acceptable to one person might not be acceptable to another. What is acceptable on a large-model AS/400 may not be acceptable on a smaller model. What is acceptable at 2:30 A.M. may not be acceptable at 10:30 A.M.

Optimizing OPNQRYF has no hard-and-fast rules. You'll find that getting a slow job to run the way you want it to is often a matter of trial and error. You have to try different variations of the job and then use whichever works the best.

Appendix D of the *Database Guide* (SC41-5701) has a very thorough discussion of query optimization that applies not only to OPNQRYF but to other AS/400 software used to query the database. Although most of the information in this chapter is taken from the *Database Guide*, this chapter won't be a rewrite of what IBM has already explained in great detail. You should read and study that appendix.

DATA RETRIEVAL METHODS

When the system executes the OPNQRYF command, it must decide how best to retrieve the data. The following sections provide brief explanations of these retrieval methods.

DYNAMIC PROCESSING

The system reads all records in the file member (including deleted ones) in arrival sequence. This method works well when more than approximately 20 percent of the records in the member are retrieved.

KEY SELECTION

The system uses an existing access path whose index matches the KEYFLD parameter. The system reads all records in the access path. Record selection is done dynamically. This method is not efficient if a large percentage of records (about 20 percent or more) is selected. OPTIMIZE(*FIRSTIO) often forces the processor to use this method. You can improve the query by specifying ALWCPYDTA(*OPTIMIZE).

KEY POSITIONING

The system uses an existing access path whose key matches the QRYSLT parameter. The system doesn't read all the records in the access path. Only those records that satisfy the QRYSLT parameter are read by the system. This is similar to the RPG technique of setting a lower limit against an indexed file (followed by READ or READE operations). Key positioning uses the primary key field only. This method is not efficient when a large percentage (again, more than approximately 20 percent) of the records is retrieved.

INDEX-FROM-INDEX

The system uses an existing access path over the QRYSLT field to build an access path in the order of the KEYFLD fields. This is one of the best access methods when less than approximately 20 percent of the records in the member are selected. This method is often chosen when the OPNQRYF command specifies OPTIMIZE(*MINWAIT) or when the KEYFLD and QRYSLT parameters conflict.

INDEX-FROM-DATA

The system must use indexes in certain cases. Most often those cases include joining files or when ordering and ALWCPYDTA(*NO) is specified. If no existing index is suitable, the system will create a temporary index from the data in the physical file. The system must read all records, including deleted ones, in the file to build the index.

SORT ROUTINE

The system can use a sort routine, rather than build an index, to order the data. To allow the system to use a sort routine, specify ALWCPYDTA(*OPTIMIZE).

THE JOB LOG

When you are trying to improve the performance of an OPNQRYF job, the job log is your best friend. Execute the commands shown in Figure 16.1 before running OPNQRYF.

```
STRDBG
CHGJOB     LOG(4 00 *SECLVL)
```

Figure 16.1: Commands to debug to a job log.

The preceding commands will fill up the job log with all sorts of messages that tell you what the system is going through to run your request. The system will tell you if it builds an access path and, if so, why it did and what fields were used as keys. The second level text will also suggest how you might speed up the process. Refer to appendix E in this book for brief explanations and comments about these messages.

IMPROVING PERFORMANCE

The process of improving the performance of OPNQRYF is not cut-and-dried. In general, good performance depends on providing access paths that OPNQRYF can use—allowing a broader use of the sort routine through ALWCPYDTA(*OPTIMIZE)—and avoiding the undesirable copying of data.

The first thing you should do is use the messages in the job log to determine which data-retrieval methods the system is using. For example, you might be joining three files and sorting on fields from each one. The system could be building an index from data fields, in order to carry out the join, and then making a copy of the data in order to sort.

Next, decide whether or not to permanently create logical files so that the system won't have to build temporary access paths. Then, if the system is copying data, decide whether or not the copy is desirable. If you are selecting 80 percent of the records in the file, and the system is using a sort routine, the copy is probably good. If you are sorting on fields from more than one join file, and sorting fields from one file only would be just as good, the copy is undesirable.

ADDITIONAL CONSIDERATIONS

Most OPNQRYF jobs will deliver acceptable results. A job will only occasionally hog the system's resources and run too slowly. You don't have to spend hours trying to optimize each OPNQRYF you write. You just need to identify the OPNQRYF commands that are taking too long to run.

Performance is not as crucial as it once was. Each new series of AS/400s is far more powerful than the previous line. Therefore, you can afford more inefficiency with each upgrade.

Running an inefficient program that gets needed results is better than running an efficient program that delivers useless information. Running an inefficient program that gets needed results is also better than running no program and getting no results. If the president of your organization asks for a report that requires you to join three files and use fields from all of them in the KEYFLD and QRYSLT parameters, are you going to tell the president that you aren't going to run that report because the report doesn't perform well?

Remember what OPNQRYF is all about. It is a tool to help provide timely information. The days are gone when a new program had to be written every time someone requested information. Most programmers don't have the time to code, debug, test, and run a program just to get another variation of the manufacturing order schedule. OPNQRYF is one of the tools you can use to satisfy the information needs of your employer. Keep that your top priority and let performance take second place.

A

❖ Common Runtime Errors

Debugging OPNQRYF commands is not difficult once you learn how to look for errors. It would be nice if the runtime error messages pointed out the exact cause of a problem. What usually happens when an OPNQRYF command abnormally ends is that you get error message CPF9899, which is probably one of the most useless error messages in OS/400.

An error in an OPNQRYF command can be caused three ways. The first way is to violate the syntax of the command. For example, you code KEYFDL instead of KEYFLD or you put a list of values into a parameter that only accepts a single value. As a result, you will probably get error message CPF0006 (which says there is an error in the CL command). Look at the job log for the cause of the error.

If you use the prompter in SEU, you won't have this problem. You probably will come up against this type of error only when you build OPNQRYF commands dynamically and execute them with QCMDEXC. Therefore, this type of error isn't detailed here.

A second type of OPNQRYF error occurs when there are invalid values in parameters. This error could happen if you have a field called CUSNM (customer name), but you misspell it as in KEYFLD(CUSNAM).

The third type of error is the logic error. The program runs to a normal end of job, but doesn't yield the correct results. Keep in mind that this type of error can be caused by the

OPNQRYF command, the CL program that runs it, or the high-level language program that reads the OPNQRYF file. The remainder of this appendix describes common errors of the last two varieties. Use the following information to help identify problems in your OPNQRYF jobs.

ERRORS CAUSED BY INVALID PARAMETER VALUES (CPF9899)

When the system halts on an OPNQRYF command, it will probably give you the message CPF9899. The CPF9899 message tells you nothing except that there is some error with your OPNQRYF command. In this case, your two best friends are the job log and program dump.

If possible, while the job is active, look at the job log on a terminal so that you can see second-level messages. Don't look only at first-level messages because they seldom give you enough information to find your problem.

The following sections describe some of the most common runtime errors encountered when using OPNQRYF and some probable causes of each. (A group of capital letters, such as XXXXX, indicates a message parameter.) See the appropriate chapter of this book or the AS/400 reference manuals for more information.

MISSING OPERAND IN THE EXPRESSION IN THE QRYSLT PARAMETER

The QRYSLT parameter contains a CL variable name such as QRYSLT('CUSZIP *EQ &ZIPCODE'). You must use the value, not the name, of the CL variable in the expression.

Presume &ZIPCODE is a character variable. If CUSZIP is a numeric field, the proper expression is QRYSLT('CUSZIP 'EQ' 'BCAT &ZIPCODE). If, instead, CUSZIP is a character field, you must also include quotation marks (or double apostrophes) as in QRYSLT('CUSZIP 'EQ' '''CAT &ZIPCODE 'CAT''').

MISSING OPERATOR IN THE EXPRESSION IN THE QRYSLT PARAMETER

You have omitted the asterisk on an operator. For example, you coded AND instead of *AND or EQ instead of *EQ.

KEY FIELD XXXXX/YYYYY NOT VALID FOR RECORD FORMAT

One of your key fields is not in the record type specified in the FORMAT parameter. (The default value of the FORMAT parameter is the value of the FILE parameter.) Even if you don't intend to use them in the high-level language program, you must include all key fields in the OPNQRYF file's record format.

FIELD XXXXXX ON THE FORMAT PARAMETER NOT FOUND

Your record format (the value of the FORMAT) parameter contains a field that isn't in any queried file (those listed in the FILE parameter) or defined in the MAPFLD parameter. The field name might be misspelled in the definition of the FORMAT file or in the MAPFLD parameter. You might have forgotten to define the field name in the MAPFLD parameter or you might have forgotten to include a file in the FILE parameter.

FIELD XXXXX/YYYYYY NOT ALLOWED IN THE RECORD FORMAT

You have included a field in the FORMAT parameter's record type that is neither a grouping field (listed in the GRPFLD) parameter nor a grouping function (listed in the MAPFLD) parameter.

FIELD XXXXXX FOUND IN MORE THAN ONE RECORD FORMAT

A field in the FORMAT parameter's record type is found in two or more input files (listed in the FILE parameter), but you didn't use the MAPFLD parameter to tell which value to use.

EXAMPLE

Assume that you are joining two files: CUSORD (customer orders) and CUSMAS (customer master). Both have a field called CUSNUM (customer number) and the FORMAT file, ORDWORK, also has a CUSNUM field. The code is shown in Figure A.1.

```
OPNQRYF     FILE((CUSORD) (CUSMAS)) FORMAT(ORDWORK) +
              KEYFLD((CUSNAM)) QRYSLT('ORDTYP=1') +
              JFLD((1/CUSNUM 2/CUSNUM))
```

Figure A.1: OPNQRYF to join two files with the missing MAPFLD command.

OPNQRYF doesn't know which CUSNUM field to pass into the high-level language program unless you add a mapped field like one shown in Figure A.2.

CHARACTER 'x' FOLLOWING STRING 'xx' NOT VALID

a) The QRYSLT string has apostrophe problems. See Figure A.3.

```
    MAPFLD((CUSNUM '1/CUSNUM'))
 or MAPFLD((CUSNUM '2/CUSNUM'))
 or MAPFLD((CUSNUM 'CUSORD/CUSNUM'))
 or MAPFLD((CUSNUM 'CUSMAS/CUSNUM'))
```

Figure A.2: MAPFLD options.

```
CHGVAR     VAR(&QRYSLT) +
             VALUE('CUSNAM *CT ''' *CAT &SEARCH *TCAT '''')
```

Figure A.3: Coding method for QRYSLT with potential apostrophe errors.

EXAMPLE

The example shown in Figure A.3 works as long as &SEARCH doesn't contain any apostrophes, but crashes when you search for a string such as CAL'S CAFÉ. To make the string able to accept apostrophes, replace the apostrophes surrounding the CL variables with quotation marks as shown in Figure A.4.

```
CHGVAR     VAR(&QRYSLT) +
             VALUE('CUSNAM *CT "' *CAT &SEARCH *TCAT '"')
```

Figure A.4: Coding method for QRYSLT to eliminate apostrophe errors.

Now the example will cancel if &SEARCH contains a quotation mark. You will have to decide which character (the apostrophe or quotation mark) you are most likely to include in a field, and use the other one as a delimiter.

If you need to use both characters in the QRYSLT expression, you'll have to double the one used as a delimiter before it gets concatenated into the expression. If you are using the apostrophe as a string delimiter and you want to search for a string that contains an apostrophe, such as CAL'S, you must concatenate CAL"S into the QRYSLT expression.

b) You have left the percent mark off an operator. For example, you coded SUM instead of %SUM.

OTHER RUNTIME ERRORS

The following sections describe some additional runtime errors encountered when using OPNQRYF.

CPF4174 OPNID(XXXXX) FOR FILE YYYYY ALREADY EXISTS

A shared open data path was already in existence when the OPNQRYF was executed.

a) A previous OPNQRYF command executed successfully, but the high-level language program canceled, which left the open data path open. Run the CLOF or RCLRSC (reclaim resources) command to close the file.

b) The file was previously opened with the OPNDBF (open database file) command. You must close the file before the OPNQRYF command can open it.

It is a good idea to code a CLOF command, followed by a MONMSG command for CPF4520 (No file open with identifier &4) at the beginning of programs (as shown in Figure A.5), especially interactive programs, to prevent this error from halting a program.

```
CLOF       OPNID(MANUFORD)
MONMSG     MSGID(CPF4520)

OVRDBF     FILE(MANUFORD) SHARE(*YES)
OPNQRYF    FILE((MANUFORD)) etc.
```

Figure A.5: Proper coding of CLOF and MONMSG to prevent existing open data path error.

LOGIC ERRORS

Sometimes an OPNQRYF job will run to completion, but give erroneous results. The following is a list of some of the most common logic errors.

1: Many Records

All records are selected, or more records than desired are selected, but the QRYSLT parameter has a record-selection expression that should select only a subset of records. For example, you specified QRYSLT('DPTNO = 4'), and yet your report contains records for the other departments as well. Possible causes are as follows:

a) Your high-level language program might not be sharing the open data path built by
   OPNQRYF. Code an OVRDBF command, with the SHARE(*YES) attribute, before the
   OPNQRYF command. If you already have an OVRDBF command, check the spelling of
   the file name.

b) If you have a compound condition, check how you used the logical operators. In English you can say "give me the records where the state code is not Mississippi or Alabama," but if you code it as shown in Figure A.6, you will get every record in the
   database.

```
QRYSLT('STATE *NE "MS" *OR STATE *NE "AL"')
```

Figure A.6: Incorrect specification for the selection of records from Mississippi or Alabama.

Instead, use the *AND operator or the %VALUES function as shown in Figure A.7.

```
    QRYSLT('STATE *NE "MS" *AND STATE *NE "AL"')
or QRYSLT('*NOT (STATE *EQ %VALUES("MS" "AL"))')
```

Figure A.7: Correct specifications for selection of records from Mississippi or Alabama.

c) There might be an error with a concatenation operator. For example, suppose you
   want to retrieve all records where the item number is greater than some value specified in the parameter &ITEM. If you code it as shown in Figure A.8, you will get more
   than you wanted.

```
CHGVAR     VAR(&SELECT) +
             VALUE ('ITMNBR *GT "' *BCAT &ITEM *BCAT '"')
OPNQRYF    FILE(...) QRYSLT(&SELECT)
```

Figure A.8: Incorrect specification for records greater than &ITEM.

To see why you'll get more data than you anticipated, let's presume &ITEM has the value
"B290". Field &SELECT becomes ITNBR *GT ' B290', which will retrieve records with items
such as "A111". The proper code is shown in Figure A.9.

```
CHGVAR     VAR(&SELECT) +
             VALUE ('ITMNBR *GT "' *CAT &ITEM *CAT '"')
```

Figure A.9: Correct specification for records greater than &ITEM.

This code yields ITNBR *GT 'B290', which will function correctly.

Looking at variable &SELECT on a CL dump or running the program under debug will help you find this type of error.

2: No Records Selected

If you have asked for records from department 4, but none were found—and yet you know there are department 4 records in the file—you have a logic error in the QRYSLT parameter.

a) If you are using a CL variable in the QRYSLT parameter, make sure the expression in it was not truncated. For example, look at the code shown in Figure A.10.

```
DCL        VAR(&SELECT) TYPE(*CHAR) LEN(10)
CHGVAR     VAR(&SELECT) VALUE('CUSNO=12345')
OPNQRYF    FILE(...) QRYSLT(&SELECT)
```

Figure A.10: Incorrect specification due to too short of a length for the variable.

You may think OPNQRYF is looking for customer 12345, but it's really looking for customer 1234.

b) If you are using a compound condition, check the logical operators *AND, *OR, and *NOT. You might have conflicting conditions.

In English, you say "list all records for Mississippi and Alabama." If you translate that like the example shown in Figure A.11, you'll never get any results.

Instead, use the *OR operator or the %VALUES function as shown in Figure A.12.

c) Check your concatenation operations. Suppose you are looking for all records with the item number equal to the value in &ITEM, and your code looks like the example shown in Figure A.13.

```
QRYSLT('STATE="MS" *AND STATE="AL"')
```

Figure A.11: Incorrect specification to select records for Mississippi and Alabama.

```
QRYSLT('STATE="MS" *OR STATE="AL"')
or QRYSLT('STATE=%VALUES("MS" "AL")')
```

Figure A.12: The correct specification to select records for Mississippi and Alabama.

```
CHGVAR      VAR(&SELECT) +
              VALUE ('ITMNBR *GT "' *BCAT &ITEM *BCAT '"')
OPNQRYF     FILE(...) QRYSLT(&SELECT)
```

Figure A.13: Incorrect specification to select on items greater than &ITEM value.

You won't get what you want. To see why, let's presume &ITEM has the value "B290". Field &SELECT becomes ITNBR *EQ " B290", which will ignore the records you want. The proper code is shown in Figure A.14.

```
CHGVAR      VAR(&SELECT) +
              VALUE ('ITMNBR *EQ "' *CAT &ITEM *CAT '"')
```

Figure A.14: Correct specification to select on items greater than &ITEM value.

This code yields ITNBR *EQ "B290", which will function correctly.

3. CPI3104 Query Result May Differ from Intended Value of &1

The usual cause of this error (CP13104) is comparing a field to values that can't fit into it. For example, as shown in Figure A.15, suppose field CLASS is a two-byte character field and &FROM and &TO are three-byte character CL variables.

You might not get the results you're after because of the difference in lengths between the field class and the variables.

```
QRYSLT('CLASS = %RANGE("' *CAT &FROM *CAT '" "' *CAT &TO *CAT '")')
```

Figure A.15: Incorrect specification to select CLASS values between &FROM and &TO.

4. The Report Has the Wrong Sequence

a) Verify the KEYFLD parameter. If the KEYFLD has the value *FILE, verify the access path of the queried file.

b) If the access path is okay, then make sure you are sharing the open data path.

B

❖ Specifying Variable-Control Breaks

In the program shown in Figure B.1, control breaks can be specified at runtime. The command can handle up to three control breaks or no control breaks at all. It can also print either detail or summary reports. This job consists of an RPG program, a CL program to run it, and a command. There are four parameters: three break fields, in major to minor order, and a switch to tell whether or not to print detail lines. The order of the control break fields is significant, but which is used is not important. In other words, if there is to be only one level of breaks, any of the three break-field parameters may be used. Here are some examples of how the sls02 command might be used. Also, see Figures B.2 through B.6.

1. SLS02: Print a detail report with no subtotals. Report totals will be printed, however.
2. SLS02 BREAK1(REP): Print a detail report with subtotals by sales representative number.
3. SLS02 BREAK2(REP) or SLS02 BREAK3(REP): Equivalent to example 2 in this list.
4. SLS02 BREAK2(CUST) BREAK1(ITEM): Prints a detail report that shows item totals within customer totals.
5. SLS02 BREAK2(ITEM) BREAK1(CUST): Print a detail report that shows customer totals within item totals.
6. SLS02 BREAK3(REP) BREAK2(CUST) BREAK1(INVOICE): Print a detail report that subtotals invoice within customer within sales representative.
7. SLS02 BREAK3(REP) BREAK2(CUST) BREAK1(INVOICE) PRTDTL(*NO): Same as example 6 in this list, but produces a summary report instead.
8. SLS02 PRTDTL(*NO): Prints report totals only.

```
/*======================================================================*/
/* Sales report with 0 to 3 variable control fields                     */
/*======================================================================*/
/* To compile:                                                          */
/*                                                                      */
/*            CRTCMD    CMD(XXX/SLS02) PGM(XXX/SLS02C) +                 */
/*                      SRCFILE(XXX/QCMDSRC)                            */
/*                                                                      */
/*======================================================================*/

        CMD         PROMPT('Sales history report')
        PARM        KWD(BREAK3) +
                    TYPE(*CHAR) LEN(7) RSTD(*YES) +
                    VALUES(' ' REP CUST ITEM INVOICE) +
                    PROMPT('Break field 3 (major)')
        PARM        KWD(BREAK2) +
                    TYPE(*CHAR) LEN(7) RSTD(*YES) +
                    VALUES(' ' REP CUST ITEM INVOICE) +
                    PROMPT('Break field 2 (middle)')
        PARM        KWD(BREAK1) +
                    TYPE(*CHAR) LEN(7) RSTD(*YES) +
                    VALUES(' ' REP CUST ITEM INVOICE) +
                    PROMPT('Break field 1 (minor)')
        PARM        KWD(PRTDTL) +
                    TYPE(*LGL) RSTD(*YES) DFT(*YES) +
                    VALUES('0' '1') +
                    SPCVAL((*YES '1') (*NO '0')) +
                    CHOICE('*YES, *NO') +
                    PROMPT('Print detail lines?')
```

Figure B.1: The SLS02 command handles zero to three control breaks.

```
/*======================================================================*/
/* Sales report with 0 to 3 variable control fields                     */
/*                                                                      */
/* Logic                                                                */
/*   Make sure no two break fields are the same                         */
/*     e.g., do not permit REP, CUST, REP                               */
/*   Concatenate 3 break fields into 1 for loop processing              */
/*     REP, blank, CUST becomes REPbbbbbbbbbbbCUSTbbb,                   */
/*     where b = blank                                                  */
/*   Loop 3 times, processing 1 control field each time                 */
/*        and building CL variable &BRK                                 */
/*     If no control break is called for, set substring                 */
```

Figure B.2: CL program SLS02C loads the control fields.

```
/*            of &BRK  to " "                                        */
/*        else set substring of &BRK to the expression              */
/*            needed for that field in the MAPFLD parm              */
/*        End loop                                                   */
/*      Split break variable &BRK into 3 variables for              */
/*        MAPFLD parm                                                */
/*      Run the program                                             */
/*===============================================================*/
/* To compile:                                                      */
/*                                                                  */
/*            CRTCLPGM  PGM(XXX/SLS02C)  SRCFILE(XXX/QCLSRC)         */
/*                                                                  */
/*===============================================================*/
        PGM           PARM(&BRK_FLD3 &BRK_FLD2 &BRK_FLD1 &PRT_DTL)
        DCL           VAR(&BRK_FLD3) TYPE(*CHAR) LEN(7)
        DCL           VAR(&BRK_FLD2) TYPE(*CHAR) LEN(7)
        DCL           VAR(&BRK_FLD1) TYPE(*CHAR) LEN(7)
        DCL           VAR(&PRT_DTL)  TYPE(*LGL)
        DCL           VAR(&BRK_FLD)  TYPE(*CHAR) LEN(21)
        DCL           VAR(&CUR_FLD)  TYPE(*CHAR) LEN( 7)
        DCL           VAR(&COUNTER)  TYPE(*DEC)  LEN( 1 0)
        DCL           VAR(&POINT_1)  TYPE(*DEC)  LEN( 2 0)
        DCL           VAR(&POINT_2)  TYPE(*DEC)  LEN( 2 0)
        DCL           VAR(&POINT_3)  TYPE(*DEC)  LEN( 2 0)
        DCL           VAR(&BRK    )  TYPE(*CHAR) LEN(75)
        DCL           VAR(&BRK_1  )  TYPE(*CHAR) LEN(25)
        DCL           VAR(&BRK_2  )  TYPE(*CHAR) LEN(25)
        DCL           VAR(&BRK_3  )  TYPE(*CHAR) LEN(25)
        DCL           VAR(&DESC   )  TYPE(*CHAR) LEN(27)
        DCL           VAR(&DESC_1 )  TYPE(*CHAR) LEN( 9)
        DCL           VAR(&DESC_2 )  TYPE(*CHAR) LEN( 9)
        DCL           VAR(&DESC_3 )  TYPE(*CHAR) LEN( 9)
/* Make sure no two break fields are the same */
        IF (&BRK_FLD3 *EQ &BRK_FLD2 *OR &BRK_FLD3 *EQ &BRK_FLD1) +
            THEN(CHGVAR  VAR(&BRK_FLD3) VALUE(' '))
        IF (&BRK_FLD2 *EQ &BRK_FLD1) +
            THEN(CHGVAR  VAR(&BRK_FLD2) VALUE(' '))
/* Concatenate 3 break fields into 1 for loop processing */
        CHGVAR        VAR(&BRK_FLD) +
                      VALUE(&BRK_FLD1 *CAT &BRK_FLD2 *CAT &BRK_FLD3)
/* Initialize loop control variables */
        CHGVAR        VAR(&COUNTER) VALUE(1)
        CHGVAR        VAR(&POINT_1) VALUE(1)
        CHGVAR        VAR(&POINT_2) VALUE(1)
        CHGVAR        VAR(&POINT_3) VALUE(1)
/* Build variable control break fields */
```

Figure B.2: CL program SLS02C loads the control fields. (Continued)

```
LOOP_10:
    CHGVAR      VAR(&CUR_FLD) VALUE(%SST(&BRK_FLD &POINT_1 7))
    CHGVAR      VAR(%SST(&BRK &POINT_2 25)) VALUE('" "')

    IF (&CUR_FLD *EQ ' ') +
        THEN(GOTO LOOP_90)
    IF (&CUR_FLD *EQ REP) THEN(DO)
        CHGVAR  VAR(%SST(&BRK   &POINT_2 25)) +
                VALUE('%DIGITS(REPNO)')
        CHGVAR  VAR(%SST(&DESC &POINT_3  9)) VALUE('SALES REP')
        GOTO    LOOP_90
    ENDDO

    IF (&CUR_FLD *EQ CUST) THEN(DO)
        CHGVAR  VAR(%SST(&BRK   &POINT_2 25)) +
                VALUE('%DIGITS(CUSNO)')
        CHGVAR  VAR(%SST(&DESC &POINT_3  9)) VALUE(CUSTOMER)
        GOTO    LOOP_90
    ENDDO

    IF (&CUR_FLD *EQ ITEM) THEN(DO)
        CHGVAR  VAR(%SST(&BRK   &POINT_2 25)) VALUE(ITMNO)
        CHGVAR  VAR(%SST(&DESC &POINT_3  9)) VALUE(ITEM)
        GOTO    LOOP_90
    ENDDO

    IF (&CUR_FLD *EQ INVOICE) THEN(DO)
        CHGVAR  VAR(%SST(&BRK   &POINT_2 25)) +
            VALUE('%DIGITS(INVNO)')
        CHGVAR  VAR(%SST(&DESC &POINT_3  9)) VALUE(INVOICE)
        GOTO    LOOP_90
    ENDDO
LOOP_90:
    IF (&COUNTER *LT 3) THEN(DO)
        CHGVAR  VAR(&COUNTER) VALUE(&COUNTER +  1)
        CHGVAR  VAR(&POINT_1) VALUE(&POINT_1 +  7)
        CHGVAR  VAR(&POINT_2) VALUE(&POINT_2 + 25)
        CHGVAR  VAR(&POINT_3) VALUE(&POINT_3 +  9)
        GOTO    LOOP_10
    ENDDO
/* Break down &BRK & &DESC fields              */
    CHGVAR      VAR(&BRK_1)  VALUE(%SST(&BRK  1 25))
    CHGVAR      VAR(&BRK_2)  VALUE(%SST(&BRK 26 25))
    CHGVAR      VAR(&BRK_3)  VALUE(%SST(&BRK 51 25))
    CHGVAR      VAR(&DESC_1) VALUE(%SST(&DESC  1 9))
    CHGVAR      VAR(&DESC_2) VALUE(%SST(&DESC 10 9))
    CHGVAR      VAR(&DESC_3) VALUE(%SST(&DESC 19 9))

/* Begin processing */
    OVRDBF      FILE(HISTWK2) TOFILE(HISTJL1) SHARE(*YES)
    OPNQRYF     FILE((HISTJL1)) +
```

Figure B.2: CL program SLS02C loads the control fields. (Continued)

```
                        FORMAT(HISTWK2) +
                        KEYFLD((BREAK3) (BREAK2) (BREAK1) +
                               (INVNO) (INVLN)) +
                        MAPFLD(+
                               (BREAK3      &BRK_3) +
                               (BREAK2      &BRK_2) +
                               (BREAK1      &BRK_1) +
                               (EXTPR       'QTYSLD * UNTPR') +
                               )
            CALL        PGM(SLS02R) +
                        PARM(&DESC_3 &DESC_2 &DESC_1 &PRT_DTL)
            CLOF        OPNID(HISTJL1)
            DLTOVR      FILE(HISTWK2)
ENDPGM
```

Figure B.2: CL program SLS02C loads the control fields. (Continued)

```
*========================================================================
* Format file for OPNQRYF processing
*========================================================================
* To compile:
*
*      CRTPF   FILE(XXX/HISTWK2) SRCFILE(XXX/QDDSSRC) +
*                 MBR(*NONE)
*
*========================================================================
A                                      REF(HISTJL1)
A          R HISTWK2R
A            REPNO      R
A            REPNAM     R
A            CUSNO      R
A            CUSNAM     R
A            INVNO      R
A            INVDAT     R
A            INVLN      R
A            ITMNO      R
A            ITMDSC     R
A            UNTPR      R
A            QTYSLD     R
A            EXTPR         8  2
A            BREAK1       10
A            BREAK2       10
A            BREAK3       10
A          K INVNO
```

Figure B.3: DDS for work file HISTWK2.

```
*===================================================================
* Sales report with 0 to 3 control breaks
*
* Parameters
*    BDESC3 - Description of major break field
*    BDESC2 - Description of middle break field
*    BDESC1 - Description of minor break field
*    PRTDTL - Detail line print flag
*             '0' - Print a summary report
*             '1' - Print a detail report
*
* If a description parameter is blank, no control total
*    is printed for that level
*
* Indicators
*    41 - L1 break is to be printed
*    42 - L2 break is to be printed
*    43 - L3 break is to be printed
*    44 - Detail lines are to be printed
*
*===================================================================
* To compile:
*
*    CRTRPGPGM  PGM(XXX/SLS02R) SRCFILE(XXX/QRPGSRC)
*
*===================================================================
FHISTWK2 IP  E           K          DISK
FQSYSPRT O   F     132      OF       PRINTER
IHISTWK2R    01
I                                             BREAK3L3
I                                             BREAK2L2
I                                             BREAK1L1
I            SDS
I                                      *PROGRAM PGMNAM
I                                      276 2810SYSDAT
I                                      282 2870SYSTIM
C            *ENTRY   PLIST
C                     PARM             BDESC3  9
C                     PARM             BDESC2  9
C                     PARM             BDESC1  9
C                     PARM             PRTDTL  1
C*
C   L3                MOVE *ZERO       AMT3
C   L2                MOVE *ZERO       AMT2
C   L1                MOVE *ZERO       AMT1
C*
C                     ADD  EXTPR       AMT1
```

Figure B.4: RPG III program SLS02R.

```
C          *IN44     IFEQ *ON
C                    MOVELINVDAT      ##Y4    4
C                    MOVE ##Y4        ##Y2    2
C                    MOVE INVDAT      ##MD    4
C                    MOVEL##MD        INVDT2  60
C                    MOVE ##Y2        INVDT2
C                    ENDIF
C*
CL1                  ADD  AMT1        AMT2
CL2                  ADD  AMT2        AMT3
CL3                  ADD  AMT3        AMTR
C*
C***********
C          *INZSR    BEGSR
C*
C          *LIKE     DEFN EXTPR       AMT1  + 1
C          *LIKE     DEFN EXTPR       AMT2  + 1
C          *LIKE     DEFN EXTPR       AMT3  + 1
C          *LIKE     DEFN EXTPR       AMTR  + 1
C*                                            HILOEQ
C          BDESC1    COMP *BLANKS             4141
C          BDESC2    COMP *BLANKS             4242
C          BDESC3    COMP *BLANKS             4343
C          PRTDTL    COMP 'O'                 4444
C*
C                    ENDSR
OQSYSPRT H  204    1P
O        OR         OF
O                             PGMNAM
O                                      72 'SALES HISTORY'
O                             SYSDATY 108
O                             SYSTIM  118 '  :  :  '
O                                     128 'PAGE'
O                             PAGE
O        H   2    1P
O        OR         OF
O                                       3 'REP'
O                                      28 'CUSTOMER'
O                                      54 'INVOICE'
O                                      69 'ITEM'
O                                     102 'QTY'
O                                     110 'PRICE'
O                                     122 'EXT'
O        D   1    L1 44
O        D   1    01 44
O                             REPNO
O                             REPNAM  + 1
O                             CUSNO   + 1
```

Figure B.4: RPG III program SLS02R. (Continued)

```
O                               CUSNAM  +  1
O                               INVNO 4 +  1
O                               INVDT2Y +  1
O                               INVLN 4 +  1
O                               ITMNO   +  1
O                               ITMDSC  +  1
O                               QTYSLDJ +  1
O                               UNTPR J +  1
O                               EXTPR J +  1
O        T    1    L1
O        T    1    L1 41
O                                       63 'TOTAL FOR'
O                               BDESC1  +  1
O                               BREAK1  +  1
O                               AMT1  J 123
O                                     +  1 '*'
O        T    1    L2 42
O                                       63 'TOTAL FOR'
O                               BDESC2  +  1
O                               BREAK2  +  1
O                               AMT2  J 123
O                                     +  1 '**'
O        T    1    L3 43
O                                       63 'TOTAL FOR'
O                               BDESC3  +  1
O                               BREAK3  +  1
O                               AMT3  J 123
O                                     +  1 '***'
O        T    1    LR
O                                       66 'FINAL TOTALS'
O                               AMTR  J 123
O                                     +  1 '****'
```

Figure B.4: RPG III program SLS02R. (Continued)

```
*========================================================================
* Sales report with 0 to 3 control breaks
*
* Parameters
*   BrkDesc3 - Description of major break field
*   BrkDesc2 - Description of middle break field
*   BrkDesc1 - Description of minor break field
*   PrintDetails - Detail line print flag
*             '0' - Print a summary report
```

Figure B.5: RPG IV program SLS02R.

```
 *               '1' - Print a detail report
 *
 * If a description parameter is blank, no control total
 *    is printed for that level
 *
 *===============================================================
 * To compile:
 *
 *       CRTBNDRPG  PGM(XXX/SLS02R)  SRCFILE(XXX/QRPGLESRC)
 *
 *===============================================================
FHistWk2    if    e          k disk       rename(HistWk2R: HistoryRec)
FSls02P1    o     e                printer  oflind(*in88)

D BrkDesc3        s             9
D BrkDesc2        s             9
D BrkDesc1        s             9
D PrintDetails    s             1n

D Amt             s            +2   like(ExtPr) dim(5)
D BreakDesc       s            35   dim(%elem(Amt))
D BreakVal        s                 like(Break3) dim(%elem(Amt))
D CurLvl          s            10I 0
D V               s            10I 0
D WrkDate         s             D

D PSDS          sds
D   PgmNam              1        10
D   SysDat            276       281s 0
D   SysTim            282       287s 0

C    *entry          plist
C                    parm                    BrkDesc3
C                    parm                    BrkDesc2
C                    parm                    BrkDesc1
C                    parm                    PrintDetails
C
C                    exsr      Init
C
C                    read      HistoryRec
C                    exsr      SaveValues
C                    dow       not %eof
C                    exsr      ProcessBreak
C                    if        PrintDetails
C                    exsr      CheckOverFlow
C    *ISO            move      InvDat    WrkDate
C    *MDY            move      WrkDate   InvDt2
C                    write     DetailLn
```

Figure B.5: RPG IV program SLS02R. (Continued)

253

```
C                         endif
C                         eval         Amt (1) = Amt (1) + ExtPr
C                         read         HistoryRec
C                         enddo
C
C                         eval         CurLvl = 4
C                         exsr         EndGroup
C                         eval         *inLR = *on
C*****
C      ProcessBreakBegSR
C
C                         eval         CurLvl = *zero
C
C                         select
C                         when         Break3 <> BreakVal (3)
C                         eval         CurLvl = 3
C                         when         Break2 <> BreakVal (2)
C                         eval         CurLvl = 2
C                         when         Break1 <> BreakVal (1)
C                         eval         CurLvl = 1
C                         endsl
C
C                         if           CurLvl <> *zero
C                         exsr         EndGroup
C                         endif
C
C                         exsr         SaveValues
C
C                         EndSr
C*****
C      SaveValues    BegSR
C
C                         eval         BreakVal (3) = Break3
C                         eval         BreakVal (2) = Break2
C                         eval         BreakVal (1) = Break1
C
C                         EndSR
C*****
C      EndGroup      BegSR
C
C      1                  do           CurLvl         V
C                         if           BreakDesc (V) <> *blanks
C                         eval         TDESC = %trim(BreakDesc (V)) +
C                                      ' ' + BreakVal (V)
C                         eval         Amt1 = Amt (V)
C                         exsr         CheckOverFlow
C                         write        BrkFoot
C                         endif
```

Figure B.5: RPG IV program SLS02R. (Continued)

```
C                       eval      Amt (V + 1) = Amt (V + 1) + Amt (V)
C                       eval      Amt (V) = *zero
C                       enddo
C
C                       EndSR
C*****
C        Init           BegSR
C
C                       eval      BreakDesc (4) = 'GRAND TOTAL'
C                       if        BrkDesc3 <> *blanks
C                       eval      BreakDesc (3) = 'TOTAL FOR ' +
BrkDesc3
C                       endif
C                       if        BrkDesc2 <> *blanks
C                       eval      BreakDesc (2) = 'TOTAL FOR ' +
BrkDesc2
C                       endif
C                       if        BrkDesc1 <> *blanks
C                       eval      BreakDesc (1) = 'TOTAL FOR ' +
BrkDesc1
C                       endif
C                       eval      *in88 = *on
C
C                       EndSR
C*****
C        CheckOverFlow BegSR
C
C                       if        *in88
C                       write     PageHdr
C                       eval      *in88 = *off
C                       endif
C
C                       EndSR
```

Figure B.5: RPG IV program SLS02R. (Continued)

```
*=================================================================
* Sales report with 0 to 3 variable control fields
*=================================================================
* To compile:
*
*       CRTPRTF    FILE(XXX/SLS02P1)  SRCFILE(XXX/QDDSSRC)
*
*=================================================================
```

Figure B.6: Printer file SLS02P1, used by RPG IV program SLS02R.

```
A                                           REF(HISTWK2)
A             R PAGEHDR                      SKIPB(4) SPACEA(2)
A               PGMNAM       10            1
A                                          60'SALES HISTORY'
A               SYSDAT        6   0       101
A                                           EDTCDE(Y)
A               SYSTIM        6   0       111EDTWRD('  :   :   ')
A                                         125'PAGE'
A                                         +  OPAGNBR EDTCDE(4)
A                                            SPACEA(2)
A                                           1'REP'
A                                          21'CUSTOMER'
A                                          47'INVOICE'
A                                          66'ITEM'
A                                         100'QTY'
A                                         106'PRICE'
A                                         120'EXT'
A             R DETAILLN                     SPACEA(1)
A               REPNO        R             1
A               REPNAM       R            +1
A               CUSNO        R            +1
A               CUSNAM       R            +1
A               INVNO        R            +1EDTCDE(4)
A               INVDT2        6   0       +1EDTCDE(Y)
A               INVLN        R            +1
A               ITMNO        R            +1
A               ITMDSC       R            +1
A               QTYSLD       R            +1EDTCDE(J)
A               UNTPR        R            +1EDTCDE(J)
A               EXTPR        R            +1EDTCDE(J)
A             R BRKFOOT                     SPACEB(1) SPACEA(1)
A               TDESC        35            71
A               AMT1         R   +1       111REFFLD(EXTPR) EDTCDE(J)
```

Figure B.6: Printer file sls02p1, used by RPG IV program sls02r. (Continued)

The loop processing in the CL program is cumbersome, but it is an attempt to use the same code for each break field. This looping would be done with arrays in high-level languages. Because CL has no array structure, the array processing is simulated by stringing and substringing. Three break levels are usually plenty, but this technique could easily be adapted to handle more levels.

C

❖ Built-In Functions

The following short summaries describe the built-in functions available to OPNQRYF on the AS/400. See Tables C.1 through C.10. For more information, see the *AS/400 CL* reference, under the topic OPNQRYF.

SECTION 1: SINGLE-RECORD FUNCTIONS

The angle value is expressed in radians. Table C.1 lists trigonometric functions. The equalities listed in Table C.2 should be helpful when you work with degrees. Table C.3 lists logarithmic functions.

OTHER NUMERIC FUNCTIONS

While %MIN and %MAX have two or more arguments when they serve as single-record functions, they have only one argument as grouping functions. See Tables C.4 through C.8.

SECTION 2: FUNCTIONS ALLOWED
ONLY IN QRYSLT AND GRPSLT PARAMETERS

The QRYSLT and GRPSLT functions may only be used as the right-hand argument of a test for equality. An example is 'AMT = %RANGE(1000 2000)'. To negate these functions, use the *NOT logical operator rather than the *NE relational operator. See Table C.9.

Arguments of the %VALUES function must be constants. Arguments of the %RANGE function can be constants or fields.

Table C.1: Trigonometric Functions.	
%COS	cosine
%SIN	sine
%TAN	tangent
%COT	cotangent
%ACOS	arc cosine
%ASIN	arc sine
%ATAN	arc tangent
%COSH	hyperbolic cosine
%SINH	hyperbolic sine
%TANH	hyperbolic tangent
%ATANH	hyperbolic arc tangent

Table C.2: Values in Degrees.
pi = 3.141592 or %ACOS(−1)
pi radians = 180 degrees
1 radian = 180/pi degrees = 57.296 degrees
1 degree = pi/180 radians = 0.01745 radians

Table C.3: Logarithmic Functions.

%LOG	common (base 10) logarithm
%ANTILOG	common (base 10) antilogarithm
%LN	natural (base e) logarithm
%EXP	power of e
e = 2.7182818	

Table C.4: Other Numeric Functions.

%ABSVAL	absolute value
%MAX	maximum
%MIN	minimum
%SQRT	square root

Table C.5: String Functions.

%AND	logical and
%OR	logical or
%NOT	logical not
%XOR	exclusive or
%DIGITS	digits of numeric value
%HEX	hexadecimal value

Table C.5: String Functions. (Continued)	
%LEN	length of value
%MAX	maximum
%MIN	minimum
%SST	substring
%STRIP	remove leading/trailing characters
%SUBSTRING	same as %SST
%XLATE	translation

Table C.6: Date and Time Functions.	
%CHAR	convert date/time to character
%CURDATE	current date (system clock date, NOT the job date)
%CURTIME	current time
%CURTIMESTP	current timestamp
%CURTIMEZONE	current time zone
%DATE	date portion of date/time argument
%TIME	time portion of date/time argument
%TIMESTP	timestamp portion of date/time argument
%YEAR	year portion of date/time argument
%MONTH	month portion of date/time argument
%DAY	day portion of date/time argument
%HOUR	hour portion of date/time argument

Table C.6: Date and Time Functions. (Continued)	
%MINUTE	minute portion of date/time argument
%SECOND	second portion of date/time argument
%MICSEC	microsecond portion of date/time argument
%DAYS	integer representation of date
%DURDAY	time duration in days
%DURHOUR	time duration in hours
%DURMICSEC	time duration in microseconds
%DURMINUTE	time duration in minutes
%DURMONTH	time duration in months
%DURSEC	time duration in seconds
%DURYEAR	time duration in years
%MAX	maximum
%MIN	minimum

Table C.7: Null Value Functions.	
%NONNULL	first non-null value in list
%NULL	null value

Table C.8: Other Functions.	
%USER	user profile name
%CURSERVER	relational database server name
%NODENAME	relational database node name
%NODENUMBER	relational database node number
%HASH	partition number
%PARTITION	partition number

Table C.9: Functions for QRYSLT and GRPSLT.	
%RANGE	range
%VALUES	list of values
%WLDCRD	wild card

SECTION 3: GROUPING FUNCTIONS

Except for %COUNT, which takes none, the grouping functions take one argument. The argument can be a field name such as %MAX(AMT) or an expression such as %MAX((%ABSVAL(AMT) * 1.55)). See Table C.10.

Table C.10: Grouping Functions.	
%AVG	average
%COUNT	record count
%MAX	maximum
%MIN	minimum
%STDDEV	standard deviation
%SUM	sum
%VAR	variance

D

❖ Generating a Date-Conversion File

This program generates a dates file that contains a record for every date between January 1 of one year and December 31 of the same year or a later year. You might want to add more fields to the file to fit your needs. Other fields you might add are:

- ❖ Day of week as a number from 0 to 6 or from 1 to 7.
- ❖ Day of week spelled out (Sunday, Monday, and so on) with uppercase, lowercase, or mixed case.
- ❖ Day of week abbreviated (SUN, MON, and so on) with uppercase, lowercase, or mixed case.
- ❖ Date spelled out (January 1, 1991).
- ❖ Month-day-year, month abbreviated (15-Jan-1990).
- ❖ Quarter of year (1, 2, 3, or 4).
- ❖ Month as a number from 1 to 12.
- ❖ Month name (January, February, and so on).
- ❖ Month name abbreviated (JAN, FEB, and so on).

This file has three primary purposes:

1. To provide a way to join files with incompatible date formats.
2. To provide a way to do date arithmetic with non-date data types.
3. To provide a way to include reference information (such as day of week) in queries.

You might prefer to create some logical files over DATEFL to build access paths over other formats. If you use Julian dates, for example, it might be a good idea to create a DATEFL1 where the key is the field JULIAN.

The field SINCE contains the number of days since a base date. This gives you a way to do date arithmetic. You can add other years to the file without having to rebuild the years that are already there.

```
*  Generate a file of dates to be using for joining and date arithmetic
*
*  Parameters
*    FromYear: First year to be added to file, as a 2-digit number
*    ThruYear: Last year to be added to file, as a 2-digit number

H DFTACTGRP(*NO)

FDateFl    o  e               disk

D ToDate          pr              d
D   FromChar                      8    value

D FourYear        pr              4
D   TwoYear                       2 0  value

D FromYear        s               2 0
D ThruYear        s               2 0
D BaseYear        s               2 0  inz(70)
D BaseDate        s               d
D CurrentDate     s               d
D FromDate        s               d
D ThruDate        s               d
D WorkDate        s               8    inz('00000101')

C     *entry        plist
C                   parm                    FromYear
```

Figure D.1: RPG IV program to add to DATEFL.

```
C                       parm                    ThruYear

C                       eval      FromDate=ToDate(FourYear(FromYear) + '0101')
C                       eval      ThruDate=ToDate(FourYear(ThruYear) + '1231')
C                       eval      WorkDate = FourYear(BaseYear) + '0101'
C         *iso0         move      WorkDate      BaseDate

C                       eval      CurrentDate = FromDate
C         CurrentDate   subdur    BaseDate          SINCE: *days
C                       dow       CurrentDate <= ThruDate
C                       eval      DATE = CurrentDate
C         *iso          move      CurrentDate   YMDN8
C                       move      YMDN8         YMDC8
C                       move      YMDN8         YMDN
C                       move      YMDN          YMDC
C                       eval      MDYC = %subst(YMDC8: 5: 4) +
C                                        %subst(YMDC8: 3: 2)
C                       move      MDYC          MDYN
C                       eval      CYMDN7 = YMDN8 - 19000000
C         *longjul      move      CurrentDate   JUL7
C                       move      JUL7          JULIAN
C                       eval      SINCE = SINCE + 1
C                       write (e) DateRec
C                       adddur    1: *days       CurrentDate
C                       enddo

C                       eval      *inLR = *on
  * ================================================================
P ToDate            b

D                     pi                    d
D    FromChar                       8    value
D WorkDate           s                    d

C         *iso0         move      FromChar      WorkDate
C                       return    WorkDate
P ToDate            e
  * ================================================================
P FourYear          b

D                     pi                    4
D    TwoYear                        2   0 value
D CharYear           s                    2
C                       move      TwoYear       CharYear
C                       if        TwoYear >= BaseYear
C                       return    '19' + CharYear
C                       else
C                       return    '20' + CharYear
C                       endif
P FourYear          e
```

Figure D.1: RPG IV program to add to DATEFL. (Continued)

```
A                                      UNIQUE
A          R DATEREC
A            DATE          L
A            YMDC          6            TEXT('YYMMDD - CHARACTER')
A            YMDN          6 0          TEXT('YYMMDD - NUMERIC')
A                                       EDTWRD('  -  - ')
A            MDYC          6            TEXT('MMDDYY - CHARACTER')
A            MDYN          6 0          TEXT('MMDDYY - NUMERIC')
A                                       EDTWRD('  -  - ')
A            CYMDN7        7 0          TEXT('CYYMMDD - NUMERIC')
A                                       EDTWRD('   -   ')
A            YMDC8         8            TEXT('YYYYMMDD - CHARACTER')
A            YMDN8         8 0          TEXT('YYYYMMDD - NUMERIC')
A                                       EDTWRD('    -   - ')
A            JULIAN        5 0          TEXT('YYDDD    - NUMERIC')
A                                       EDTWRD('  -   ')
A            JUL7          7 0          TEXT('YYYYDDD    - NUMERIC')
A                                       EDTWRD('    -    ')
A            SINCE         5 0          TEXT('DAYS SINCE BASE DATE')
A          K YMDC
```

Figure D.2: DDS for DATEFL.

E

❖ Optimization Messages

The following informational messages used by the database manager are sent to the job log with some explanation of what they mean and how to improve the performance of the query. For more information, see the *SQL/400 Programmer's Guide* and the description of the messages themselves found in message file QSYS/QCPFMSG.

CPI4321 (ACCESS PATH BUILT FOR FILE &4)

The system built a temporary access path from the data field(s) in the file. This message gives a reason code that explains why the system chose to build an access path and what the key fields are. To build the access path, the system reads all records in the file, including the deleted records. Use the RGZPFM (reorganize physical file) command to remove the deleted records. If this query is frequently used, you might want to create a logical file with these key fields.

CPI4322 (ACCESS PATH BUILT FROM KEYED FILE &1)

A temporary access path was built from an existing access path. The text for this message tells you why the system chose to create an access path, what the key fields of the temporary access path are, and how long it took to create an access path.

This message is a good sign that your OPNQRYF job is already performing well. If more than 20 percent of the records are being selected, however, you might get better results with ALWCPYDTA(*OPTIMIZE).

CPI4325 (TEMPORARY RESULT FILE BUILT FOR QUERY)

The system copied the data from the queried files into a temporary physical file. This message occurs when you do group processing, when you use key fields from more than one file, when the fields used for grouping are not the same ones used for ordering, and when a sort routine is used. In the second case, verify that you really do need key fields from more than one file.

CPI4326 (FILE &1 PROCESSED IN JOIN POSITION &2)

OPNQRYF treated the file as a secondary join file. If there is no existing access path over the join field(s), you might improve the query by creating one.

CPI4327 (FILE &1 PROCESSED IN JOIN POSITION 1)

This file was treated as the primary join file.

CPI4328 (ACCESS PATH &4 USED BY QUERY)

OPNQRYF used an existing access path in retrieving the data. This message is often a sign of good performance.

CPI4329 (ARRIVAL SEQUENCE ACCESS USED FOR FILE &1)

The system processed all records in the file. This is good if the percentage of records retrieved is greater than approximately 20 percent. If fewer than 20 percent of the records are retrieved, the query will probably perform better if you create a suitable access path over a field in the QRYSLT parameter.

CPI432A (QUERY OPTIMIZER TIMED OUT)

The query optimizer did not have time to consider all access paths over the file before it decided the best way to retrieve the data. You can force it to consider all access paths by specifying OPTALLAP(*YES). However, before you do that, verify that you still need each access path. If a file has 30 access paths, does it still need them all? Are there some which were created for programs that no longer exist?

You also can try to combine access paths so that the system shares access paths. For example, suppose you create a logical file (LFILE1) over physical file PFILE keyed on FIELDA. A few months later you create LFILE2 keyed on FIELDA and FIELDB. You first should consider whether or not LFILE1 is still needed. If all programs that use LFILE1 can use LFILE2 instead, you can change the programs and delete LFILE1. If for whatever reason you decide you still need LFILE1, you can delete it and then recreate it. The system will make LFILE1 share the existing access path of LFILE2.

The optimizer considers the most recently created access paths first. If you decide you must retain all the logical files over a physical file, you can delete and recreate any logical files OPNQRYF uses. Doing this will cause OPNQRYF to consider them first (before the optimizer times out).

CPI432C (ALL ACCESS PATHS CONSIDERED FOR FILE &1)

The system did consider all the access paths available in deciding the best way to retrieve the data.

CPI432D (ADDITIONAL ACCESS PATH REASON CODES USED)

The limited size of message descriptions did not permit all reason codes to be included in message CPI432A or CPI432C. The additional reason codes are found in this message.

Index

A

K